BEAT THE ODDS

BEAT THE ODDS
SURVIVAL MANUAL

TIM MACWELCH

Illustrations by
TIM MCDONAGH
and Conor Buckley

weldonowen

CONTENTS

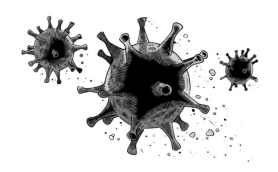

HISTORY REPEATS

 # PRESENT TENSE

THE FUTURE

YOUR LUCKY DAY

When it comes to matters of belief, we all wrestle with the same questions: Where did we come from? Why are we here? What are we supposed to do? These are complex issues, yet one thing is clear—no matter how complicated our views may be, they can divide us into two simple groups. The first group consists of people who believe that everything happens by random chance. The second is those who believe we are all part of a predetermined plan. You may have randomly picked up this book with the goal of increasing your chances of survival and your success during the unpredictable risks of the future. It's your lucky day. And if you believe the universe is governed by something larger than us, then maybe you were meant to learn the skills in this book. So, did you pick up this book by sheer chance? Or was this all part of your fate? There are questions here that we can't answer today, but there's one thing that's clear and I think we can all agree upon it. Whether you picked up some survival skills as part of the cosmic plan or you just got lucky, when push comes to shove and your back is up against the wall, you'll be the one who takes care of yourself, your family, and your friends. So, in the myriad of different emergency scenarios that could unfold in our lifetime, how can we effectively become the protector in every situation? Well, don't lose too much sleep over it. Instead, read on! We're going to study the past, look to the future, determine the most likely threats and gain the practical, real-world skills to fight those threats. Learning survival skills is a lot like investing in a life insurance policy, though in some ways it is much better. For one thing, you get to use it while you're still alive; and for another, you can use it to keep your loved ones alive too. Whether you picked up this book out of sheer luck or whether it was meant to be, we're here to help you.

TIM MACWELCH

SURVIVAL BASICS

ESSENTIAL SURVIVAL KIT

Having an abundance of self-reliance skills and knowledge is a beautiful thing. You'll walk around with greater confidence, knowing that you can provide for yourself and your loved ones. With the right skills and knowledge, you could even make the things you'd need in a crisis–if you have enough time. YFor example, you may know exactly how to improvise a tourniquet. That's great, but will you have enough time to cobble together the pieces and apply the tourniquet before it's too late? Wouldn't it be better to have a first-aid bag that contains a ready-to-use tourniquet? Of course it would! If you want to be serious about survival, you'll need the right combination of skills, knowledge, experience, and supplies.

EDC Being prepared for anything is the whole point of Every Day Carry gear, also referred to as EDC gear. Don't get caught empty handed. Carry the minimum, and add to it when you need to.

- **Your mobile phone** To call for help and get information.
- **A flashlight** To find your way and for signaling.
- **Knife or multitool** For a multitude of tasks and defense.
- **Fire** At least carry a lighter.
- **Defense** This could be a discrete handgun for concealed carry, or pepper spray or a stun gun.

BOB A bug out bag is a collection of goods that you would need to survive if you had to flee your home with no guarantee of shelter, food, or water during an emergency. Think of the BOB as your survival insurance policy for any disaster or mayhem. There may not be one perfect, universally agreed-upon set of equipment, but with a core set of items you can put together a BOB for a wide variety of situations. Fill a backpack or duffle bag basic survival essentials and a few irreplaceable items. Your BOB should contain at a minimum the following supplies, with most items sealed in zip-top bags or dry bags to prevent water damage:

- **Defense** A firearm, knife, pepper spray, or stun gun.

- **Shelter** An ultralight tent, pad, and sleeping bag, with a space blanket for backup.
- **Water** Buy 2 large bottles of water, as they will keep for a while.
- **A water filter** This will help keep you in safe drinking water.
- **Personal care** First aid, hygiene, and sanitation supplies.
- **Food** Pick ready-to-eat foods that you can eat while walking, and carry a lot!
- **Digital backups** A portable thumb drive or similar with your bank info, insurance documents, wills, and family photos and videos.
- **Garb** Walking shoes and seasonally appropriate clothes and outer wear
- **Tools** Duct tape, trash bags, a head lamp with spare batteries, and a multitool.
- **Odds and ends** Cash in small bills; waterproof matches; a lighter; hand sanitizer; a compass; a local map; and an old cell phone, fully charged.

SHELTER-IN-PLACE KIT You may need to survive on your own after an emergency. This means having your own food, water and other supplies to last for at least 72 hours.

- **Water** One gallon of water per person per day for at least three days, for drinking and sanitation
- **Food** At least a three-day supply of non-perishable food, and a manual can opener.
- **Battery-powered or hand crank radio** and a NOAA Weather Radio with tone alert
- **Flashlight** and extra batteries
- **First aid kit**
- **Whistle** To signal for help
- **Dust mask** Plus plastic sheeting and duct tape
- **Moist towelettes**, garbage bags, and plastic ties
- **Wrench or pliers** to shut off utilities
- **Local maps**
- **Cell phone** with chargers, inverter, or solar charger.

HISTORY REPEATS

What are the odds that you'd start reading a book like this, learn some new skills, and put them to good use within your lifetime? We think the odds are excellent that you'll find some useful information—and maybe even some fun—between the covers of this book. Survival isn't always about fighting predators in the wilderness or battling your way through a zombie horde. More often than not, survival challenges involve dealing with much more pedestrian issues, like figuring out how to stay safe during civil unrest or learning how to prepare for a food shortage. In this first part of the book, we'll take a look at some of the events that have rattled our forebears. These occurrences may be ordinary or unusual, but they shouldn't be unexpected. For the most part, it's all been done before. Take heart in the fact that so many of our ancestors faced these situations and prevailed. Our hardy predecessors serve as a great example, and they give us hope that we can survive too.

LET'S KEEP IT CIVIL

IS IT LIKELY TO HAPPEN?

A "Fall of Rome" scenario is pretty unlikely, but smaller civil unrest is common, such as mobs forming after sports events or political upset, or long-lasting civil turmoil.

HOW BAD COULD IT REALLY BE?

Most of these events are regional, so you may not feel a thing if you live far from the scene—but it could be really bad if you're at "ground zero" for the upheaval.

CAN I IMPROVE MY ODDS?

Get out of the hot spot if the event is localized—and even if the event is civilization-wide, you can still find ways to survive and move out of harm's way.

FOR A SUPPOSEDLY SOCIAL SPECIES, WE HUMANS CERTAINLY SPEND A LOT OF TIME ENGAGING IN ANTISOCIAL ACTS. WE TALK ABOUT OUR DESIRE FOR PEACE, BUT WE ARE ALSO QUICK TO SEEK CONFRONTATION. WILL WE LIVE TO SEE A COMPLETE FAILURE OF CIVILITY IN OUR LIFETIMES?

We all get a bit hot under the collar from time to time. It seems to be part of our very nature. It's usually no big deal, and we typically move on after we have some time to cool down. Certain issues, however, just don't go away. They grow (or fester) in people's hearts and minds, becoming a rallying point that brings people together—sometimes for beneficial change, and for self-destruction at other times. History is full of examples of both extremes, but this section is more than just a history lesson; it's a lesson that history can repeat itself. These scenarios will almost certainly play themselves out again in the future (although maybe not in your lifetime or your location, if you're lucky).

DETERMINE THE DANGER What's the threat? Maybe it's something mild, like unwittingly entering the wrong bar. Or maybe you attend a peaceful protest that turns ugly. Or maybe this is the start of the Second American Civil War.

SMALL-GROUP THREATS This is usually the "wrong place, wrong time" kind of commotion. Prevention is usually the best approach, so figure out where you're not supposed to go—and then don't go there.

THE SPONTANEOUS MOB Everything was fine, but then the crowd went nuts! Pay attention to the people around you. Situational awareness is key to escaping tricky scenarios—or, better yet, avoiding them.

RAUCOUS RALLIES Work your way to the edges and find a path that leads away from the crowd. Just make sure that you don't get pushed up against a wall or fence, where you'd risk being trapped or even crushed by the crowd, especially if there's a stampede.

CIVIL UNREST Some issues affect a culture deeply, causing hurt, creating anger, and inspiring citizens to act. You'll have to make a moral decision. Do you want to show up, or will you hide away in safety?

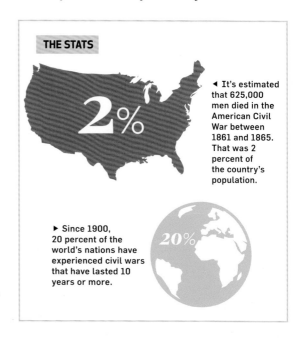

THE STATS

2%

◄ It's estimated that 625,000 men died in the American Civil War between 1861 and 1865. That was 2 percent of the country's population.

► Since 1900, 20 percent of the world's nations have experienced civil wars that have lasted 10 years or more.

20%

IS IT TIME FOR US TO PANIC YET?

Panic is defined as uncontrolled fear leading to thoughtless behavior. For example, a possible panic reaction is to run off screaming in a random direction. Panic occurs when fear takes over. So is it time to panic about civil unrest? In a word, no. At the time of this writing, political tensions are high around the world, rights are being infringed, and people all along the political spectrum are angry. But that means we should not flee, but rather speak up instead. Historically, nonviolent protest has been twice as successful as armed conflict.

So how can you tell when a seemingly isolated act of violence is just the first step toward something worse? Unfortunately, it's not our lot in life to know the future, but we can try to predict it, based on the past. By staying aware of both history and current events, we can remain vigilant about developing threats and stay ahead of certain problems. And the following ideas and skills in this book aren't just useful in a full-blown civil war; they could also help you minimize your risks in less apocalyptic scenarios.

HIT THE BOOKS History is full of great lessons. We can study the civil wars of the last century, and determine their causes and the conditions they created. We can look up all the attempts that people have made (successful or otherwise) to overthrow their government. Just remember that history is written by the victors. When unrest and warfare lead to a group's success, the events get nice names like "the Peasant's Revolt" or the American Revolution. And when the uprisings aren't so successful, they are often looked upon in a different light.

STAY INFORMED With the past as a guide, we can keep a close eye on current events and make predictions about the course they will follow.

BREAK FREE What can you do if you happen to find yourself being swept up in a riot? When the situation feels like it's getting dangerously out of control, there are a few things you can do to get into a safer position. If you're in a moving crowd, you run the risk of getting trampled; plenty of mass gatherings in history have resulted in just such a thing, especially when the crowd has been pushed to panic. Your best bet is to stay on your feet, avoid resisting the movement of the crowd, and keep your hands up near your chest to create a little space for yourself. Gradually work your way toward the edge of the mob, and stay as far as away as possible from hot spots of violence and destruction if you notice any. Once you're safely away from the crush of the crowd, you can begin to assess the larger situation and make your best guesses about the way it will all play out.

Benjamin Lay

The Quaker dwarf who fought slavery in colonial America

Benjamin Lay was many things: an immigrant to the New World, a devout Quaker, and a dwarf with very thin legs and a hunched back. Most notably, he was morally outraged by the practice of slavery in America and the cruel treatment of slaves. He never led an angry mob, but one of his dramatic acts of civil disobedience jolted a packed Quaker meetinghouse in 1738. Before the gathering of "weighty Quakers," Lay reminded the room that God loves everyone equally, regardless of wealth, gender, or color. He then proclaimed that slavery was the greatest sin of humankind, and threw off his long coat to reveal a sword and a book (with a hidden animal bladder full of red berry juice). He shouted at the crowd, "Thus shall God shed the blood of those persons who enslave their fellow creatures!" Lay stabbed the sword through the book, and to the dismay of all present, it began to "bleed" down his arm. He proceeded to fling "blood" at the slave owners present; the room erupted in chaos, and women fainted. Lay stood solemnly, "like a statue," as his work was done that day. Benjamin Lay didn't live to see the end of slavery in America, but remained an outspoken opponent to slavery, in word and deed. He even wrote an antislavery booklet published by his famous friend, Benjamin Franklin of Philadelphia. Lay was fortunate enough to see Quaker reformers undertake a "purification" campaign in 1758, disciplining and even disowning Quakers who traded slaves. The first major move toward abolition had begun, and he had been part of it. Benjamin Lay died a year later, at the age of seventy-seven.

UNDERSTANDING CIVIL WAR

When does daily rioting become a full-scale civil war? There's some gray area, but in general, routine conflict escalates to civil war when a significant percentage of the population organizes and fights with another group within the same state or country. Often, the fighting is over who holds power, or to change policies, and leaders may organize fighting over legitimate grievances or a hunger for power (or both).

THE FIRST REAL CIVIL WAR One of the earliest recorded civil wars was in ancient Rome. Even the word *civil* comes from the Roman word for citizen (*civilis*). This ancient conflict occurred over 2,000 years ago, started by generals Gaius Marius and Lucius Cornelius Sulla in 88 BCE. Over the next 400 years, several other civil wars threatened the Roman Empire, but these were neither isolated conflicts, nor the biggest of their kind.

CENTURIES OF WARFARE The Old World saw many civil wars during the Dark Ages and later periods. England had many in the 1100s and 1200s, while the Byzantine wars of the 1300s and Japanese civil wars of the 1400s preceded many more wars in Europe from the 1500s to the 1700s. The New World later became the battleground for the world's largest civil war to date, the American Civil War.

AMERICA AT WAR Stemming from complex issues, including slavery and states' rights, the American Civil War started in 1861 and ended in 1865. This bloody conflict caused at least 1 million casualties in total (roughly 3 percent of the population), with at least 620,000 dead soldiers, and perhaps as many as 850,000.

EXPECT THE UNEXPECTED

If your nation descends into civil war, the economy will falter or collapse. There will be interruptions in supply chains, communications, utilities, and other basic resources. Travel may be restricted; as things ramp up and the battlegrounds are chosen, you may even be in the line of fire. We don't really know what a civil war in a high-tech country will be like. Most conflicts since World War II have been very one-sided, technologically, and conflicts may look very different when weapons such as drones are deployed widely by both sides.

DO I HAVE TO PICK A SIDE? During the Civil War, many chose to muddle through their lives as best they could, praying that fighting never reached their homes. Still, at least 50,000 civilians died; some fled, while others picked a side, risking everything to fight. It's a sobering question—what you'd be willing to fight for and die over. Let's hope we never have to discover the answer the hard way.

10 THE DARK

Maybe it's the lack of visual stimuli, or maybe it's more deeply rooted and primal. Either way, fear of the dark isn't just something that affects children, and the results can be incapacitating. Humans aren't nocturnal creatures, and since we can't see in the dark, it makes sense that being in the dark can be uncomfortable. Some of our ancestors who were naturally fearless in the dark were possibly killed by accidents or predators at night, leaving those who stayed by the fire, and conveying fear of darkness as a genetic trait.

Profound fear of the dark is known as nyctophobia. It's believed to stem from the brain's misconceptions about potential threats in the dark, and the harm they can cause. This fear can be amplified or triggered when a person is already frightened, by recent events or by scary entertainment (such as horror films). Numerous researchers believe the phobia is linked to separation anxiety, especially in children. Symptoms can manifest as sweating, faster breathing, nausea, dry mouth, trembling, heart palpitations, trouble speaking or thinking clearly, and a sense of detachment. Nyctophobia can be debilitating, especially when symptoms do not improve over time.

11%

◀ Clinical psychologist John Mayer, PhD has stated that fear of the dark is "very common." Roughly 11 percent of adults are afraid of the dark.

▶ In a recent UK survey, 17 percent of adults admitted to sleeping with a light on most nights.

17%

2:30 A.M.

▲ According to the research, the most fearful and worrying time of the night for adults is 2:30 a.m.

IMPROVE YOUR ODDS

Nyctophobia can be managed by both therapy and medication. Exposure therapy is the most common, involving exposing a patient to darkness in a controlled and positive setting. Cognitive behavioral therapy is another option, involving a positive nighttime routine, with supportive thoughts and behaviors. When all else fails, antianxiety medication may be needed for severe symptoms. Don't feel bad or broken if you need help dealing with this fear; we've faced dangerous things in the dark for ages. Focus on the positives: At least dire wolves and saber-toothed cats are now extinct.

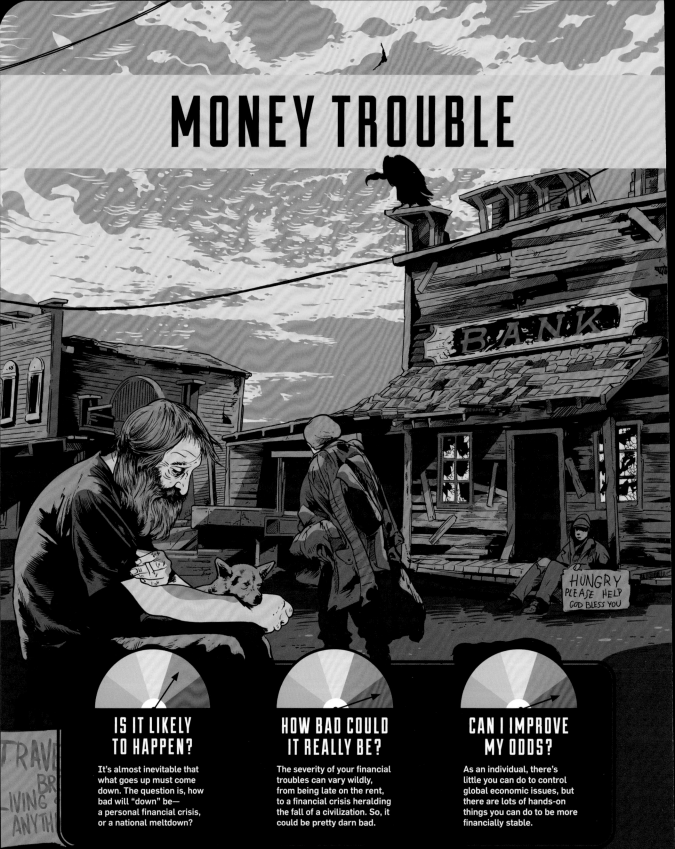

MONEY TROUBLE

IS IT LIKELY TO HAPPEN?

It's almost inevitable that what goes up must come down. The question is, how bad will "down" be—a personal financial crisis, or a national meltdown?

HOW BAD COULD IT REALLY BE?

The severity of your financial troubles can vary wildly, from being late on the rent, to a financial crisis heralding the fall of a civilization. So, it could be pretty darn bad.

CAN I IMPROVE MY ODDS?

As an individual, there's little you can do to control global economic issues, but there are lots of hands-on things you can do to be more financially stable.

EVERYONE HAS MONEY TROUBLES, EVEN BILLIONAIRES. (IT'S EASIER FOR THEM TO MAKE ENDS MEET, BUT THOSE GOLD-PLATED TOILETS AREN'T CHEAP.) BUT WHEN A NATION—OR WORSE, THE ENTIRE WORLD—HAS MONEY TROUBLES, THE STAKES SUDDENLY GET A LOT HIGHER.

You can't crack open the history books without finding sections on epic financial downfalls. Maybe you've seen those scary old black-and-white photos of starving people standing in long lines during the Great Depression just to get some free soup. More shocking still, you may have seen photos of a wheelbarrow full of cash it took to buy a loaf of bread in Weimar Germany in 1923. Thanks to hyperinflation, a loaf of bread that cost one Deutschmark in 1919 would cost 100 billion just four years later. There are many different ways in which financial difficulties can strike a region, nation, or continent or the globe—these are three of the most common situations.

RECESSION When spending is reduced and the economy shrinks, you're facing a recession: a period of negative economic growth, which often worsens other issues such as unemployment. Negative spirals are one of the risks of a recession; for example, demand for goods and services falls when spending decreases. If demand falls too much, companies lay off workers, jobless consumers spend less money, and the economy spirals further.

DEPRESSION When a recession worsens and lasts for years, then it can be classified as a depression. The technical definition of a depression is a decline in real GDP (gross domestic product) that exceeds 10 percent, or a recession that lasts more than two years. Or both. The American Great Depression is the most iconic example.

HYPERINFLATION Some inflation is normal, but when it increases by 50 percent or more each month, you're suffering from hyperinflation. This situation causes a rapid drop in the value of a local currency, which in turn causes the price of all goods to increase dramatically (and sometimes daily).

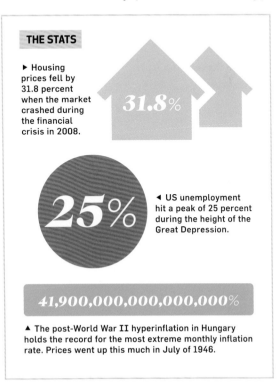

THE STATS

▶ Housing prices fell by 31.8 percent when the market crashed during the financial crisis in 2008.

31.8%

25%

◀ US unemployment hit a peak of 25 percent during the height of the Great Depression.

41,900,000,000,000,000%

▲ The post-World War II hyperinflation in Hungary holds the record for the most extreme monthly inflation rate. Prices went up this much in July of 1946.

RIDE OUT A RECESSION

Recessions typically last for just a few months, and are nothing new. In fact, there have been thirty-three recessions in the US since 1854. But just because the most recent recessions didn't lead to total financial collapse doesn't mean that the next one will follow the trend. As global marketplaces become increasingly connected, ripples are felt faster and farther away. Oddly enough, recessions don't spell doom for everyone. The right person in the right place may seize an opportunity and end up making a lot of money while others struggle. Here are a few ways you can ride out a recession.

SAVE WHILE YOU CAN The perfect time to beef up your savings account is when money is flowing in, since you likely won't have extra income during tough times. Start with enough savings to cover a month's expenses if you lost your job, then add more each month. Pay yourself with each paycheck, then the bills, then waste your fun money. Saving up enough to last you six months is a powerful tool for financial survival.

START NETWORKING NOW A common rural saying is "Make hay while the sun shines." It's true in the literal sense: You need a stretch of good warm weather to make dry hay (otherwise, the grass ends up molding). But it also means that we should take advantage of good opportunities when they present themselves because we know the next rainy day is coming. Network now with old colleagues, members of your community, and others who might be able to assist you—don't wait until you're desperate to reach out.

GET OUT OF DEBT I know this is easier said than done, but your goal should be to pay interest only on a home (not on goods).

DO THE MATH Track your spending and see where your dollars go. In most cases, simple, healthy foods from the grocery store are a fraction of the cost of restaurant meals. As for the gym membership, try switching to a cheaper gym or going for runs outside.

DEAL WITH A DEPRESSION

If really bad times come, and they will, you'd better be prepared.

FIND NEW INCOME STREAMS Working a side hustle is a great way to pick up some extra cash when times are good, and it might become a critical pursuit during a depression. Find other ways to make money and supplement your income.

LIVE ON A BUDGET Control your spending carefully—otherwise, your spending might end up controlling you. Cut the obvious wastes of money in your household, then cut some more.

DON'T QUIT YOUR DAY JOB Even if you're asked to take a pay cut, keep the job you have. You won't be the only one looking for a new job, and there's always someone else who is willing to work for less than you.

PLAY THE LONG GAME It's vital to stay positive during a financial disaster (or any other disaster) and ride it out until better times come. And while you may find that hard to do, realize that money troubles are one of the more mild calamities you could face. Seriously, you're alive, there are no zombies, the Earth isn't heaving up lava, the aliens haven't taken over—you're just broke.

HANDLE HYPERINFLATION

When the costs of your normal goods and services rise more than 50 percent in a month, you're feeling the pinch of hyperinflation. This can be caused by several things, though the most common is a government that prints extra money to pay for its own spending. It can also occur when a surge in consumer demand outstrips the supply. The short supply can be exacerbated by people stockpiling goods, fearful that the prices will be even higher tomorrow. As hyperinflation climbs, that currency of the country experiencing it loses its value.

DIVERSIFY If you're trying to protect personal wealth, diversified assets are the way to go. International stocks and bonds,

ROLL THE DICE

IT MIGHT SOUND CRAZY The economy in freefall seems less like a time to buy into the market, and more like time to convert assets into canned foods and Krugerrands. Recent studies show that 25 to 35 percent of Americans pull their money out of the market in a downturn or crash, on the principle that it's better to lose some of your money (by selling stocks at a loss, for example) than all of it. But, in fact, markets almost always rebound, and reward those who rode it out. The NerdWallet website has a fascinating tool that lets you play with different historical scenarios. For instance, if you'd had $50,000 invested in a diversified portfolio heading into the oil crisis of 1973, your investment would have dwindled to $26,000 at the bottom of the recession. A lot of people cashed out then, and locked in those losses. If you'd managed to ride it out, those investments would be worth over a million dollars today.

hard assets (like gold), and real estate can preserve a great deal of your assets.

OR DO WITHOUT For those of more modest means, find your own contingency plans to get the bare necessities, and try to live without the rest. This may mean stocking up on long-term food storage items and everyday supplies before hyperinflation hits. Learning how to grow food and cook from scratch couldn't hurt either.

BARTERING

KNOW YOUR HISTORY

You've bartered before, and it's not rocket science. You traded those home-baked cookies in your school lunch for candy. So you see, bartering isn't some alien economic system; it's something we've been doing for at least 8,000 years. Trade goods like wine, grain, salt, spices, metals, and even human skulls have been bartered back and forth throughout history. And even after money came into use, bartering still continued. During the Great Depression, bartering kept families fed and allowed people to eke out a simple existence. Even in the modern world, bartering resurfaces in times of economic hardship. After the Greek bank shutdown in June of 2015, a large part of the Greek population fell back on the barter system to acquire food and even pay some of their bills.

GET STARTED

Before you can set up your postcrisis trading post, you'll need to be prepared with desirable (but not too desirable) trade goods. Choose things that are useful, currently inexpensive, and long-lasting. Liquor never goes bad, and neither does toilet paper. Bar soap, butane lighters, candles, tampons, tea, and "how-to" books on gardening, foraging, first aid, and security (like this book) would all be great items for your desperate neighbors. Think about the supplies you'd personally want to have after a crisis, and the things that you'll use (even if no one else wanted them or conditions were too hostile for trading). Stock up at the first sign of economic trouble, since you can't trade what you don't have.

TEST IT OUT

During a crisis setting in which monetary exchange isn't practical or possible, you can try your hand at the ancient art of bartering. Start off easy, by bringing up the subject with a neighbor or someone with whom you already have a good relationship. Ask them what they would think about trading some items that they might not need for some supplies that would be more useful to them. Find out what they could use, make them an offer, and listen carefully to their counter. You may strike a bargain at the first suggestion, but more likely, you'll both have to work back and forth to come up with an amicable trade. It's best not to overwhelm the situation with too many choices or variables. Mention a few things you'd be willing to trade, and bring up a small list of things that you could use. Think of your first trade as an icebreaker, more for the purpose of building a trade relationship than getting everything you want in one transaction. Just trade a few items to get the ball rolling, then let the situation evolve naturally. If you get stuck, uncertain of the comparative worth of goods or items, consider their former price tag and then adjust your calculations based on need and scarcity. You could also look at other data on the items, like the calorie counts on food, to help you establish fair equivalency. With the bargain struck and hands shaken, it's time to swap the items, and then you're done. Welcome to the legacy skill of bartering!

ADVANCE YOUR SKILLS

As we've seen, bartering is the act of trading goods and/or services, but bartering itself isn't really a skill. It's a commerce system. The skill comes into play as you develop your talent in haggling. Also known as quibbling, bargaining, wrangling, and horse trading, haggling is an informal style of business negotiation. While personal charm and friendliness are useful personal traits, the most important part of haggling is communication. You'll need to listen carefully to your potential trade partner and effectively explain what's in it for them in order to make the trade. It also helps to be proficient in establishing a basis of value for the goods or services (in other words, determining what something is worth to another person).

AVOID THESE MISTAKES

Most of us are not accustomed to trading and bartering in modern times, so don't be surprised when your first few trades are inelegant or downright clumsy. Still, there are a few things you can avoid so that you don't look like a total noob during your first trade session.

DON'T BRING JUNK

Your undesirable items won't help anyone. Leave your junk at home. No one is going to want your pickled pigs' feet, stone arrowheads, copper trading wafers, or any of the other weird stuff you bought at a prepper expo. You're going to be standing there alone if you bring things that no one wants, and no one will want to trade with you again if you con them into trading for broken, ready-to-break, or useless items during a time of economic turmoil.

DON'T IGNORE WORK TRADES

It's easy to fall into the trap of thinking that you can only barter with tangible goods. Take a lesson from history, though, and you'll see that our ancestors often traded labor or services, in addition to physical commodities. You might be able to trade professional services for goods, offering your skills in medical, dental, mechanical, or carpentry fields. You could also stack the deck in your favor by trading both goods and high-value skills.

DON'T FORGET THE DANGER

In a crisis setting, never forget that there will be desperate people out and about. And the more cool stuff you drag out onto your trade blanket, the more of a target you paint on your household. Similarly, if a trade turns out badly, don't expect anyone to forget about it. Only bring trade goods out in public when they have a low likelihood of inspiring murderous envy in onlookers.

IF ALL ELSE FAILS

You tried so hard, but you just couldn't come to an agreement. It happens in the business world today, and you should expect disagreements to be even more common during the stress of an economic upheaval. Don't show your emotional investment while bartering, no matter how desperate you may be. You have to be willing to walk away. This is a good standard for any trading situation, and it may be your only option in a failed transaction. Walk away, and have someone else try to make the deal on your behalf. Whether you miscommunicated somehow during the deal, or they just didn't like you, a fresh face can make the mood lighter, and it may even secure the barter deal. Remember that wanting or needing something very badly doesn't mean you should pay an unbearable price. A good trade should leave both parties happy and eager to trade again.

LEARN FROM THE PAST

When most of us hear about booms and busts, we tend to think of the stock market crash of 1929, and then to the most recent financial disaster our nation has experienced. It might be somewhat encouraging to look back, and see that what goes up has come down again over and over throughout history. This is just the latest loop of that roller coaster. Here are some of the more dramatic market corrections of days gone by.

TULIP MANIA The tulip flower was introduced into the Netherlands around 1554, as a gift from the Ottoman Empire. By the end of that century, tulips had become much-coveted by royalty and the wealthy. Since new tulip colors and patterns take several years to develop, the Dutch unknowingly cultivated an early futures market along with their beloved flower bulbs. Once the bulbs had reached unbearable prices—and a plague outbreak occurred in a tulip-trading hot spot—their prices dramatically crashed in February 1637.

SOUTH SEA BUBBLE Even though their economy was bustling, Britain's national debt was a shocking £9 million in 1711 (that's €2.1 billion and $2.27 billion in modern terms). So, Britain created

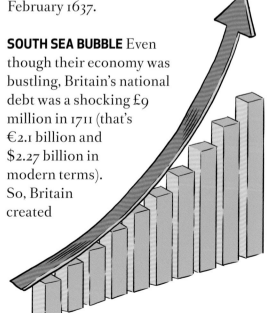

the South Sea Company and promised shareholders that they'd become rich through monopolized trade in South America. Unfortunately, the company couldn't trade in South America at the time, due to the nation's conflict with Spain. The company imploded, leaving both the country and starry-eyed private investors in even worse shape than before.

CREDIT CRISIS OF 1772 In the mid-1760s, Britain had rebuilt its wealth through holdings and trade in colonial America, and banks expanded credit widely. This easy money came to a halt in June 1772. One of the partners at an influential British banking house fled the country to avoid repaying his debts. Word spread like fire, creating a financial panic in Britain. Patrons formed long lines in front of British banks, demanding their cash immediately. The domino effect quickly spilled over to Scotland, other parts of Europe, and even the British-American colonies, perhaps becoming a factor in the Boston Tea Party and the subsequent American Revolution.

PANIC OF 1873 Uncontrolled speculation, a huge drop in the value of shares, panicked selling in the stock market—these seem like modern problems, but they're all the factors behind the crash of the Vienna Stock Exchange of May 1873. With its reserves drained, Austria's National Bank was unable to provide support, and the economy took the hit. From the imperial court and the bankers to the little people, the market crash affected people locally— and eventually, it impacted the whole of Europe.

THE GREAT DEPRESSION OF 1929-39 The Roaring Twenties were a time of great prosperity—until they ended horribly with the Wall Street crash in the autumn of 1929. Starting in September and ending in late October 1929, this event kicked off the worst economic disaster of the 20th century, the Great Depression. For a humber of reasons, the depression lasted nearly ten years, during which it affected the world economy, caused massive unemployment, and resulted in incalculable income and production losses worldwide.

THE OPEC OIL PRICE SHOCK OF 1973 In the early 1970s, OPEC (the Organization of the Petroleum Exporting Countries) chose to strike back against the United States and its decision to support Israel by halting oil exports to the United States and several allies. The significant shortage of oil and the accompanying price hike led to an economic crisis—to make things worse, the oil shortage was accompanied by very high inflation. The crisis took many years to correct, but thankfully, inflation eventually dropped back to normal levels.

ASIAN CRISIS OF 1997 Beginning in Thailand in 1997, then rapidly spreading throughout East Asia, this crisis began when speculative capital flows led to unfounded optimism, inspiring an overextension of credit and debt. This time, it happened in Hong Kong, Indonesia, Malaysia, Singapore, South Korea, and Thailand. With billions of dollars of foreign investment reversed, fears of a worldwide financial meltdown spread. In the end, thanks to the help of IMF (International Monetary Fund) bailout packages, the countries that were hardest hit were able to avoid default, and global financial trouble was averted.

ARGENTINE GREAT DEPRESSION (1998-2002) A short period of significant economic growth was followed by a crash in late 1998, followed by massive unemployment, rioting in the streets, and the collapse of the government. Likely triggered by Russian and Brazilian financial troubles, the Argentine economy shrank by 28 percent by 2002. During the crisis, more than half of Argentinians could be considered poor, and one-quarter were homeless. Things turned around in 2003, and the GDP surpassed precrisis levels in 2005.

FINANCIAL CRISIS OF 2008 Unless you lived in a cave, you felt the impact of the largest financial crisis since the Great Depression. This event centered around the collapse of the US housing bubble, which in turn took down one of the world's largest investment banks (Lehman Brothers). Key financial institutions and big businesses required government bailouts to stay afloat. It took nearly a decade to get back to "normal."

MONEY MATTERS

5 STOCKS THAT SURVIVED THE 1929 CRASH

Exxon — FOUNDED 1882
Coca-Cola — FOUNDED 1893
Stanley Black & Decker — FOUNDED 1891
P&G — FOUNDED 1891
PPG — FOUNDED 1899

PRICE OF TULIP BULBS (1636-1637)

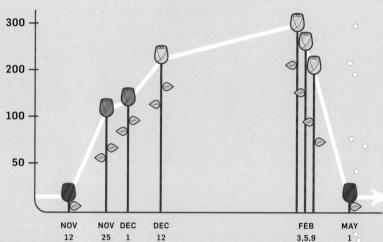

NOV 12 — NOV 25 — DEC 1 — DEC 12 — FEB 3,5,9 — MAY 1

WORST CASES OF HYPERINFLATION

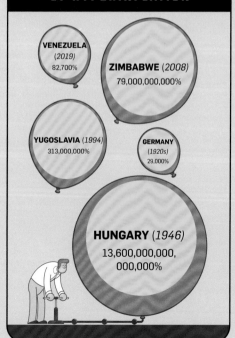

VENEZUELA (2019) 82,700%

ZIMBABWE (2008) 79,000,000,000%

YUGOSLAVIA (1994) 313,000,000%

GERMANY (1920s) 29,000%

HUNGARY (1946) 13,600,000,000,000,000%

If you had invested $40 into a single share of Coca-Cola in 1919 during the IPO and reinvested all of your dividends, your investment would be worth over $10 million in 2020.

COST OF BREAD IN POST-WW2 GERMANY

1918	0.25 Reichsmark
1922	3 Reichsmarks
JAN 1923	700 Reichsmarks
JUL 1923	100,000 Reichsmarks
SEP 1923	2,000,000 Reichsmarks
NOV 1923	80,000,000,000 Reichsmarks

PEOPLE WHO GOT RICH DURING THE GREAT DEPRESSION

JOHN DILLINGER
Bank Robber

JOSEPH KENNEDY
Stock Speculator

BABE RUTH
Baseball Star

MICHAEL J. CULLEN
Inventor of the Supermarket

CHARLES DARROW
Inventor of Monopoly

JAMES CAGNEY
Movie Star

J. PAUL GETTY
Oil Baron

GENE AUTRY
Singing Cowboy

GLENN MILLER
Band Leader

HOWARD HUGHES
Aviator, Film Producer, Stone Cold Weirdo

In the USA the average CEO earns 450 times as much as the average worker. In the UK it's 22 times, in Germany 12.

In one of the most impressive flameouts of the dot-com era, Pets.com's stock went from $14/share at its IPO in 2000 to 22 cents before it closed after only 9 months.

AVERAGE MINIMUM WAGE UNITED STATES

Actual Money/Today's Money

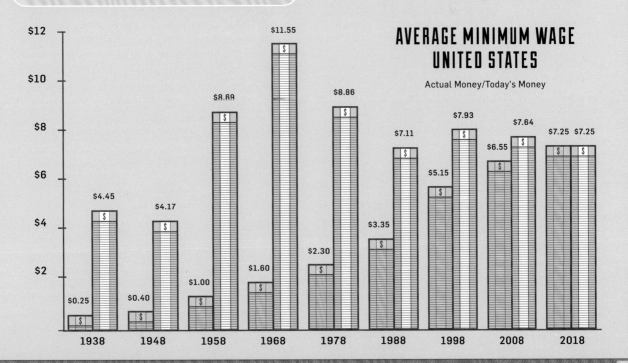

Year	Actual Money	Today's Money
1938	$0.25	$4.45
1948	$0.40	$4.17
1958	$1.00	$8.69
1968	$1.60	$11.55
1978	$2.30	$8.86
1988	$3.35	$7.11
1998	$5.15	$7.93
2008	$6.55	$7.64
2018	$7.25	$7.25

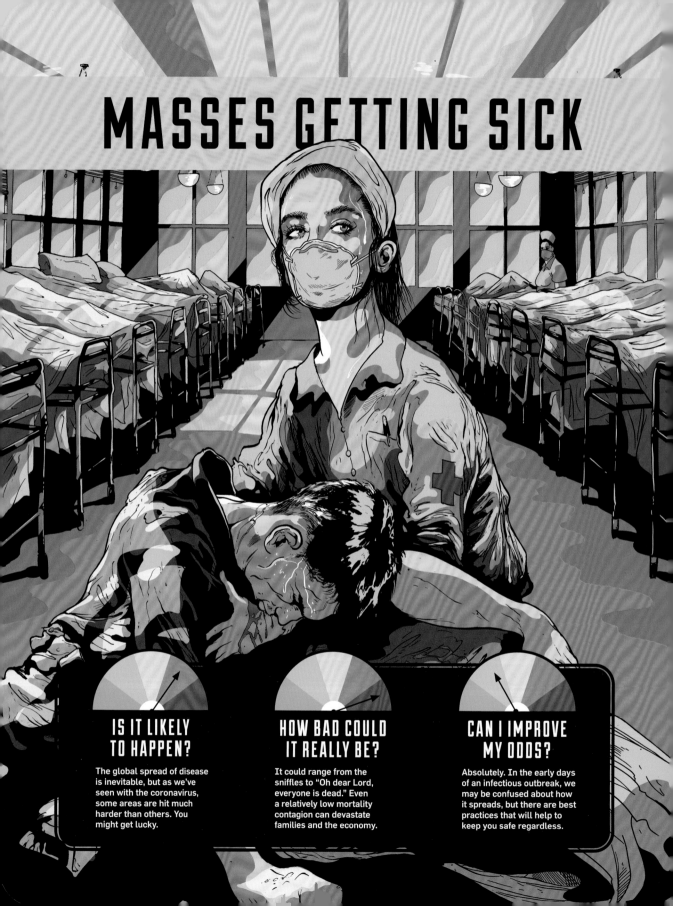

MASSES GETTING SICK

IS IT LIKELY TO HAPPEN?

The global spread of disease is inevitable, but as we've seen with the coronavirus, some areas are hit much harder than others. You might get lucky.

HOW BAD COULD IT REALLY BE?

It could range from the sniffles to "Oh dear Lord, everyone is dead." Even a relatively low mortality contagion can devastate families and the economy.

CAN I IMPROVE MY ODDS?

Absolutely. In the early days of an infectious outbreak, we may be confused about how it spreads, but there are best practices that will help to keep you safe regardless.

PLAGUES AND PANDEMICS HAVE ALWAYS BEEN WITH US, FROM THE BLACK DEATH OF THE MIDDLE AGES ALL THE WAY UP TO TODAY'S LATEST CRISIS. IS A NASTY BUG GOING TO WIPE OUT A GIANT SWATH OF HUMANITY AGAIN, OR WILL MODERN MEDICINE SAVE US BEFORE IT GETS TOO BAD?

Throughout history, all kinds of things have made people sick. Some we now know how to avoid or mitigate. (Cook that pork thoroughly, kids, and for the love of God, wash your hands!) But some diseases are still a threat—how severe it is depends on where you're located, how strong your immune system is, and what kind of medical care is available. Sometimes the flu just makes you feel yucky for a few days. But in 1918, a flu killed over 50 million people worldwide, many of them young and strong. And as the world has learned all too recently with the COVID-19 pandemic, new diseases pop up with surprising frequency, often after incubating in an animal population.

As this book was being written and sent to press, the coronavirus was spreading across the globe, making everything we might write about it likely obsolete. So, instead of trying to predict exectly how this latest challenge facing humanity will go, let's look at pandemics of the past. One thing you can pretty much count on is that we will get through this, and history often has some useful lessons as we ponder how.

The flu is a useful comparison, as a disease we're more familiar with: According to the World Health Organization (WHO), 3 million to 5 million cases of severe flu each year result in between 291,000 and 646,000 deaths worldwide. Of course, these numbers vary widely from year to year, but even on the low end, that's a tremendous number of lives lost. And it's not the flu virus itself that's doing all the killing, as we see with other viruses as well.

Sometimes you're killed by your own body's immune responses, not to mention secondary infections that attack while the immune system is already struggling. Roughly one-third of flu-related deaths are caused by the virus overwhelming the immune system. Another one-third of victims die from the body's response to secondary bacterial infection, like pneumonia in the lungs. The rest are lost due to single or multiple organ failure.

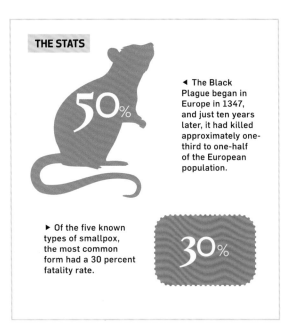

THE STATS

◄ The Black Plague began in Europe in 1347, and just ten years later, it had killed approximately one-third to one-half of the European population.

50%

► Of the five known types of smallpox, the most common form had a 30 percent fatality rate.

30%

KNOW YOUR ENEMY

Germs are all around us, but even in the grip of a global pandemic, we're often uncertain about exactly what related terms mean, let alone best practices for improving the odds of survival. Here are some essentials everyone should know for now, and for whatever comes next. (And if history tells us anything, it's that something will come next. You can bet your germy wad of cash on it.)

LEARN THE TERMINOLOGY You might be wondering when a disease turns into a pandemic. In short, outbreaks are a widespread occurrence of an infectious disease within a community. An epidemic is an outbreak with higher mortality rates than were expected for the disease. Finally, a pandemic is an epidemic that occurs across several countries and affects a large percentage of the population in each. The last influenza pandemic, prior to the late-2000s H1N1 outbreak, happened between 1968 and 1969: the Hong Kong flu, which killed over 33,000 Americans.

PREP FOR A PANDEMIC The two main things that make a pandemic so alarming are communicability and lethality. The definition of a pandemic is "an infectious disease that had spread around the globe"—which happens only when the organism is easy to spread (highly communicable). Something that is strictly blood-borne is not likely to jump out of a carrier and all over the other passengers at the international airport, for example. Yet something that's

easily spread in the air—by droplets from coughing and sneezing, breath, bodily fluids, or other close contact—can spread across the globe in a few days, due to the speed of modern international travel. If this wide-spreading ailment is just a common cold, it doesn't matter too much. But when it is an illness with a higher-than-normal mortality rate? That's when things get ugly.

LIMIT YOUR RISK So, what should you do if an outbreak happens in your area or a pandemic sweeps the globe? The most important thing is to limit your exposure to public places, people that have been to public places, and people who are known to be ill. This is hard to do, for example, when you're a parent taking care of your sick child, but avoidance is the best solution—for everyone. Stay home and let the organism burn itself out without spreading. When this isn't possible, like when you run out of groceries, take steps to protect yourself and your loved ones. Wear a mask in public places, and maybe even gloves if things are really bad. Wash your hands well and often. Take off your shoes at the door so you don't track in organisms and spread then all over your home. And don't be stingy with the Lysol or bleach disinfectant.

MASK UP Your doctor isn't likely to hand out prescriptions for medicines so that you can stock up ahead of time—if they'd even work. After all, our latest pandemic is one that had no vaccine or treatment, making preparing for it particularly challenging. But what you can get before an outbreak is disinfecting spray and masks. Keep from spreading your germs and block some of the incoming ones with a supply of masks. The basic surgical mask is the cheapest and most common form of disease-preventing mask. The next-higher quality of mask is the N95. It protects against 95 percent of particulates larger than 0.3 microns. The next level of protection is the N99 mask (99% effective) and the N100 mask (99.97% effective). The average N100 mask is five times more expensive than the common N95 mask. None of these can guarantee the filtering of viruses (which are smaller than 0.3 microns), but they can catch droplets from coughing and sneezing, so they still do offer some protection in a viral outbreak. If you and the people you come in contact with mask up, it can help. In the most recent pandemic, masks ran short in many places, and people were forced to get creative—in some cases, perhaps more creative than practical, like gentlemen wearing lacy thong underpants over their faces. While this hack is arguably better than nothing, a paper dust mask or simple bandana over your mouth and nose will block more contagions, if less sexily.

WASH LIKE A SURGEON Nothing fights germs like frequent and thorough hand washing. Sure, you've been washing your hands since childhood, but likely not as thoroughly as doctors recommend.

STEP 1 Turn on the warm water and wet your hands. Apply soap to the palms, and backs of your hands. Rub your soapy palms together.

STEP 2 Rub each palm on the back of your other hand, threading your fingers together. Rub your palms together, interlacing your fingers and scrubbing them.

STEP 3 Cup your hands together with fingernails against the opposite palm and swivel your hands back and forth.

STEP 4 Wash each thumb by twisting the opposite hand around it. Using your fingernails, scrub the palm of each hand in a circular motion.

STEP 5 Rinse both hands with warm water. Dry your hands with a disposable paper towel. Turn off the water, using the paper towel to touch the faucet handle.

DIY ISOLATION ROOM

1 GUEST ROOM The ideal space for an isolation room is a guest room that has its own bathroom and windows for ventilation, and is located away from the main traffic areas of the home. Since most of us don't live in a palace, you may have to settle for an out-of-the-way bedroom with a bucket for a toilet.

2 AIR VENTS If your home has central air conditioning and/or heating, you'll need to block off the air flow to the isolation room. Cover the floor and wall vents tightly with duct tape. Never make an isolation room out of a space with an air return for the AC or heating system. This could suck in bacteria and viruses, and spread them throughout the home.

3 SAFETY GLASSES Don't forget about eye protection when you're shopping for masks. All of the breathing protection on Earth won't help you if an infected person sneezes into your eyes. Lab goggles or work goggles are the best choices, especially ones with an antifog coating and vents.

4 BUCKET TOILET If you don't have a bathroom in the isolation room, turn a bucket into a toilet by lining it with a trash bag and adding a little cat litter. Make sure it has a tight-fitting lid that stays on between uses. Consider having a second bucket designated as a barf bucket.

5 TYVEK OVERALLS These are tough, tear-proof, and almost waterproof. They're available at most hardware stores, and can be purchased with head and shoe covers.

6 MASKS A variety of standard medical masks, N95 masks, or even a few N100s could be invaluable. Buy a giant box of them at one of those warehouse stores, and you'll have plenty extra for trade goods.

7 GLOVES A case of nitrile gloves will protect your hands—without causing latex allergies.

8 PLASTIC SHEETING AND DUCT TAPE These can seal off doors, windows, vents, and more. They're also handy for covering mattresses and dead bodies.

9 LARGE TRASH BAGS Take out the trash, wear them as aprons, or turn them into barriers—there are hundreds of uses.

10 DISINFECTING SPRAY A case of disinfecting spray cans could save your family. You could also mix together nine parts water and one part bleach in a spray bottle to make a DIY version.

11 HAND SANITIZER Everyone should be using this—very often—during any infectious event.

12 CHLORINE BLEACH Bleach can be a great disinfectant for laundry and for making sanitizing solution.

13 THERMOMETER Get several inexpensive thermometers. Check each patient's temperature with their own unit. Don't share. Disposable forehead thermometers are an option, though not as easy to read.

14 ADULT DIAPERS For those too sick to get out of bed, adult diapers can contain incontinent mess and keep you from having to wash bedsheets or blankets all day, every day.

15 COMMUNICATION Your patient should have an easy way to signal for help, as they may be too weak to call out. A bell, rattle, or other similar noise-making gizmo should be within your patient's reach.

16 FOOD AND WATER Your patient will need plenty of food and water (if they can keep it down), so keep water bottles and snacks available in the room. To limit your cooking and avoid spreading germs through dishes, provide disposable packaging and ready-to-eat foods.

In the event of a hospital-swamping epidemic, you may have to care for a friend or loved one at home. Since you probably won't be able to set up an army tent in the backyard as a quarantine zone, you can set up a sick room in your house.

Of course, the real answer is no, you should never panic. Not when we consider that true panic is defined as acting irrationally, forgetting everything you learned, and maybe even behaving in suicidally dangerous ways. So, no, never panic. But should you be just a little more paranoid than usual? That, friends, may be the thing that saves you.

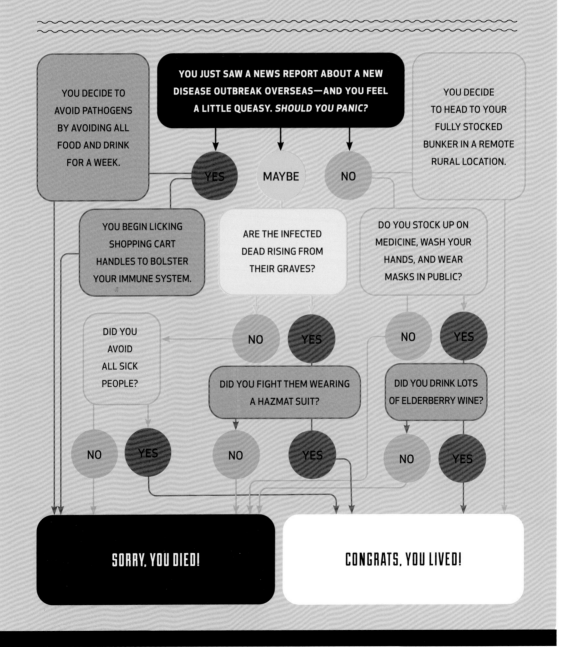

YOU JUST SAW A NEWS REPORT ABOUT A NEW DISEASE OUTBREAK OVERSEAS—AND YOU FEEL A LITTLE QUEASY. *SHOULD YOU PANIC?*

YOU DECIDE TO AVOID PATHOGENS BY AVOIDING ALL FOOD AND DRINK FOR A WEEK.

YOU DECIDE TO HEAD TO YOUR FULLY STOCKED BUNKER IN A REMOTE RURAL LOCATION.

YES   MAYBE   NO

YOU BEGIN LICKING SHOPPING CART HANDLES TO BOLSTER YOUR IMMUNE SYSTEM.

ARE THE INFECTED DEAD RISING FROM THEIR GRAVES?

DO YOU STOCK UP ON MEDICINE, WASH YOUR HANDS, AND WEAR MASKS IN PUBLIC?

DID YOU AVOID ALL SICK PEOPLE?

NO   YES

NO   YES

DID YOU FIGHT THEM WEARING A HAZMAT SUIT?

DID YOU DRINK LOTS OF ELDERBERRY WINE?

NO   YES

NO   YES

NO   YES

SORRY, YOU DIED!

CONGRATS, YOU LIVED!

28 DAYS LATER

There are plenty of nondisease hazards that may arise as knock-on effects during and after an outbreak. During and right after the 1918 flu pandemic, the economy and the supply chain took a major hit. Ports were closed and trade was crippled. Stores weren't even allowed to have sales, for fear that they'd draw too many people to one place. Churches and schools were shuttered, and morgues became grisly body banks—stacked to the ceiling with corpses, in some cases. Morticians worked day and night to process the incoming dead, and special trains were used to carry away the bodies. Some large cities (like Chicago) actually banned funerals since the death toll was so high. For those who were lost, their suffering was over, but for those who survived, the hardships and loss only continued.

Once the pandemic has been settled, and you've presumably survived, what's next? You'll have to build a new normal in your world. You may be forced to avoid doctors and hospitals in order to avoid being exposed to the disease (if you've dodged it thus far). If you were sick and survived, you'll have to regain your strength (which may be hard, as food resources will likely be limited). You may even have the hard work of burying (or burning) your dead friends and family members in the event that local funeral homes refuse to take in more remains. It's bitter and brutal work to rebuild a society in the wake of a cataclysmic event, but it's better than wallowing in grief and wasting your time wishing for a different outcome. You survived, and it's your job to help yourself and the other survivors put the pieces back together again.

T / F

SECRET VIRUS LABS ARE LIKELY TO CAUSE THE NEXT PANDEMIC

LIKELY FALSE Even supervillain-style bad guys are aware that it's impossible to have germs spread only to their enemies. The very nature of an infectious disease is that it's, well, infectious. That doesn't mean that governments don't study horrible contagions, either in the hopes of finding some way to weaponize contagions that wouldn't also wipe out the government using them against a foe or to learn how they work as a defense in case the other guy decides to release something nasty first. And then there are all those labs studying deadly diseases for perfectly positive reasons, as was very likely the case with the bat-virus labs in China that raised suspicions when the coronavirus started spreading around the world. After all, our technologically advanced society is not invulnerable to screw-ups any more than it is immune to diseases. Case in point: Anthrax spores were accidentally released at a military research compound in the town of Sverdlovsk, Russia, in April 1979. The incident was later dubbed the "biological Chernobyl," and it caused over 100 deaths.

SHINE ON I have long been a believer in colloidal silver, but it's had some bad press over the years. You can't search for it online without coming up with pictures of people who have turned themselves blue (permanently) from consuming massive overdoses of tainted products. Scrupulously made colloidal silver is safe for topical use in wound care, and it's also safe when consumed in reasonable doses. Silver is a biocide, killing viruses, bacteria, and other microbes with little to no ill effect on a host. The healthful effects of silver are nothing new. Our wealthier forebears believed that eating from silver dishes and cutlery kept them healthier, and silver is still being used in dental work, veterinary care, and even against antibiotic resistant infections. Today, you can purchase a form of silver remedy (colloidal silver) as a metallic-tasting water in health food stores (don't buy cheap stuff online unless you dig the Smurf look), or you can make your own.

COLLOIDAL SILVER

Supplies:

A clean glass canning jar

Two 4-inch pieces of ultrafine pure silver (.999) wire

A water meter that tests for dissolved solids

Distilled water that's tested 0.0 for dissolved solids (this water can be purchased from grocery stores or produced yourself)

Three fresh 9-volt batteries

Slender insulated electrical wire

Electrical tape

Two small alligator clips (available at electronics shops)

Directions:

Pour your distilled water into the jar. Check your water with the meter to ensure that it is free of dissolved solids. If not, find a purer source of water.

With a knife or electrician's wire stripper, cut your insulated electrical wire into two 1-foot pieces. Strip 1 inch of insulation on each end of each wire.

Connect the alligator clips to one end of each wire, using tape if needed.

Connect one of the free ends of the electrical wire to the positive terminal of one battery, and connect the other free end to the negative terminal. Secure with electrical tape.

Clip the silver wire pieces into each alligator clip without touching them. Then insert the silver wires into the water jar—without the alligator clips touching the water, and so that the wires are parallel in the water (about ¾ inch apart). Secure with tape so nothing slides out of position.

Once the wires are in the water, silver ions will begin to strip off the wires and suspend in the water. Run the "silver generator" until the water takes on a slight yellowish tint (30–45 minutes).

Pull the wires out of the water. Disconnect the batteries and bottle your colloidal silver water in a dark glass bottle. Use within one month, for best results.

The silver wires will last for ages, and the batteries will work for many uses (but should be replaced when they drop to 8 volts each, which can be tested with a small-voltage electrical meter). Improve your immune system by taking a spoonful or two daily during an outbreak or illness.

AN OUNCE OF PREVENTION

Legend says that "thieves' oil" was created by a group of 15th-century thieves to protect themselves from illness while robbing the homes and bodies of plague victims. Whether the tale is true or not, the essential oils in this blend are truly antiseptic and antiviral, with a high kill rate against airborne bacteria. I use it every year during cold and flu season, and it even smells nice. Blend together 40 drops clove bud essential oil, 35 drops lemon essential oil, 20 drops cinnamon bark essential oil, 15 drops eucalyptus essential oil, and 10 drops rosemary essential oil. Mix this blend with a generous amount of olive oil to dilute it, and wipe it on your skin. You can also use the undiluted essential oils in a diffuser.

GET TO KNOW ELDERBERRY

A common shrub that grows in fields and in shade, elderberry is found throughout the northern hemisphere. The purple-black berries are each about half an inch diameter, and they form large, umbrella-shaped clusters of fruit. Not only can these musky-scented berries be cooked as part of a wide variety of tasty beverages and dishes, they are also widely regarded as a potent virus-fighting supplement. They contain high amounts of dietary fiber, vitamin C, vitamin A, vitamin B6, iron, and potassium. Just keep in mind that elderberry has caused allergic reactions in some people. Furthermore, always collect dark purple or nearly black fruits. The unripe fruits are toxic enough to cause nausea and vomiting, even after cooking. Finally, elderberries should be consumed only after cooking or drying, as they are slightly toxic raw.

RECIPE FOR SUCCESS

MAKE YOUR OWN Often growing as a weedy bush in rural areas, elderberries are loaded with compounds that aid the immune system, especially when dealing with colds and flu. Elderberries (commonly seen in the US as *Sambucus canadensis* and *S. nigra*) have been used to make a pungent fruit wine for centuries. My family and I also take elderberry elixir anytime we fear the flu or feel like we're coming down with something. Elderberries have been known to fight influenza and other viral ailments since at least the 5th century. Syrups, lozenges, and other products can be purchased in drugstores and health food shops, or you can make your own.

ELDERBERRY ELIXIR

Supplies:

3 cups water

1 ½ cup of fresh or frozen black elderberries

2 tablespoons of freshly grated ginger

1 teaspoon of ground cinnamon

½ teaspoon of ground cloves

1 cup of raw honey

Directions:

Add the water, elderberries, ginger, cinnamon, and cloves to a pot and cover it. Bring the mixture to a boil, then reduce heat and simmer for 30 minutes. Next, turn off the heat and allow the pot to sit another 15 minutes. Take the mixture out of the pot while still warm, and crush the berries with a spoon or some other mashing implement. Strain the resulting liquid through cheesecloth or a fine-mesh strainer. Add the raw honey and blend while the liquid is still warm. Bottle the elixir in clean glass containers and store refrigerated for up to 6 months. Take 1–2 tablespoons daily during cold and flu season, or several tablespoons if someone in your household is sick.

MEDICINAL PLANTS

People have been collecting and cultivating all of these helpful plants for centuries or millennia. In an outbreak situation, doctors may be overwhelmed or unavailable or you may wish to avoid being around other sickly people to avoid potential contagions. While none of these home remedies should take the place of any professional medical care, it's still nice to have a sense that you are not helpless, should you end up having to fend for yourself.

ALOE VERA Very soothing to burns and scalds, this tender plant is best grown in a container so that it can be brought inside for the winter (unless you live in an area with very mild winters).

BLACKBERRY Yes, the berries are delicious, but did you know that blackberry leaves are helpful for diarrhea? Make an infusion (like a tea) by pouring near-boiling water over the leaves and let steep 5 to 10 minutes. The usual amount to use is about 2.5 ounces (75 g) of fresh leaf, or 1 ounce (30 g) of dried herb to one cup (240 ml) of hot water. The infusion must be taken same day.

BIRCH Birch bark, particularly the bark of the sweet birch, can be an effective analgesic. The bark is scraped from the tree's twigs before being brewed into a tea. Add ¼–½ teaspoon (1–2 g) of bark to about 7 ounces (200 ml) of water and then boil for 10 minutes. This tea can be taken up to five times per day.

BORAGE The flowers can be soaked in alcohol to make a mood-boosting tonic.

BURDOCK The roots and leaves make an excellent liver tonic and help to purify the body and blood. Make a tincture of the dried root in alcohol and consume 10–20 drops daily. You could also eat the fresh leaves and roots (after boiling in water and discarding the water to remove bitterness).

COMFREY Cooked, mashed roots are a topical treatment for arthritis, bruises, burns, and sprains. (Don't eat it; this herb can potentially damage the liver if ingested.) Simmer the fresh peeled or dried root, about 3.5 ounces (100 g), in 1 pint (500 ml) of water for 10 to 15 minutes, then mash into a paste and apply to the injury.

ECHINACEA If consumed at the first sign of cold symptoms, this can reduce the effects and duration of the common cold in adults.

JEWELWEED This stuff is a great cure for poison ivy, poison oak, or poison sumac. Crush the juicy, purplish stalk into a paste, and briskly scrub it all over the affected skin. After two minutes, wash it off with

clean water. If you do this within 45 minutes of exposure to ivy, oak, or sumac, you should have little to no reaction.

LAVENDER Used since ancient times for bug bites, burns, and skin disorders. To relieve itching, rashes, and swelling, apply crushed fresh leaves to the affected area. You can also make an infused oil for skin problems. Fill a jar with dried leaves and cover with olive oil. Allow it to soak for six to eight weeks, then decant. Not for use by pregnant or nursing women, or small children.

LEMON BALM This makes an outstanding topical agent for cold sores. Crush the fresh leaves and bind them over the sores.

MULLEIN An unparalleled herb for respiratory congestion, clearing lung and bronchial air passages, cough, and bronchitis. It's also used for pain with infused oils for earaches or ear mites, and as an antibacterial and antifungal.

PENNYROYAL This great-smelling mint relative can be crushed and applied to the skin as a very effective bug repellent. The leaves can also be crushed and then applied to wounds as an antiseptic, or brewed as a tea to settle upset stomachs. Stronger brews of the tea may help regulate menstruation; however, pregnant women should avoid it.

PLANTAIN While not quite strong enough to tackle snake bites, plantain can still help neutralize the venom of bees, wasps, scorpions, or other pain-inducing creatures. Just keep the paste of plantain

DON'T DIE FROM DIARRHEA Our bowels can stage a revolt for a wide variety of reasons. A viral infection, tainted food, bad water, or unsanitary living conditions can each cause a dangerous case of diarrhea; during an emergency situation, you will likely have enough problems without worrying about colon control and dehydration. Luckily, relief is close at hand in the world of traditional medicine: You can brew an antidiarrheal tea. Woody canes in the genus Rubus (such as blackberries) produce thorny leaves that are often used as an herbal tea. This tea also contains at least one compound that can help to dry up diarrhea. Make a strong tea from the dried leaves, and drink 1 cup (240 ml) every couple of hours until you notice a positive change. If this isn't strong enough, then you can also use blackberry roots for a tea, sipping it in comparable amounts to the leaf tea.

leaf on the wound and replace as it dries out. Relief should be swift.

ST. JOHN'S WORT Used internally and topically for pain, swelling, inflammation, burns, bruises, muscle damage, and nerve damage/neuralgia, and consumed as an antiviral and antidepressant.

YARROW Crushed leaves and flowers can be placed on cuts and scratches to stop bleeding and reduce the chance of infection.

WIDESPREAD FAMINE

IS IT LIKELY TO HAPPEN?

In an industrialized nation, the likelihood of a famine in modern times is pretty low, but it exists on a regular basis in some of the more challenged countries.

HOW BAD COULD IT REALLY BE?

Famines are often springboards for disease, political unrest, crime, and economic distress. Food shortages can also be a side effect of other disasters.

CAN I IMPROVE MY ODDS?

By stocking up on food (when it is available) and learning to grow your own food, you can keep the specter of famine from looming too large.

FAMINE WAS ONE OF THE FOUR HORSEMEN OF THE APOCALYPSE FOR A REASON. TODAY WE TEND TO THINK OF FAMINE EITHER AS A LONG-AGO PART OF HISTORY, OR IN TERMS OF TRAGIC IMAGES FROM FAR-OFF LANDS. BUT THAT HORSEMAN MAY BE CLOSER THAN YOU THINK.

Remember the last time you were really hungry? Now multiply that by a thousand, and add in the despair you'd feel as you notice that your children's bones are visible—even through their clothing. The textbook definition of famine just doesn't convey the real horror of a prolonged and pervasive food crisis. A famine is defined as a food crisis in a specific area or region that causes mass starvation and fatalities. According to the United Nations, any food shortage is upgraded to a famine when it meets the following criteria:

- More than 20% of households are facing major food shortages and have little to assist them.
- More than 30% of children suffer from acute malnutrition.
- Mortality is higher than two people per 10,000 people per day.

While the term *famine* doesn't guarantee any response from the UN or its member states, the use of the word does draw global attention to the event.

This form of food crisis is nothing new. The Christian Bible and other books of faith chronicle famines in the ancient past. Famines have continued to impact cultures around the world, and despite our best technological advances, there's no end in sight for vulnerable nations across the globe. From the Dark Ages until today, famines have been a common accompaniment during periods of political or military conflict. They've also been spawned by droughts and other crop-destroying weather conditions, overpopulation, crop blights, and even plagues of insects. Throughout recorded history, every inhabited continent has faced famine at some point. Europe and Asia were hardest hit by famine in the 19th and 20th centuries, and today, African nations like Nigeria, Somalia, and south Sudan are still suffering from famines (with more than 20 million at risk).

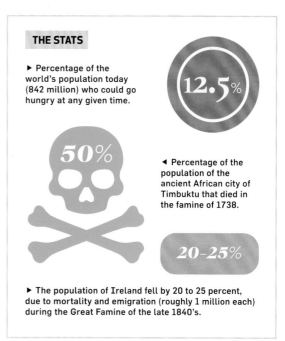

THE STATS

▶ Percentage of the world's population today (842 million) who could go hungry at any given time.

12.5%

50%

◀ Percentage of the population of the ancient African city of Timbuktu that died in the famine of 1738.

20-25%

▶ The population of Ireland fell by 20 to 25 percent, due to mortality and emigration (roughly 1 million each) during the Great Famine of the late 1840's.

RABBIT STARVATION Even if you feel like you're getting enough to eat, you could still be dying of malnutrition. Protein poisoning, also called rabbit starvation, is a threat in survival situations. Mountain men and fur trappers during the last few centuries—and anyone who was stuck on a life raft for a long period of time—have been at risk from this ailment, which is caused by a diet of nothing but lean meat. This form of acute malnutrition is caused by excess consumption of any lean muscle meats, coupled with a lack of other sources of nutrients. It is often aggravated by other factors like cold or dry environments and the stress of emergency situations. The symptoms include diarrhea, headache, fatigue, low blood pressure and heart rate, and a hunger that can be satisfied only by eating fat or carbohydrates. The cure for rabbit starvation is simple: Just add carbs or fat to your diet until the symptoms fade.

UNDERSTAND THE REASONS Even though the advancement of farming knowledge throughout history has usually meant advancement in food security, we have still been at the mercy of the environment and our own mismanagement—as we still are today. Famines have historically occurred as a result of unfavorable weather, and bad behavior on the part of human beings. Less commonly, nature hit our agrarian ancestors with a sucker punch, as with the potato blight that spawned the Great Famine in Ireland, or a swarm of plant-devouring locusts.

PREDICT THE FUTURE Full disclosure: Humans are terrible at predicting the future. Numerous studies have shown that even laser-focused "experts" in a particular field are bad at both short-range and long-range forecasting of events. So, who makes the best predictions? The same studies have shown that well-read people with diverse interests have been better able to predict future events. Are there ways for a layperson to predict the likelihood of a famine? As an expert who understands his limitations, I give you a resounding "Maybe." If livestock start dropping dead from a virus, or freakish weather patterns destroy massive amounts of crops, you should stock up on some staple foods before their price or availability are impacted. Furthermore, you could take a more proactive approach and stock up now. Since we have no idea what tomorrow may bring, what's the harm in providing your family with a little extra security?

10 RAJPUTANA FAMINE OF 1869

1.5 million dead

In what was then the region of Rajputana, India, tens of millions of people were impacted and 1.5 million died after monsoon rains were lighter than normal. The region's troubles magnified in 1869, as the food shortage was accompanied by a cholera outbreak, a locust swarm, and a malaria epidemic.

9 GREAT PERSIAN FAMINE OF 1870-71

1.5–2 million dead

The 1870 drought in Persia led to a poor crop of wheat and barley, which were both Persian staple crops. This shortage caused unbearable inflation on grain prices, which led starving people to begin to eat grass, pets, and possibly even other human beings.

8 RUSSIAN FAMINE OF 1601-03

2 million dead

The Russian famine of 1601–03 was the result of a combination of political unrest (dubbed the Time of Troubles) and record cold temperatures (due to a Peruvian volcano eruption cooling the atmosphere). Crops failed, leading to political instability and, ultimately, the deaths of some 2 million Russian citizens.

7 JAVA FAMINE OF 1944-45

2.4 million dead

In World War II, the Japanese occupation of the Dutch East Indies led to slave labor, torture, execution, and starvation, along with many other war atrocities. Between 1944 and 1945, around 2.4 million people died as a result of the famine in the region.

6 RUSSIAN FAMINE OF 1921

5 million dead

Overwhelmed by the aftermath of World War I and impacted by the Civil Wars of 1918–20, the famine in Bolshevik Russia claimed approximately 5 million lives between 1921 and 1922.

5 SOVIET FAMINE OF 1932-1933

3–8 million dead

Just a decade after the Bolshevik famine, the main grain-producing territories of the Soviet Union experienced a famine that was felt across the USSR, with a death toll estimate of 3 million to 8 million.

4 PERSIAN FAMINE OF 1917-1918

8–10 million dead

Persia suffered a second famine less than 50 years after the Great Persian famine. Far more severe, this catastrophe killed as many as 8 to 10 million (one-quarter of the population of northern Iran). The Persian government placed the blame on the British, though the matter is still disputed.

3 GREAT BENGAL FAMINE OF 1770

10 million dead

The lack of monsoon rain in 1769 left the region of Bengal, India, with a critically low rice harvest. That, combined with the policies of the Mughal Empire and the British East India Company, created a famine that killed as many as a third of Bengal's population.

2 CHALISA FAMINE OF 1783-84

More than 11 million dead

An unusual El Niño weather pattern is believed to be responsible for the Chalisa Famine of 1783–84, which affected South Asia and India. India was hit hardest, with losses greater than 30 percent in communities around Delhi.

1 GREAT CHINESE FAMINE OF 1959-61

Up to 43 million dead

The most lethal famine in recorded history had an official death toll reported at 15 million, though unofficial estimates place it between 20 and 43 million people. A combination of bad weather, worse political reforms, and economic malpractice devastated urban and rural populations alike.

MAKE ADJUSTMENTS What do you do if you find yourself in a famine? How can you maximize your nutritional intake and minimize loss of energy? Any dieter knows that when you restrict your calories, your body goes into a thrifty mode for some time. This is our ancient protection from the cycles of feast and famine, and you don't even have to think about it. Your body naturally wants to adapt. You can also try the technique of "super chewing" your food. This has been done for centuries in situations with limited food. Simply chew each mouthful of food for as long as you can (until it's liquefied and there's nothing left). By grinding each bite into the smallest particles possible and incorporating excessive amounts of digestive enzymes from your saliva, you can increase your nutrient intake from each meal.

SIDE EFFECTS MAY VARY Historically, violence and theft are the companions of famine. As people become desperate, looting, robbery, and home invasions emerge as quick solutions to the problem of hunger. While these acts may dial down as the energy levels of the population plummet, the threat of violence in any disaster is a real and unsettling possibility.

DEFEND YOUR CALORIES They can't steal it if they can't find it. Among the many options for defending yourself and your calories, camouflage may be your best bet. It's nonconfrontational and it works. If you have limited room, fill the space under your bed with food. You could also think about the empty spaces in your walls. Interior walls—walls between rooms—that are

BAD IDEA

DON'T EAT PEOPLE It's true that people have fallen back on cannibalism in order to survive in desperate times, but it's a terrible idea. Even leaving aside the very real moral issues, this is not a healthy or sustainable source of calories for you. How much meat is really on a starving person? Someone who perished from starvation would likely be very thin and in poor condition. They may also be a source of diseases that you could easily contract in your weakened state. So how about attacking the problem of hunger from a different avenue? At the time of writing this, Kenya is experiencing the worst plague of crop-destroying desert locusts it has seen in 70 years. So, rather than eating people (victims of famine), how about eating the cause of famine (bugs)? Just 100 grams of cooked grasshopper contains 20.6 grams of protein, 6.1 grams of fat, and 3.9 grams of carbohydrates, plus essential micronutrients like iron and zinc.

covered in drywall or paneling usually don't have insulation. These hollow spots can store quite a bit of food. Open up the wall, load in your stuff, and do your best repair job. Tell only a trusted few about it.

If you have more room, consider using waterproof storage containers or even metal boxes (which have the benefit of being rodent-proof). Carefully packaged white rice, jars of honey, and many other grocery store items can fit the bill for nutrition and longevity.

GET YOUR VITAMINS A number of diseases can result from a deficiency in vitamins, minerals, and other essential nutrients. Your odds of survival increase when you know the signs, and know what to eat to address these terrible conditions.

NAME OF ILLNESS (MISSING NUTRIENT)	SIGNS/SYMPTOMS	HELPFUL TREATMENTS
XEROPHTHALMIA (VITAMIN A)	BLINDNESS FROM CHRONIC EYE INFECTIONS, POOR GROWTH, DRYNESS AND KERATINIZATION OF EPITHELIAL TISSUES	LIVER, FORTIFIED MILK, SWEET POTATOES, SPINACH, GREENS, CARROTS, CANTELOUPE, APRICOTS
RICKETS (VITAMIN D)	WEAKENED BONES, BOWED LEGS, OTHER BONE DEFORMITIES	FORTIFIED MILK, FISH OILS, SUN EXPOSURE
BERIBERI (THIAMIN)	NERVE DEGENERATION, ALTERED MUSCLE COORDINATION, CARDIOVASCULAR PROBLEMS	PORK, WHOLE AND ENRICHED GRAINS, DRIED BEANS, SUNFLOWER SEEDS
PELLAGRA (NIACIN)	DIARRHEA, SKIN INFLAMMATION, DEMENTIA	MUSHROOMS, BRAN, TUNA, CHICKEN, BEEF, PEANUTS, WHOLE AND ENRICHED GRAINS
SCURVY (VITAMIN C)	DELAYED WOUND HEALING, INTERNAL BLEEDING, ABNORMAL FORMATION OF BONES AND TEETH	CITRUS FRUITS, STRAWBERRIES, BROCCOLI
IRON-DEFICIENCY ANEMIA (IRON)	EXTREME FATIGUE, REDUCED GROWTH, INCREASED HEALTH RISK IN PREGNANCY	MEAT, SPINACH, SEAFOOD, BROCCOLI, PEAS, BRAN, WHOLE AND ENRICHED GRAINS
GOITER (IODINE)	ENLARGED THYROID GLAND, POOR GROWTH IN INFANCY AND CHILDHOOD, POSSIBLE MENTAL IMPAIRMENTS, CRETINISM	IODIZED SALT, SALTWATER FISH
KWASHIORKOR (PROTEIN)	AFFECTS INFANTS, PRODUCING A SWOLLEN BELLY DUE TO EDEMA , POOR GROWTH, FATAL DIARRHEA, APATHY, HAIR DISCOLORATION, AND SKIN SORES THAT WON'T HEAL	EASY-TO-DIGEST PROTEIN

TOP 10 FOODS TO STORE

1 WHITE RICE Most of the following supplies are nicknamed "forever foods," as they will virtually last forever when stored in airtight containers with oxygen absorbers to keep them fresh. These foods should be kept in a cool, dry, dark location and protected from pests. One of the crown jewels of the collection is white rice. This carb-rich food provides almost 1,700 calories per pound (uncooked), and doesn't need any preparation besides boiling. Don't try to go the heathy route by storing brown rice; it will last only a short time before it goes rancid, thanks to its higher fat content. Stick to the white rice, and you'll have food for years.

2 SALT Today, salt is very common and cheap, but long ago, certain cultures traded salt as literally worth its weight in gold. It was so valuable, in fact, that Roman soldiers were paid with salt (and it's from this custom we still use the word *salary* for payment). In modern times, iodized salt is used as flavoring—necessary to help you get down the more unappetizing options you might be stuck with in a survival scenario. Salt also provides necessary nutrients — specifically, sodium and iodine; they're available in other foods, but you can die withou them, so, why not have a supplement? Lastly, you can also use salt to preserve many foods, like meat and vegetables, extending their life spans.

3 SUGAR Your doctor, your dentist, and I all agree: Ordinary white table sugar is bad for your heath and your teeth. But the infinite shelf life and high calories of this sweet substance do make it a great staple food item. You can dump a little sugar in almost anything to improve the taste and boost the calorie content. You can also turn that table sugar into many different things, including candy and alcohol. Every pound of sugar will provide over 1,700 calories, and it will last for decades if you keep it dry and out of the reach of pests. Even if your sugar turns into rock-hard brick, it's still good; just chisel off little pieces as needed and think of them as your end-times sugar cubes!

4 ENRICHED FLOUR No, it isn't wholesome like whole-wheat flour or whole-kernel wheat seeds (aka wheat berries). But do you really want to choke down "health food" during doomsday? Not me—give me the bleached and enriched all-purpose flour. Just shy of 1,700 calories per pound, this stuff can be turned into gravy and dumplings with only boiling water for preparation. If baking is an option, try bread, cookies, and other baked goods. The hardest part about working with flour is learning to cook from scratch. This can be very challenging, especially on an uneven heat source (like a fire), but it's worth the trouble.

5 PASTA There's no need to cobble together some kind of postapocalyptic oven when the grid goes down—not if you have water, fire, a big pot, and some pasta. Comparable to the other staple carbohydrates listed here (at, like flour or rice, almost 1,700 calories per pound), dried pasta is a great long-term storage food. Choose varieties that pack down tightly. A pound of squiggly noodles will take up a lot more room that a pound of spaghetti or couscous. Add some spice to your meals by storing oils, jarred sauces, and herbs that will make the pasta tasty and familiar for you and family members. Don't store these flavorings in your food buckets, as they won't last as long, and be sure to rotate them frequently for freshness.

Your doomsday pantry isn't just a bulwark against the end times. Situations such as a power outage or a blizzard can often strand us in our homes in need of nutrition. And, in an unexpected supply disruption due to epidemics or other issues, you'll have supplies to fall back on.

6 **DRIED BEANS** Dried beans provide welcomed dietary variety and nutrients, but not all beans are equal. Read the package. White beans (aka navy beans) will generally provide the most calories (about 850 a pound), but a mixture of different legumes will diversify your diet nicely. As with the pasta and rice, all you need is a pot of boiling water to prepare them, though they do perform better when soaked prior to cooking. In addition to protein and fiber, beans contain many micronutrients like copper, folate, iron, magnesium, manganese, phosphorus, potassium, and zinc.

7 **POWDERED MILK** While it isn't the best-tasting beverage, powdered milk does provide good nutrition. Some companies produce a powdered whole milk that is packaged for long-term storage, but when shopping at the local grocery store, choose powdered nonfat milk for the longest storage life. Use it to make plain milk for drinking, stir in chocolate milk mix to make it taste better, or add it to recipes where milk is needed. For the diehard prepper, pack a 5-gallon bucket with little Mylar bags of powdered milk with oxygen absorbers, rather than using one big Mylar bag. Powdered nonfat milk provides 1,600 calories per pound.

8 **HONEY** Honey is a very strange food—most people know that it comes from bees, but few people actually know the how: Through a careful series of processes, bees suck up flower nectar, digest it, regurgitate it, and evaporate it to make honey. That's right, honey is bee barf. You're welcome. That aside, honey is also a superfood, with an indefinite life span. One pound of honey provides 1,360 calories. It can be eaten as food, applied to wounds to prevent infection, or turned into mead (a sweet, honey-based wine). Just don't give it to babies, as it can cause infant botulism.

9 **POTATO FLAKES** Often forgotten and remarkably versatile, instant potato flakes can be transformed into many delicious comfort foods. With just boiling water, potato flakes can become mashed potatoes or potato soup. By blending them into flour, you can make dense and tasty potato bread. Add some water and onions to make stiff potato "dough," pat it out into flat disks, and you can sizzle up some little fried potato cakes like Mom used to make. While dry potato flakes contain about 100 calories per ounce, comparable to pasta, sugar, and flour, potato flakes are a very fluffy staple food (meaning that you won't get too many pounds in each storage bucket). But this staple is so useful, why not stock additional buckets of it?

10 **OIL** Of our top ten, salt, sugar, and honey last indefinitely—even without oxygen absorbers or desiccant. Even if the salt and sugar solidify into a brick, just chop some off. It's still good. Similarly, the honey can get hard and crystallize, but it's still safe to use (just heat it to melt it into a familiar form). The other six foods can last for three decades or more when packed in Mylar bags with enough oxygen absorbers (1,500 cc to 2,000 cc in 5-gallon volumes). That brings us to number ten, which is oil. This has the shortened life span of the foods on this list, and you'll need to rotate your jugs of oil annually, but this stock food is too valuable to ignore. A gallon of veggie oil has almost 32,000 calories!

COMPANION GARDENING Back in World War II, communal Victory gardens often meant the difference between having fresh food and going without. These gardens were so successful that, despite other hardships, many folks were actually healthier than ever, due to rationing of meat and an abundance of vegetables. If you have trusted neighbors, consider banding together to turn a vacant lot or shared yard space into nature's own produce department. If that's not an option, grow your own. This chart lists some common veggies for your own garden that which can be planted together (or not) depending on factors such as growing periods, or competition for resources.

PLANT	FRIEND	FOE
BEANS	CORN, CABBAGE, CUCUMBERS	GARLIC/ONIONS
CARROTS	LETTUCE, PEAS	STRAWBERRIES, CABBAGE
CELERY	BEANS, CABBAGE FAMILY, SPINACH, TOMATOES	POTATOES
CORN	BEANS, CUCUMBERS, MELONS, PEAS, PUMPKINS, SQUASH	CABBAGE, TOMATOES, CELERY
CABBAGE FAMILY	POTATOES, BEETS, CELERY, GARLIC/ONIONS	TOMATOES, BEANS, PEPPERS, STRAWBERRIES
GARLIC/ONIONS	CARROTS, BEETS, STRAWBERRIES, TOMATOES, LETTUCE, CABBAGE	PEAS, BEANS
POTATOES	BEANS, CORN, CABBAGE, EGGPLANT	PUMPKIN, CUCUMBER, SQUASH, MELONS, SUNFLOWER
SQUASH	CORN	POTATOES
TOMATOES	ONION, CARROTS, CELERY	CABBAGE FAMILY, POTATOES

CONTAINER-FRIENDLY PLANTS

Some plants need lots of room underground in order to develop their massive root systems, while others just don't need that much footprint. In general, you should skip tall vegetables such as corn and those with trailing vines, such as pumpkins. Focus on herbs, tough perennials, root crops, and salad plants for the best results in your urban Eden.

WHAT YOU PLANT	WHAT THEY NEED
CILANTRO, CHIVES, BASIL, AND PARSLEY	HAVE TO BE REPLANTED EACH YEAR
ROSEMARY, MINT, THYME, AND SAGE	PERENNIALS THAT LAST FOR YEARS.
POTATOES, BEETS, AND RADISHES	DO BETTER IN COOL CONDITIONS
SWEET POTATOES	IDEAL FOR VERY WARM AREAS
LETTUCE AND SPINACH	CAN HANDLE SHORT DAY LENGTH OR LOW LIGHT
CUCUMBER AND CHERRY TOMATOES	DO WELL IF THEY HAVE ENOUGH SPACE AND LIGHT
GREEN BEANS AND PEPPERS	CAN HANDLE HEAT AND DRY CONDITIONS
PEAS AND KALE	CAN HANDLE VERY COLD WEATHER

RECIPE FOR SUCCESS

NATURAL PEST CONTROL Insect pests have plagued farmers since the very first patch of crops were planted. It often feels like you have a choice between eating poison-covered food or losing crops to hungry pests. But you can take a third option by mixing up a nontoxic, DIY pest-control spray from easily obtained ingredients. If you search for "nontoxic pest control" online, you'll find dozens and dozens of recipes. This is one of my favorites for most nasty critters.

ORGANIC ORANGE SUPER SPRAY

Supplies:

1 spray bottle

3 tablespoons (44 ml) of liquid organic castile soap

1 ounce (30 ml) of organic orange oil

1 gallon (3.8 l) jug of water

Directions:

Mix the liquids in a 1-gallon (3.8-l) jug. Shake well, and pour some of the mix into the spray bottle. Spray hard-shelled insect pests with extreme prejudice. Add 1 Cup (237 ml) of diatomaceous earth to the mix in a non spray container for soft-bodied invaders, such as slugs and caterpillars.

AUTOMATIC WATERING SYSTEM Most gardens are happier when watered regularly and in the early morning. But who has time for that when there are so many other chores to do at your off-grid ranch? This is where timers and other automatic devices can come in handy when attached to soaker hoses or drip lines for watering. These can be programmed for specific times on daily or multiday schedules. Morning is best, since water droplets at midday can act like magnifying lenses, actually burning the leaves. The a.m. shower is also better for disease prevention. Evening watering can promote fungal disease in plants susceptible to these ailments. To conserve water, set up your self-watering garden with soaker hoses or drip lines. This wastes less water than sprinkler systems, and delivers the water right where it's needed—at the roots.

THE SECRET GARDEN

Obviously, tomatoes, peppers, and sweet corn taste great, but they are obviously food to anyone wandering by. In a time of crisis, it would be easy for almost anyone to justify stealing the fruits of your hard labor. One solution is to grow a secret garden of just root crops. Only a savvy gardener will know what these plants look like above ground, and root crops are a relatively high-calorie food that can be stored in the ground where they grow. This can be a great benefit if you feel that break-ins, robberies, or home lootings are likely in your area during an emergency, as your food will be safely hidden in the ground.

HIDE A SUBURBAN FOOD PLOT One of the best ways of hiding your garden in a suburban or urban backyard is to grow some food that won't even look like food to the casual passerby—and don't just plant them inside a traditional garden plot. Plant your crops in flower beds, containers, and other places throughout your property that look like ornamental plantings rather than proper garden beds. Avoid rows and orderly planting. Make it look random and weedy for some camouflage. You can even scatter them on property edges to blend in with local weeds and brush. Another added benefit to using this dispersed planting strategy: By avoiding a dense concentration of the same plant type, the unique scent of those plants is dispersed. This may make individual plants harder for pests to find, for natural, pesticide-free bug control.

GO UNDERGROUND Another way that you can disguise your crops is by going underground—literally! If you focus your efforts on growing high-calorie root crops, your food will remain safely hidden under the dirt instead of growing tall and tempting hungry passersby—especially if the plants that you grow are not set in orderly rows, but each sprouting up from a different random spot. Consider planting white potatoes, sweet potatoes, peanuts (in warmer climates with sandy soil), turnips, rutabagas, parsnips, carrots, and Jerusalem artichokes. (These plants look like tall flowers but hide tasty edible tubers stealthily underground.

Start planting your sweet potato slips and peanuts in mid-spring, once the last frost is gone. The other plants are hardier and can be planted in early spring. Plant these hidden crops in places with at least eight hours of uninterrupted sunlight each day. Water the veggies regularly if rain is scarce and monitor them for pests.

EAT YOUR WEEDS Many common weeds are actually perfectly edible wild plants. Chickweed, purslane, lamb's quarters, dandelion, curly dock, amaranth, wild onion, plantain, and plenty of other wild edibles pop up in my garden beds throughout the year. Those weeds have parts that are edible raw or cooked, each packed with nutrition. When appropriately prepared, many are even delicious. Dandelion flowers that are battered and deep-fried are one of my favorite wild treats, and they are loaded with vitamin A. Chickweed and purslane are excellent in salads and full of important minerals. You might start to wonder why you're not just growing weeds, since they are so wholesome and prolific. Once you learn to positively identify these persistent weeds, you'll see them throughout the year in your garden and virtually everywhere else.

WARD OFF CRITTERS Even if you cleverly hide or defend your bounty from human pests, deer and rabbits aren't so easily bamboozled. For hungry deer and rodents, the nonstealthy solution is tall fences (with sunken chicken wire to keep out digging varmints). Or try peeing around the perimeter (yes, really). The scent will scare off most critters.

LEARN TO FORAGE You'll start to see food everywhere when learning to identify wild edible plants. This fascinating—and savory—field of study is a great companion to your gardening skills, since so many garden weeds are actually food too. In its most basic form, learning to forage is learning how you can identify safe foods, differentiate them from common look-alikes, and prepare them as food. Of course, you'd need to pay attention to details and have 100-percent positive identification of the plant. This is usually safest when done with a good field guide. These books often contain keys which group and differentiate plants by flower color, leaf patterns, or branch patterns. They may also be grouped by season. Whatever you do, be sure that the plant is the species you believe it to be. If you have any doubts, don't eat it!

chickweed   purslane   lamb's quarters   dandelion

curly dock   amaranth   plantain   wild onion

RECOVER FROM FAMINE WITH 'ATMIT'

Famine victims and relief organizations have used highly nutritious porridge to fight famine—and it works. This thin gruel is high in calories and protein, and easily digestible. Originally from Ethiopia, its recipe frequently uses staple foods such as oat flour, powdered milk, and sugar, supplemented by vitamins and minerals. Easy to prepare and eat, *atmit* can be digested by those who are so severely malnourished that they cannot take in solid food. Frequently adjusted for better nourishment, the formula was revised in 2009, and that same year, the Church of Jesus Christ of Latter-day Saints sent 700 tons (1.4 million pounds) of the new formula to Ethiopia. The new recipe is simple: 51 percent oat flour, 25 percent sugar, 23 percent nonfat dried milk, and 2 percent powdered micronutrient blend. Just add clean water and stir.

COUNT CALORIES (NO, NOT LIKE THAT) When you're growing your own food, it all comes down to calories. You can't live off salad. There simply aren't enough calories and nutrients in leafy veggies to sustain a human being. And the really tasty stuff isn't the answer either. Tomatoes, peppers, and similar flavorful plants are disturbingly low in calories. Rather than growing a bunch of space-hogging, low-cal vegetables, try these healthy, higher-calorie crops instead. Peanuts and sunflowers will be your highest-calorie crops (around 160 calories per ounce), followed by soybeans, navy beans, chickpeas, kidney beans, black-eyed peas, and dry shelling beans (around 100 calories per ounce). Let the beans fully form and dry out for maximum calories. Potatoes are another high-calorie crop (providing around 200 calories per spud).

DON'T WORRY THAT WINTER IS COMING
Unlike Ned Stark, you're going to be a survivor (so long as you don't lose your head!). But once the temperatures begin to drop, your garden will also need to adapt. While most plants require warm weather in order to grow, some veggies can move the water out of their vulnerable cells as the temperature approaches freezing. The ice crystals form in open spaces between cells, then melt and reabsorb into the plant cells when the temperatures rise again. Only a prolonged deep freeze can kill the sturdiest of these cool-weather crops. Agriculturalists divide veggies into categories depending on how well that crop is likely to hold up when the mercury drops. Light frost-tolerant plants can handle temperature ranges as low as 28 to 32 °F (-2 to 0 °C). These include artichokes, arugula, beets, carrots, peas, and chard. Hard frost-tolerant veggies include broccoli, cabbage, garlic, kale, spinach, and more.

9 ZOMBIES

Why are zombies so feared? Whether they come from necromancy, chemical weapons, or a mutated virus, our morbid fascination with the mindless cannibals may reflect our fear of the unknown, our discomfort in crowds, or our collective worry about an impending disaster. Perhaps it's simpler, based in zombies' uncanny knack at sensing outsiders in their midst or, simpler yet, because of the idea that our loved ones could turn on us.

According to a 2019 YouGov survey, the younger generation seems to take the threat more seriously than their elders. Nearly a quarter of millennials have a zombie apocalypse plan—10 percent more than Gen Xers, and almost 20 percent more than baby boomers; naturally, people in urban zones (21%) worry more about zombies than those in rural areas (11%). The most common plan involves gathering weapons, followed by holing up in a secure location. Other plans include rallying with friends and family, relocating, and fighting back. Alarmingly, 12 percent surveyed refused to share their secret plans, and just under 2 percent suggested that they would "switch sides" (either helping the zombies as a human or intentionally turning into a zombie).

◀ Twenty-two percent of America's postgrads have a zombie plan (8% higher than those with a four-year degree).

▶ The percentage of Americans who would stock up on weapons and ammo as their main zombie survival strategy.

▲ The average number of Americans who claim to have a zombie-apocalypse plan.

IMPROVE YOUR ODDS

On the off chance that I'm wrong and zombies become an actual problem, isolating yourself from the undead hordes would be a key tactic for your survival. They can't bite you if they can't reach you. Consider taking up residence on a deserted island (providing you have the resources to grow your own food until the crisis is over). You might also want to head to a colder climate. If the undead are really dead, they shouldn't be able to keep warm in a deeply cold climate. By that thinking, a field of frozen-solid zombies would be a good sign that you've reached a safe zone—but stay armed!

THE EARTH MOVES

IS IT LIKELY TO HAPPEN?

At any given time, there's a volcano erupting somewhere and quakes are a daily event in certain areas. It's unlikely that one will ruin your day (or life!), but it's possible.

HOW BAD COULD IT REALLY BE?

Little tremors and oozing lava are no big deal, but the biggest quakes have killed tens of thousands, and a super volcano could mean global catastrophe.

CAN I IMPROVE MY ODDS?

Besides moving to a more geologically stable part of the world, form a plan and note evacuation routes, both around your hometown and as you travel.

THE EARTH SEEMS SOLID ENOUGH—UNTIL IT ISN'T. SOMETIMES YOU'RE IN THE WRONG PLACE AT THE WRONG TIME, WHEN A VOLCANO BLOWS OR A BIG QUAKE STRIKES, BUT THERE ARE OFTEN WARNING SIGNS, AND YOU CAN ALWAYS DO SOMETHING TO INCREASE YOUR CHANCES OF SURVIVAL.

When good ol' terra firma isn't as firm as we'd like, it can be anywhere from terrifying to deadly. But what actually causes quakes? Earthquakes are the result of one of four different events: tectonic movement, volcanic activity, underground collapses, and huge explosions.

TECTONIC These quakes occur due to movement in the tectonic plates of the Earth's rocky crust. When the tectonic plates shift quickly or slide over each other, an earthquake can result.

VOLCANIC This type of earthquake is the result of geological movement caused by volcanic activity.

COLLAPSE These small earthquakes are the caused when underground voids—like caverns or mines—collapse and create seismic waves in the earth's surface.

EXPLOSION Another small earthquake type, these tremors are caused by something blowing up, either aboveground (such as a building demolished by charges) or belowground (as with historic nuclear weapons testing exercises).

In earthquakes caused by explosions or collapses, the minor trembling of the ground doesn't pose much danger—we'd actually be at much greater risk of falling in a sinkhole or being vaporized by the nuke. In the other two scenarios, though, the quake does pose a serious threat. Seismic damage can destroy the structures and landscape around you, cause buildings to collapse, topple trees, and set off landslides.

Earthquakes kill roughly 8,000 people yearly—an estimated 13 million deaths over the last 4,000 years. The deadliest known earthquake hit Shanxi, China, in 1556, and resulted in the deaths of an estimated 830,000 people. If that's not bad enough, earthquake-induced tsunamis pose a serious risk to those near large bodies of water. Remember Fukushima?

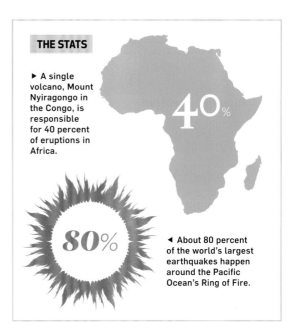

THE STATS

▶ A single volcano, Mount Nyiragongo in the Congo, is responsible for 40 percent of eruptions in Africa.

40%

80%

◀ About 80 percent of the world's largest earthquakes happen around the Pacific Ocean's Ring of Fire.

CONTROL YOUR KITCHEN It's never a bad idea to disaster-proof your home—especially in earthquake country. The same cabinet latches used for childproofing kitchen cabinets and drawers do a great job keeping dishes, canned food, and other supplies from flying out during a quake.

STRAP THE TALL STUFF Bolt or strap tall items (like bookcases and water heaters) to the wall studs that lie behind them; this will keep them from falling over.

DODGE DANGEROUS DECOR Don't place any potential hazards loose in a high location. Don't use picture frames with a glass covering, and secure hanging pictures to studs, not just the drywall.

PREPARE YOUR PANTRY Avoid using glass jars and bottles in your emergency food and water storage. They break too easily, bumping into each other or falling to the floor in an earthquake. That soggy heap of spoiling food and broken glass isn't going to help anyone after a disaster.

STOCK UP NOW In addition to stocking the normal supplies you'd need in a disaster (like nonperishable food, bottled water, and a first aid kit), it's smart to have earthquake-specific supplies in place. Purchase a utility shutoff wrench and keep it in a handy place. Get a medium-sized pry-bar, a bright flashlight, and some heavy gloves.

Keep these (and a sturdy pair of shoes or boots) beside your bed. The pry bar can be essential when trying to open windows and doors that are stuck shut thanks to the house shifting. The flashlight can give you valuable light in the event that the earthquake knocks out the power at night. The footwear and gloves can protect you from getting injured by broken glass and other hazards.

ASSESS THE HAZARDS Imagine that there's a major earthquake right now. What would be happening in your immediate surroundings? Your imagination can be a useful tool as you earthquake-proof your home. Imagine the things that would fall, and figure out either a way to keep them from falling or a better place they could be. Imagine the things that would be damaged by the movement of floors, walls, and ceilings, and determine the safest spot you could take shelter. For example, near the windows would be a terrible place to seek shelter. Glass moves and breaks in strange patterns during earthquakes, and these broken pieces can be deadly if they fall on you—or if you fall on them. Similarly, staircases can be a deathtrap in an earthquake. If you're on top of a staircase, the treads can cut into you if the building collapses—and if you're underneath, the stairs can detach from the landing and crush you.

DROP, COVER, AND HOLD So, where should you shelter during an earthquake? If you're outside and away from anything that could fall on you, stay there. If you're indoors, drop, cover, and hold. Drop to the ground and take cover under the nearest protective surface—such as a desk or table—and away from hazards such as windows and loaded shelves. The majority of deaths in earthquakes are due to falling objects or debris, so taking cover is essential. Once you've done that, hold onto something to stay anchored, bend over to protect your internal organs, and cover the back of your neck with your spare hand. Don't leave until the shaking has stopped completely.

LIVE ON A BUDGET Just the word *budget* is painful to most people, but it's a necessary tool to use during tough times. Control your spending carefully—otherwise, your spending might end up controlling you. Cut the obvious wastes of money in your household, then cut some more.

DON'T HUNKER IN A DOORWAY The old advice of standing in a doorway during an earthquake is no longer the right approach. In former times, doorways were built with heavier and stronger framing around them. Today, doorframes are built into walls with the cheapest, lightest, and most minimal lumber allowed. They are essentially a big hole in your wall. If the door jamb falls forward or backward, you will still get crushed by the ceiling. And should the door jamb fail horizontally, people have actually been cut in half by a collapsed doorway. In any event, don't stay under any doorways in a quake!

T / F

EARTHQUAKES ARE LINKED TO THE WEATHER

FALSE While I've never stuck my head out the window and said, "Wow, those clouds sure look like an earthquake is coming," some people in the past have thought exactly that. People have believed that there is a link between earthquakes and the weather since at least the 4th century BCE. Our forebears were convinced not only that they would see strange lights in the sky before or during an earthquake, but also that certain weather patterns were "earthquake weather." While there is some anecdotal evidence that hurricanes have caused tremors, and there is a long-held belief that hot weather can play a role in quakes, most geologists reject the idea of earthquake weather—both as a cause of earthquakes and a result of them.

TURN IT OFF You're not out of danger when the quake ends. You have to worry about aftershocks (additional earthquakes), and ensure that damaged utilities aren't a threat. Find out where your electrical, gas, and water shutoffs are located in your home or business. Keep the necessary tools near them, so that you can turn them off quickly in case of quake damage to the lines.

If you suspect a relationship between earthquakes and volcanoes, you're right. Volcanic eruptions are sometimes caused by quakes—such as in the case of the 1980 Mount St. Helens eruption—and volcanoes can create their own earthquakes. That said, they are different geological phenomena. An active volcano is a vent from below the Earth's crust that is currently erupting, or has signs of erupting soon: small quakes beneath the volcano, landform swelling, and increased heat and gas from volcanic vents. Scientists define active as "having erupted within the last 10,000 years."

When volcanoes erupt, rock, lava, gases, and ash are ejected, varying from a slow and quiet stream of liquid rock flowing outward, to violent explosions of volcanic materials. With about 1,500 active volcanoes worldwide, there's plenty to go around, and these quiet giants usually show little of their potential threat. In fact, many volcanoes are so placid that nearly one in twenty people live within the danger zone of an active volcano. (That's 300 million people paying little mind to their explosive neighbors.) So, how are the threats different for a volcano than for an earthquake?

The heat, gases, and explosive power of volcanoes are deadly if you're close to an eruption, which can happen with little to no warning. Regardless of the type of eruption, you need to get away. Forget walking or running; drive away from the area if you can unless authorities notify you otherwise (such as in congested areas around Mount Vesuvius in Italy). It's usually best to head upwind and uphill, if possible. Aside from pyroclastic flows, choking ash, and lava bombs, you're trying to avoid the volcanic

SUPERVOLCANOES What makes a volcano a "supervolcano"? It's not the flowing cape or the colorful tights. A supervolcano is a high-powered volcano with eruptions of gargantuan proportions. Think "nuclear bomb with lava"—and with a near-nuclear ice age, thanks to all the ash expelled. Though incredibly rare, these eruptions are far more dangerous than any other seismic or volcanic events. And supervolcanoes lurk where most people don't realize— Yellowstone National Park in Wyoming contains an enormous crater formed after the blast of a supervolcano about 640,000 years ago. Since then, smaller eruptions have filled the caldera with lava and ash—including a sizeable eruption about 70,000 years ago. While that might seem like very old news, Yellowstone's caldera has been rising recently, and some experts suggest that it's not a matter of "if" the supervolcano will blow again, but "when."

gases. The most common one is carbon dioxide; the same stuff you breathe out can reach dangerously high concentrations after an eruption. A mere 3 percent carbon dioxide concentration causes dizziness, headaches, and trouble breathing. When the air has more than 15 percent CO_2, you can quickly lose consciousness and die. Other dangerous gases can be released in an eruption, including sulfur dioxide and hydrogen sulfide, which can both be deadly in even smaller amounts than CO_2.

VOLCANOES

Most eruptions can be cone shaped and grow over time (as material is ejected and it accumulates), though other volcano shapes are sometimes formed. Some volcanoes are even underwater. Sleeping or dormant volcanoes are those that were active in the past but are inactive—though they are capable of erupting again.

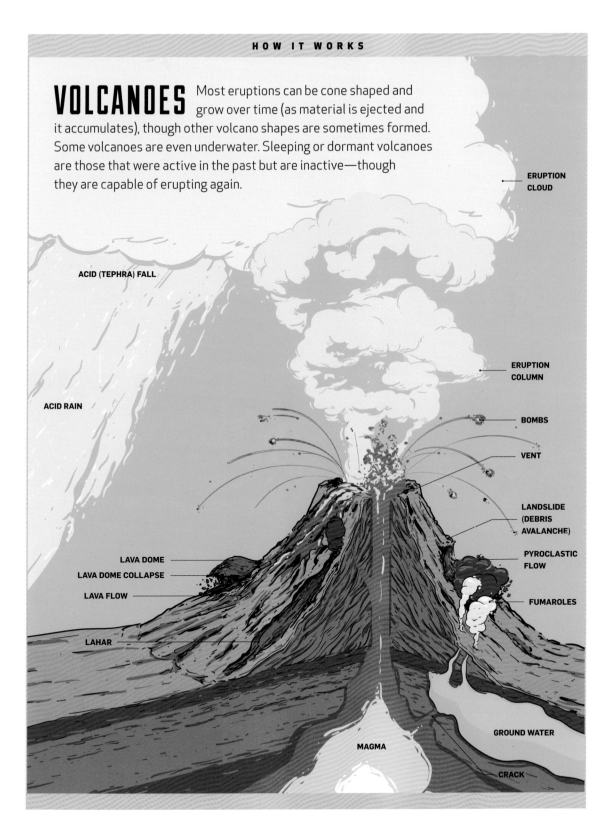

ERUPTION CLOUD

ACID (TEPHRA) FALL

ERUPTION COLUMN

ACID RAIN

BOMBS

VENT

LANDSLIDE (DEBRIS AVALANCHE)

PYROCLASTIC FLOW

LAVA DOME

LAVA DOME COLLAPSE

LAVA FLOW

FUMAROLES

LAHAR

GROUND WATER

MAGMA

CRACK

HOT SPOTS

Among the 1,500 or so active volcanoes or seismic regions around the world are these ten of the most potentially dangerous locations or recent eruptions.

1 MOUNT MERAPI—INDONESIA The most active volcano in Indonesia, which has spewed forth more lava than any other volcano on Earth.

2 MOUNT NYIRAGONGO—CONGO One of the largest, most active volcanic threats in Africa, with a huge lava lake in its main crater. Since 1882, it's erupted thirty-two times.

3 MOUNT VESUVIUS—ITALY Buried the city of Pompeii in 79 CE, but that doesn't stop people from living nearby. Naples is just nine miles away, boasting a population of 1 million people.

4 EYJAFJALLAJOKULL—ICELAND One of the world's most famous volcanoes right now, thanks to the 2010 eruption which affected more than 100,000 international flights. It's pronounced "EY-A-FYAT-LA-YO-KUTL."

5 MAUNA LOA—HAWAII The world's largest volcano, which has been erupting regularly for the past 700,000 years.

6 SANTA MARÍA—GUATEMALA Responsible for one of the three largest eruptions in the 20th century.

7 SAKURAJIMA—JAPAN The most active volcano in Japan, Sakurajima has erupted every year since 1955 and has caused thousands of deaths in the area.

8 GALERAS—COLOMBIA Rising 14,000 feet above sea level, Galeras has been active for millions of years. In 1993, it ironically erupted during a volcanology conference, killing six scientists who were attending.

9 SAN ANDREAS FAULT LINE—CALIFORNIA If the Big One ever hits California, it will be because of the San Andreas Fault—one of the longest fault lines in the world. The San Andreas is made up of many fault lines and runs more than 800 miles through California and Mexico.

10 NEW MADRID SEISMIC ZONE—EASTERN UNITED STATES An earthquake hot spot away from America's West Coast, this zone runs from Missouri and Arkansas, up toward southern Illinois. This area creates the most earthquake activity east of the Rocky Mountains.

ALEUTIAN TRENCH

RING OF FIRE

HAWAIIAN "HOT SPOT"

JAVA TRENCH

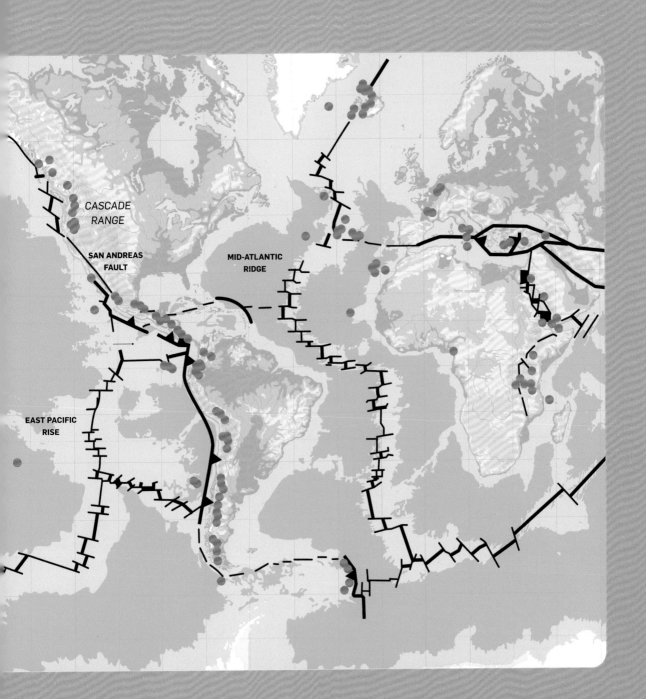

CASCADE
RANGE

SAN ANDREAS
FAULT

MID-ATLANTIC
RIDGE

EAST PACIFIC
RISE

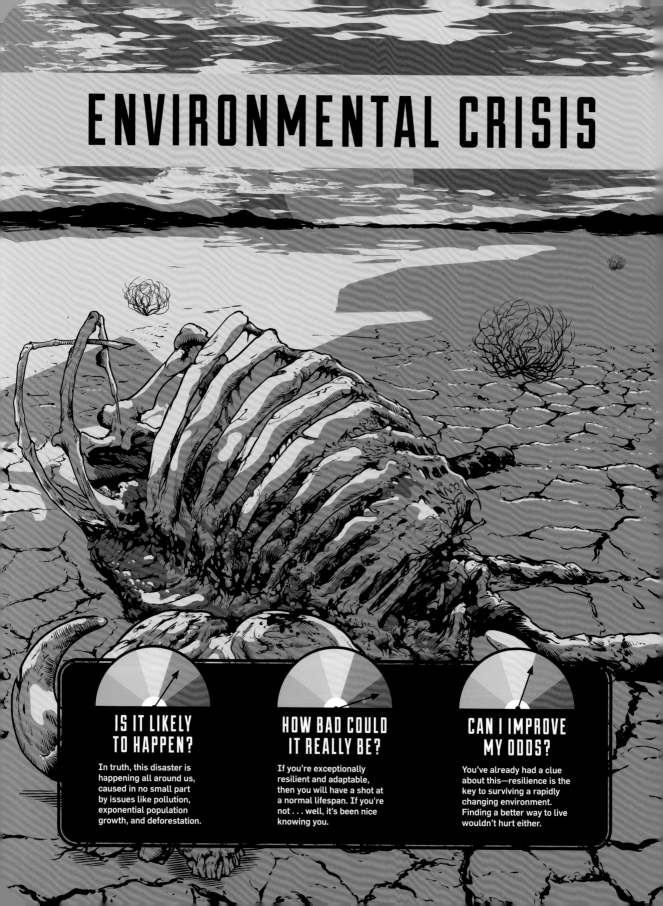

ENVIRONMENTAL CRISIS

IS IT LIKELY TO HAPPEN?

In truth, this disaster is happening all around us, caused in no small part by issues like pollution, exponential population growth, and deforestation.

HOW BAD COULD IT REALLY BE?

If you're exceptionally resilient and adaptable, then you will have a shot at a normal lifespan. If you're not . . . well, it's been nice knowing you.

CAN I IMPROVE MY ODDS?

You've already had a clue about this—resilience is the key to surviving a rapidly changing environment. Finding a better way to live wouldn't hurt either.

AN ENVIRONMENTAL DISASTER IS A RUINOUS EVENT CAUSED BY HUMAN ACTIVITY, ONE THAT CREATES LONG-TERM ECOLOGICAL HAVOC. LOCALIZED SITUATIONS LIKE OIL SPILLS AND NUCLEAR MELTDOWNS CAN ALTER AN ECOSYSTEM QUICKLY YET CREATE LONG-LASTING DAMAGE.

Even though our species appears to be doing well, with an ever-expanding population that is spread across the globe, the planet's rapidly dwindling resources and increasingly polluted environment tell another story altogether. The cost of our success can be seen in damaged biomes throughout the planet, especially in the wake of an environmental disaster. The after-effects of these events can include the loss of plant, animal, and human life, as well as ecosystem disruption so severe that the area is no longer habitable to humans (for example, the area becomes radioactive or turns into a desert). But wait, it gets worse.

We currently live in what's now known as the Anthropocene era, where human activity has strongly affected how the natural world functions. Some have contended that people cannot possibly cause damage of this scope. But this is, in fact, not a new concept: As early as 1873, the Italian geologist Antonio Stoppani described an "anthropozoic era," acknowledging the growing influence of humans on nature.

By now, the effects on atmosphere, ocean, and more are all definitely observable, and in some cases, even self-reinforcing (such as temperature increases from air pollution leading to drier, hotter weather, to less rain or snowfall, and thus to severe droughts). Even environments that have endured for thousands of years are going through such upheaval: Major rivers such as the Upper Missouri are drying up in a way not seen in over a millennium, even worse than the Dust Bowl period of the 1930s.

Animal and plant life are dying off rapidly as a result; according to the UN Environment Programme, an estimated 150 to 200 species of mammals, amphibians, birds, fish, insects, and plants are going extinct every day. Changing environments around the globe mean rare species are disappearing forever. We're losing another every eight or nine minutes; this extinction is nearly a thousand times the "normal" rate of loss—the greatest loss in biological diversity since the dinosaurs died out nearly 65 million years ago.

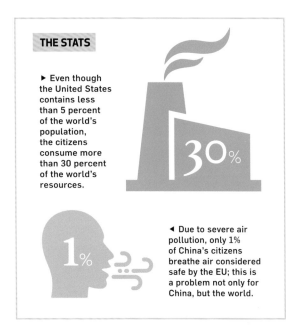

THE STATS

▶ Even though the United States contains less than 5 percent of the world's population, the citizens consume more than 30 percent of the world's resources.

30%

1%

◀ Due to severe air pollution, only 1% of China's citizens breathe air considered safe by the EU; this is a problem not only for China, but the world.

It's been said that the greatest civilizations aren't murdered by outsiders; they end up committing suicide instead. For one example, the mighty Western Roman Empire fell because it couldn't sustain its own expansion and consumption indefinitely, and its military forces were spread too thin, trying to control land from Britain to the Middle East. Plagued by religious discord and civil wars, as well as actual plagues, the Eternal City of Rome itself was sacked by the Vandals in 455, and the Empire was gone by 476, broken into smaller eastern and western empires that disintegrated in the decades and centuries after. But Rome did not fall due to military losses or plagues alone. Around this period in the early 500s CE, the climate also cooled, impacting agriculture, leading to crop shortages, and thus to starvation for many across Europe.

GOOD TO KNOW

THE "SEVEN GENERATIONS" PRINCIPAL

Looking back on history, it's possible to see some very thoughtful principals to live by. One of my favorites is the Native American concept of "Seven Generations." In this system of thinking, we consider the impact of our actions in our own lifetime, and the subsequent lives of seven generations of our descendants. So if we cut down a sapling today to make a bow, are we making the forest better or worse in our own generation, and then next, and the next, seven times removed from us. Before we reach a "point of no return", can we avert disaster by thinking about our legacy as much as we think about ourselves?

Rome isn't the only civilization to fall after overextending itself and then overconsuming resources during a period of unfavorable weather. The fall of the Anasazi people in the American Southwest, the Mayan civilization in Central America, the Tiwanaku people in South America, the Moai builders of Easter Island in the Pacific, and many other cultures have all coincided with abrupt changes in climate—typically leading to drought conditions. Since humanity is now supported by a global economy with a global reach for resources, are we immune to the vulnerabilities that our ancestors faced? Or are we all headed for a fall that will take everyone down together?

FACE THE PROBLEM

We can handle this problem the hard way or the harder way, now or later, but at some point we'll have to face facts: As a species, we can't live out of balance with our home planet. We can either make a worldwide shift in our stewardship of the Earth to limit further damage or keep up business as usual and run the world into the ground. Many experts say that we're in the six mass-extinction event in history. From the laundry list of things needing attention, here are some of the worst offenders.

FAILING BIODIVERSITY Every species matters, and as mentioned earlier, the loss of more than 100 species each day can have ramifications that can last forever. As plants and animals disappear, the balance of nature begins to disappear. We can fight back against the loss of biodiversity by focusing our spending on local foods and products and drastically reducing our consumption of unsustainable goods.

DIRTY WATER One of our world's most precious resources is water. Oil spills, garbage, and toxic chemicals are just a few of the unsavory materials that enter our waterways, by accident and deliberately. Protect our lakes, rivers, and oceans by getting educated about the causes and effects of water pollution, and demanding tougher environmental laws.

DEFORESTATION Trees provide oxygen, many of the foods we eat, medicines, lumber, and other vital resources across the planet. Wildfires, illegal logging, and excessive consumption all take a toll on the

MAKING A DIFFERENCE FOR THE FUTURE

It's not your fault if an asteroid hits our planet or a lethal strain of the flu emerges. This section, however, has a very different feel. It's people who cut down rain forests and spill oil, and it's consumers like us setting up the demand that leads to these disasters. How can you make a difference? If there was one thing you could do regularly, often, or daily to improve your odds of survival (and that of the world), it would be to conserve. That's right: Ese less of everything. "Reduce, reuse, and recycle" should be your daily mantra. Buy, eat, and throw away less. Eat locally grown food. Take fewer frivolous trips in your car, avoid eating foods shipped from half a world away, and think about the environmental impact of the things you buy. The Anthropocene era doesn't have to end bitterly for us if we plan for a future over the conveniences of today.

world's forest lands. Reduce your impact by seeking out recycled and organic products, and limiting the forest products you use (like paper and cardboard).

TOP 10 USES FOR A SHOVEL

1 **THE OBVIOUS: DIGGING!** The humble shovel dates to antiquity, with shovels made of animal shoulder bones appearing in the late Stone Age, and metal shovels originating in the Bronze age. The familiar shape of shovels today can be seen in China, as far back as 3,000 years ago. In all this time, shovels have been used for digging, scooping, and lifting materials. From dirt and poop, to snow and rocks, shovels allow us to move materials with greater ease than using our bare hands. In a survival setting, use your trusty shovel to dig a latrine, a grave, a garden, a cache, a cooking pit, an in-ground shelter and countless other fixtures that can improve your situation.

2 **CHOPPING** The sharp edge of a shovel and the leverage of the tool's handle can allow you to chop with a shovel, as if you were using a crude axe. When chopping soft materials, like live roots in the ground, you can stab downward with the shovel (like a spear) to chop off the unwanted woody growth. You can also swing it in an overhanded chop, much like an axe, to cut into harder materials. Flat-bladed shovels are often better at this off-label use than curved shovel blades, but beggars can't be choosers. While it's nowhere near as effective as a real hatchet, a sharp shovel can do a passable job when the right tools are lacking.

3 **COOKING** We mentioned digging of a cooking pit already, and while that's cooking adjacent, it's still digging. But when cookware is in short supply, a shovel can also serve as a cooking surface. This is best done with an unpainted steel shovel. Don't try to heat up a painted surface unless you intend to burn off the paint. Depending on the shovel's shape, it may make a passable baking surface for cooking thin breadlike cakes, or you can use it as a griddle to fry meats and vegetables. Keep in mind that heating the steel like this will soften it, but you can reharden it by heating the edge until it glows, and then quenching it in water.

4 **PRYING** With a long lever, even a small-framed person can move heavy items. Though it isn't meant to be used as a pry bar, a shovel can do a fair bit of pry work. The shovel handle provides the leverage and a rounded blade can be the pivot point. From prying stones out of the ground, to maneuvering logs into position, prying with a shovel can assist you in construction projects and many other tasks. Of course, all this comes with a warning. I've broken many shovels in my lifetime, and the vast majority have been broken while using them as pry bars. Be careful when you decide to use a shovel instead of an actual pry bar!

5 **FIGHTING** In a pinch, a shovel can be an effective close-range weapon (wielded like a spear or an axe). Modern military entrenching shovels still keep this function in mind. From American entrenching tools to the sharp-edged shovels of Russia's Spetsnaz special-forces units, these "blades on a stick" aren't just for digging. This is hardly a new concept: The idea of a slashing or chopping blade on a stick is ancient. The Japanese *naginata* and the European glaive are just two examples of pole arms from the postclassical warfare of Asia and Europe, which extend the fighter's range and striking power (thanks to the long shaft).

6 **WEDGING** Mechanical advantage is the secret behind the shovel's effectiveness. The shovel's sharp edge cuts into the soil, driven by body weight when a user steps on the blade's

The shovel came from the even more humble digging stick—literally just a sturdy branch or similar sized piece of wood used to jab into the soil and break it up to be moved out of the way by hand, or put to use elsewhere. But its simple origins don't limit its many possible utilities!

other end. Then the handle uses leverage to pop a chunk of soil out of the ground or lift a scoop of gravel. But a shovel is more than just a fancy lever. It's a wedging tool. When placed flat on the ground, a rounded shovel presents a ramp shape, which acts as an inclined plane. Jam the tip of the shovel under a door to wedge it shut for security or use it like a wheel chock to keep a cart or vehicle from rolling downhill.

7 EXTINGUISHING FIRES Whether you use the shovel to fling dirt on a fire and smother it, or you choose to beat the fire to death with the blade, this ancient digging tool can quickly kill a fire that's getting out of control. For best results, dig a fire pit to contain your fire, and leave a loose pile of dirt nearby. If the wind kicks up dangerously, blowing sparks up and out and threatening to start a wildfire, fling some of the dirt onto the blaze to drop its flames back down. Pour water, if necessary, onto the fire to finish it off. If the dirt doesn't smother the fire, you can dispatch the flames by striking the fuel with the shovel blade.

8 CUTTING It's big, broad, and awkward, but a sharpened shovel edge can do some rough cutting tasks, acting as a backup for your knife. Make sure the shovel is clean before attempting to cut up food or to open food packaging—other than that, slice away! Keep in mind that knife covers a broad category of tools, so it can be used in many ways. For example, the native Inuit people above the Arctic Circle have been transforming the large bones of whales and walruses into shovels for centuries. These bone shovels can be used by skillful crafters to carve blocks of snow used for building igloos, and for other carved snow and ice projects.

9 PADDLING We're not suggesting that you paddle your errant children with a shovel; that's cruel and excessive. Your shovel can, however, be a workable paddle for watercraft. The world's oldest canoe remnants were found in the Netherlands and are nearly 10,000 years old, though watercraft and their accompanying paddles may be tens of thousands of years old. The shovel is not an ideal propeller for your canoe or raft, but when you're up the creek without a paddle—well, you get the idea. Paddles aren't just for rowing along on the waterways, either: A medieval wooden paddle called a "beetle," among other names, was used to smack the dirt out of soapy laundry, well before washboards or washing machines were invented. Similarly, even up to the modern era, people have hung up their carpets or rugs on laundry lines, and have used beaters made of cane or wood to thrash the dust and debris out of them. Grab your shovel and get to swinging!

10 ANCHOR Speaking of watercraft, a shovel on the end of a rope can make a serviceable anchor for very small rafts and canoes. A shovel can also be driven into the ground to act as an anchor for ropes or cord, taking the place of a tent stake. This holds well in most soil types, but you may need something stronger for conditions such as loose sand and dry, shifting snow. The strongest anchor is nicknamed a deadman: Start by using the shovel to dig a small trench, perpendicular to the direction that your rope will be pulling. Tie the rope around the middle of the shovel, drop it in the trench, and then backfill it with your hands. Buried under dozens or hundreds of pounds of soil, this shovel-based anchor line will hold very well.

CATASTROPHIC EFFECTS

Ecological disasters can impact more than just plants and animals. Human health, economy, and agriculture can all be impacted for decades or longer by pollution, contamination, and the depletion of natural resources affected by such events.

CHERNOBYL DISASTER (1986) The meltdown and subsequent explosion at the Chernobyl Nuclear Power Plant in 1986 is considered the worst nuclear disaster in history. The official Soviet death toll of 31 is disputed, since approximately 50 emergency workers died of radiation poisoning and 4,000 people living in the three most contaminated former Soviet states near the facility have already died from radiation-induced cancers.

HANFORD NUCLEAR POLLUTION (1986) The Hanford Site near Richland, Washington, was once a plutonium manufacturing and processing facility. According to declassified US government documents, this site allowed radioactive waste to be released into the air, and worse still, released thousands of gallons of radioactive waste into the Columbia River during its operation between 1946 and 1986.

EXXON VALDEZ OIL SPILL (1989) A reportedly tired crew and an allegedly drunken captain may have played major roles in the *Exxon Valdez* oil tanker spill, which occurred in the Prince William Sound of Alaska on March 24, 1989. After the ship struck a reef, an estimated 10.8 million gallons of crude oil spilled into the pristine and remote waterway.

PRESTIGE OIL SPILL (2002) A structurally deficient oil tanker spilled 20 million gallons of heavy fuel oil off the coast of the region of Galicia, Spain, on November 13, 2002, after being struck by a storm.

KINGSTON FOSSIL PLANT SLURRY SPILL (2008) When the wall of a holding pond outside Kington, Tennessee, ruptured, 1.1 billion gallons of ash slurry spilled onto 300 acres, contaminating rivers and destroying homes.

DEEPWATER HORIZON OIL SPILL (2010) An explosion on an oil rig in the Gulf of Mexico killed 11 men and injured 17. It took five months to seal the well after spilling nearly 210 million gallons of crude oil.

FUKUSHIMA DAIICHI NUCLEAR DISASTER (2011) In the worst nuclear disaster since Chernobyl, an earthquake and tsunami on March 11, 2011, caused nuclear meltdowns, fires, and explosions, releasing radioactive material into the air and the Pacific Ocean. One death and 18 injuries were reported; more than 150,000 residents nearby also had to be evacuated. It is estimated that the cleanup will take 30 to 40 years.

8 STRANGERS

We get the word *xenophobia* from two Greek words, *xenos* ("stranger" or "foreigner") and *phobos* (which means "fear"). But is this a fear like the others on our list? Not really. This phobia doesn't give us the heebie-jeebies, like our fear of spiders or snakes. This condition can be a blend of both fear and hatred, focusing on individuals or groups that we perceive as strange, alien, or foreign.

The strong ties between xenophobia and racism are hard to ignore, but at the root of this "fear" is discrimination. It's a sense of "us" versus "them," and it's often based on physical appearances and national identity. Xenophobia can manifest itself as suspicion or revulsion, and it can escalate to open racism and hate crimes. This desire to eliminate the presence of outsiders is more common in certain cultures than others, but recent examples prove that this old human flaw is in no danger of going away. In September of 2019, South Africa made it into world news as twelve people were killed and hundreds arrested after mob violence broke out in Johannesburg and Pretoria. The attacks targeted foreign-owned shops and resulted in reprisal attacks in many places.

> **40%**

▲ In a multinational survey in 2013, many Indians (43.5%) and Jordanians (51.4%) did not want racially different neighbors.

▼ Only 6.5 percent of Pakistanis objected to a neighbor of a different race, making them more racially tolerant than even the Germans or the Dutch.

6.5%

< **5%**

▲ In a 2013 *Washington Post* report, the US, Canada, Australia, and many Latin American countries were the most tolerant; less than 5 percent were xenophobic.

IMPROVE YOUR ODDS

If you're worried about being the victim of a xenophobic or racist attack, it's smart to do your research before traveling. Some nations welcome strangers from other lands, as their economy may have a large benefit from tourism. Other countries, however, may have a less friendly welcome (or even a hostile attitude). If you're looking to quell feeling of xenophobia in yourself, consider the source. The root word *xeno* can be interpreted as "stranger," but people are no longer strangers after you get to know them. By looking for common ground with others, you might be surprised by all the things you share.

DEATH FROM ABOVE

IS IT LIKELY TO HAPPEN?

It's unlikely that a satellite will smash your car or a meteorite will land in your house, but sooner a later, a stray "bullet" may have your name on it.

HOW BAD COULD IT REALLY BE?

Threats can range from funny (like being smacked in the face with a fish pulled from the sea by water spout) to deadly (like the meteor that killed the dinosaurs).

CAN I IMPROVE MY ODDS?

With an asteroid strike, there's little to do about it. But if it's not close enough kill you on impact, your disaster-preparedness supplies and skills can help.

EVERY SCHOOLCHILD IS TAUGHT THAT AN ASTEROID KILLED THE DINOSAURS, AND THAT ALL HAPPENED A LONG TIME AGO. SO WE'RE SAFE NOW, RIGHT? (SPOILER ALERT: NOPE, WE ARE NOT, AND ASTEROIDS ARE JUST ONE OF THE MANY THINGS UP THERE THAT MIGHT RUIN YOUR DAY).

For such an empty place, outer space is awfully crowded with things that can kill us. Just for starters, there are asteroid impacts, gamma ray bursts, supernovae, coronal mass ejections, falling nuclear satellites, and the possibility of threats that are currently unknown to us. (We won't say it could be aliens. Although . . .) There are plenty of things that can strike out of the blue, and very few will improve your day if you happen to be there when they do.

ASTEROID STRIKE Asteroids and comets can penetrate our atmosphere at unimaginable speed and strike the Earth with massive power. From the asteroid strike that wiped out the dinosaurs to more recent events, the threat is small on any given day, but another major strike is almost inevitable. Our ability to survive would depend on the size of the object, the location of the strike, and our proximity to it. The current hope is that we can nuke an incoming body before it hits our atmosphere. Fingers crossed!

SOLAR FLARE Our sun is both a source of life and a source of peril, especially for technology-dependent societies. While it will be billions of years before the sun grows to a size that will burn away our atmosphere and ruin our world as a vacation spot forever, we do have to be concerned with solar flare eruptions now.

There are three classes of solar flares, C-class (weak and harmless), M-class (stronger but harmless), and X-class (the strongest, likely to disable communications and power grids). These are strong enough to disrupt satellites and communication systems here on Earth and potentially overload electrical grids. The event would be survivable but awfully inconvenient.

SPACE JUNK With more and more objects being sent into space, there's an increasing risk that these objects will fall back down. So far, there has been only one legitimate case of space junk striking a person. But who knows—today might be your lucky day!

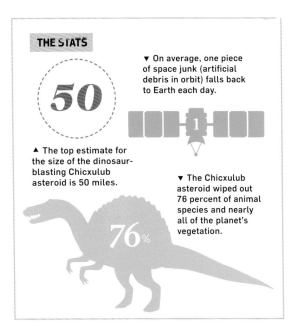

THE STATS

50

▼ On average, one piece of space junk (artificial debris in orbit) falls back to Earth each day.

1

▲ The top estimate for the size of the dinosaur-blasting Chicxulub asteroid is 50 miles.

▼ The Chicxulub asteroid wiped out 76 percent of animal species and nearly all of the planet's vegetation.

76%

WHAT IS AN ELE? Not every asteroid impact or exploding star will reset the Earth's dominant species and climate, but some do. It's happened before, and it's nearly inevitable that it will happen again. When the chessboard of life is swept clean, this is called an Extinction-Level Event, or ELE. Also known as a mass extinction, this is widespread drop in biodiversity in a short span of time. There appear to have been five (though some experts count as many as twenty) major mass-extinction events in the past 540 million years. The most recent event was the Cretaceous–Paleogene extinction event about 66 million years ago. Contenders for future ELE events include supervolcano eruptions, massive tectonic plate shifts, an asteroid strike, a nearby star going nova or supernova, a gamma ray burst, and human activity. The current mass extinction, driven by human activity, has been dubbed "the sixth great extinction."

WATCH OUT BELOW!

Our little blue planet has seen its share of major asteroid impacts over the eons, and while the evidence of the earliest strikes has long since eroded away, the evidence of more recent strikes can be seen around the world. The Tunguska event was the large explosion of an asteroid or comet over a wilderness area in Russia, on June 30, 1908. It's believed that this object was a few hundred feet in diameter and it exploded a few miles above the ground, flattening trees over an area of 830 square miles (2,150 sq. km) and equal to the power of 1,000 atomic bombs dropped on Hiroshima. Much larger than Tunguska, the Chicxulub asteroid was a celestial body believed to be between 7 and 50 miles (11–81 km) in diameter, that struck the Earth roughly 66 million years ago. Named after the present and nearby town of Chicxulub, Mexico, this asteroid strike is probably the reason you are a mammal and not a reptile today. What's the takeaway from these impact examples? The impact of a large celestial body striking our planet would be devastating. Asteroid and comet impacts present a danger, not just from being hit but also from the heat, radiation, debris, shockwaves, tsunamis, acid rain, volcanic eruptions, and related events that a strike would set in motion. This is why NASA and other groups carefully monitor near-Earth objects.

GET TO KNOW YOUR FRIENDLY LOCAL SPACE ROCKS

Not all spaceborne objects are created equal. These objects come in a wide range of sizes and materials. Here's the difference between meteors, meteorites, comets, asteroids, and other cosmic debris.

ASTEROID These are rocky objects that orbit our sun. Asteroids are much smaller than planets, but larger than meteoroids. Formed when our solar system was created, most of these ancient rocks float in an asteroid belt between Jupiter and Mars. A few, however, roam the system on orbits around the sun that bring them near Earth.

Asteroids range from a little larger than a pebble to several miles across.

METEOROID When two asteroids love each other very much, sometimes they crash into each other and pieces break off. These pieces, called meteoroids, can also be released by comets. Meteoroids are typically pebble-sized or smaller.

METEORS If a meteoroid enters the Earth's atmosphere, it is considered to be a meteor. Also known as shooting stars, these objects usually vaporize in the atmosphere and create a streak of light as they burn up. During certain times in the Earth's orbit around the Sun, our planet passes through meteor-rich areas in the solar system. On nights when see more meteors than normal, you're seeing a meteor shower. And when these meteoroids don't burn up completely in the atmosphere, the pieces of rock that strike the Earth's surface are called meteorites.

COMETS These objects orbit the Sun like asteroids, but instead of being composed of rock, they are made from ice, bits of rock, and dust. When their orbit moves toward the Sun, the vaporizing materials can be seen as the comet's tail. This is different

SHIFTING MAGNETIC POLES EQUAL DEATH

FALSE A geomagnetic reversal is a shift in the Earth's magnetic field, essentially flipping our magnetic north and south pole (but not affecting the geographic north and south poles). In other words, we're still spinning like a top in the same direction, but our protective magnetic field has experienced a shift. According to the geological record, the Earth has seen 183 reversals in the last 83 million years. The latest shift happened about 780,000 years ago, and these aren't quick changes. The average geomagnetic reversal takes approximately 7,000 years (though it may be as long as 12,000 years). While some hypotheses have been offered that the Earth's field disappears entirely during reversals or that volcanic activity intensifies during these periods of change, the fossil record doesn't offer any direct connection between magnetic shifts and mass extinctions.

than the short-lived tail of a meteor. The streak behind a comet is outside our atmosphere and long lasting, while meteor streaks are inside the atmosphere and brief.

TOP 10 FALLING OBJECTS

① A REALLY, REALLY BIG PREHISTORIC ROCK We've name-checked it already, but still no Top 10 Things that Fell to Earth list could be complete without the most famous space rock, the Chicxulub asteroid (or maybe comet), estimated to have been 50 miles (80 km) across, that hit us 66 million years ago, ending a pretty good run for the dinosaurs. The impact crater, in the water off what is now the Yucatan, is more than 90 miles (145 km) across and 12 miles (20 km) deep. But signs point to some even older impacts from the early days of our planet. One of the oldest we know of is the Vredefort Dome in South Africa, which is some 2 billion years old. At over 185 miles (300 km) across, it's also one of the largest.

② CHUNKS OF MEAT Okay, this one is just weird. Weird enough to tell the tale here, at any rate. On March 3, 1876, a farmer's wife named Mrs. Crouch was making soap on her front porch in rural Kentucky when what appeared to be raw meat began to rain from the sky. The decent-sized flakes—measuring approximately 2 by 2 inches (5 cm × 5 cm), with at least one being 4 by 4 inches (10 cm × 10 cm), fell from the sky in a 100-by-50-yard (91 x 46 m) area for several minutes. Just in case you're wondering what Mrs. Crouch might have been smoking that fine morning, the results of this strange shower were witnessed by a number of other residents, including several hunters who sampled the meat and proclaimed that it tasted, variously, of bear, beef, or venison. The shower remains a mystery (the Crouches saw it as a sign of God's displeasure), though the prevailing theory is that a flock of vultures may have flown overhead vomiting up their lunch for some reason.

③ TUNGUSKA ASTEROID On the morning of June 30, 1908, something exploded 3 to 6 miles (5–20 km) above a sparsely populated area of eastern Siberia. It's estimated that the dramatic explosion's destructive force was equal to the blast of a ten-megaton bomb. In an unusual turn of events, no major impact crater was ever found, leading to all sorts of theories, ranging from the scientific to science fiction. Most likely, according to scientists is that a small asteroid or comet, some 160 to 620 feet (50–190 m)across, entered our atmosphere at great speed, but exploded in midair before making impact. Nonetheless, the force flattened some 80 million trees over an area of 830 square miles (2,150 sq km). It was sheer chance that this event occurred in such a remote place—but even so, the sonic booms from this strike injured roughly 1,100 people and hospitalized 48 more. Had the object entered at a very slightly different angle, much of European civilization could have been devastated. And don't forget, a hundred or so years is nothing in geological time. We could be due for another of these any day now—right after the murder hornets arrive, perhaps.

④ GOLF BALLS You've probably heard cautionary tales about golf ball–sized hail, but what about actual golf balls cascading down from the heavens? Well, dozens and dozens of them fell from the sky in Punta Gorda, Florida, one afternoon in 1969 after a heavy rainfall. No nearby golf course reported balls missing; the best theory was that a passing waterspout scooped up years' worth of errant balls from the nearby waterways and rained them on the land below. Fore!

Mostly, what we're worried about is giant rocks, and those are definitely out there. But that's just the beginning of what might be in the forecast. Plenty of odd things have plummeted from the sky before, and it's a sure bet more will fall in the future. Cloudy with a chance of spiders, anyone?

5 SKYLAB The first space station, NASA's Skylab was launched on May 14, 1973, and briefly occupied for a total of 14 weeks in 1973 to 1974, by a series of three three-man teams. (In case you were wondering, they were all men, it being the '70s and all). The structure was relatively badly damaged in the launch process, meaning that the first mission was largely dedicated to patching the poor thing back together as best they could. The original plan was for the Space Shuttle to service Skylab; unfortunately, the shuttle program hit some delays with NASA, and Skylab became increasingly unstable. In 1979, it lost the ability to maintain its orbit. A report commissioned by NASA as the station deteriorated calculated that the odds were 1 in 152 of debris hitting any human and 1 in 7 of debris hitting a city of 100,000 people or more. In the summer of '79, the whole world watched as the station eventually fell into our atmosphere, burned up on reentry, and scattered its debris over Western Australia and the Indian Ocean.

6 SPACE JUNK We keep putting stuff up in space, and while physics has a lot of ways of explaining that what goes up won't necessarily come down, sometimes it does. With literally hundreds of items falling to Earth each year, it appears that only one person has actually been hit by space junk. Scientists tell us that your odds of actually getting hit are about one in a trillion. Which must have made Lottie Williams of Tulsa, Oklahoma, feel incredibly special when a 6-inch-long piece of blackened metal that fell out of the sky and hit her shoulder on January 22, 1997, turned out to be part of a fuel tank from a rocket that had been launched the prior year. Luckily, she was uninjured.

7 FROZEN SQUID In 1997, a Korean fisherman who had been plying his trade in the water off the Falkland Islands spent two days in a coma after a single frozen squid dropped out of the sky, and rendered him unconscious.

8 SPIDERS Yep, you read that right. In 2007, a rain of thousands of spiders, each about 4 inches (10 cm) across fell in Argentina's Salta province. Apparently these spiders like to hang out high in the trees, and the right (or very wrong) wind can send them sailing. And yes, there is a YouTube video of the 2007 event. You're welcome.

9 CHELYABINSK METEOR This space rock exploded in the sky over Russia on February 15, 2013. Although it was "only" 66 feet (20 m) in diameter, its power was estimated about equivalent to 500 kilotons of TNT—thirty times that of the A-bomb dropped over Hiroshima.

10 TREASURE At last, here's something you might want to be showered with! Well, metaphorically speaking, anyway, since a conk on the noggin from a solid-gold brick isn't going to feel very good at all. Anyway, that was the scene in Siberia in March 2018, when an old transport plane carrying an estimated $378 million in gold, platinum, and diamonds accidentally spilled its cargo while taking off from Yakutsk Airport. The plane's cargo hatch ripped open during takeoff, causing nearly 200 solid-gold bricks to tumble onto the runway and nearby snow. (If you're thinking of booking a flight to Yakutsk and going treasure hunting, hold off on that ticket; all the loot was recovered soon after by the local authorities.)

COSMIC DOOM So, how do all these big rocks and killer plasma rays stack up? What's most likely to get you, and what can you do to up your odds? Glad you asked—this is the kind of thing we love thinking about!

EVENT		HISTORY	HOW LIKELY?	HOW DANGEROUS?	SURVIVAL TIPS
CORONAL MASS EJECTION	A BLAST OF PLASMA AND MAGNETIC ENERGY FROM OUR SUN. SMALL EJECTIONS HAPPEN ALL THE TIME; BIG ONES ARE RARE.	SEE THE SOLAR STORM OF 1859.	SCIENTISTS PREDICT THE LIKELIHOOD OF A STORM AS BAD AS 1859'S EVENT AT ABOUT 12% IN A GIVEN DECADE.	A BAD ONE COULD FRY ELECTRONICS WORLDWIDE.	SHIELD YOUR ELECTRONICS WITH FARADAY CAGES, OR LEARN TO PLAY WITH STICKS AND ROCKS INSTEAD OF YOUR PHONE.
ELECTROMAGNETIC PULSE	AN EMP CAN DESTROY COMMUNICATIONS, POWER GRIDS, AND POSSIBLY OTHER TECHNOLOGIES.	THERE ARE A LOT OF UNKNOWNS AS NO ONE'S TRIED USING ONE AS A WEAPON.	AS DEPENDENCE ON TECHNOLOGY INCREASES, THIS TYPE OF WEAPON SEEMS MORE LIKELY.	AN EMP SHOULDN'T HURT US ONE BIT, UNTIL THE GRID COLLAPSE CAUSES PEOPLE TO GO NUTS.	LEARN THE SKILLS THAT WOULD ALLOW YOU TO LIVE WITHOUT POWER AND COMMUNICATIONS. STORE EQUIPMENT IN FARADAY CAGES.
FALLING SPACE STATION	NASA MONITORS 1,000 ABANDONED SPACECRAFT OR SPACECRAFT PIECES IN ORBIT.	SKYLAB BURNED UP IN THE SKY OVER AUSTRALIA IN 1979.	YOU'RE MORE LIKELY TO BE HIT BY ROCKS FROM SPACE THAN SPACE STATIONS.	GETTING HIT BY ANYTHING TRAVELING FASTER THAN A BULLET IS NOT GOOD.	PAY ATTENTION TO THE MEDIA AND GET OUT OF THE WAY WHEN AN IMPACT IS PREDICTED.
COSMIC RADIATION	A GAMMA RAY BURST LESS THAN 6,000 LIGHT-YEARS AWAY WOULD FRY THE OZONE LAYER.	A NEARBY SUPERNOVA OR GAMMA RAY BURST MAY HAVE CAUSED EXTINCTION.	GAMMA RAY BURSTS ARE FAIRLY RARE, OCCURRING ONLY A FEW TIMES EVERY MILLION YEARS.	GAME OVER, MAN!	UNLESS YOU CAN MUTATE QUICKLY AND LIVE UNDERGROUND LIKE MOLE PEOPLE, BUY YOURSELF A ONE-WAY TICKET TO MARS.
ASTEROID	THESE ARE ROCKS FROM SPACE, WHICH POSE A THREAT WHEN THEY STRIKE THE EARTH.	SEE ANY SAURO SAPIENS AROUND? NOPE. BYE-BYE, DINOS.	ANOTHER LARGE STRIKE IS A 100% CERTAINTY, UNLESS WE FIND A WAY TO DESTROY THEM FIRST.	SO MANY FACTORS, BUT IN GENERAL THE BIGGER THE ROCK, THE BIGGER THE THREAT.	THAT UNDERGROUND BUNKER ISN'T LOOKING SO CRAZY NOW, IS IT?

Let's say that the worst has happened. In the case of a space-strike event, the likelihood of survivability is going to be based on the scale of the event. Obviously, a small, localized asteroid impact would be survivable for the Earth. Something larger, like our Sun going nova or becoming a red giant a few billion years early, we'd have no chance of survival (unless we can flee the solar system). But what if it's somewhere in the middle? What would it take to survive such a disaster? The biggest hurdle might be damage to the electrical grid. Or it might be growing enough food for the survivors, if the atmosphere was shrouded in dust and smoke from a major impact. With so many variables, it's hard to even speculate how long it would take to create a "new normal." So, what are we supposed to do to prepare?

The megapreppers in their bunkers are well situated to such long-lasting disasters (as long as no one finds them or their stash). But this plan is expensive, and that stockpile is not mobile. If evacuation is necessary, these preppers won't be much better off than the well-stocked apartment dweller—that is, they are limited to what they can carry. In an evacuation situation, that stockpile preparation is far less helpful than adaptability and the ability to react quickly in a disaster. This "reactionary" person focuses on training rather than hoarding and is highly mobile. Which prepping style is best in an end-times scenario? I'd say you need a little bit of both. Those food stocks could get you through a long, cold (nuclear) winter. I don't care how good your skills are—you can't make food appear where there is none. And being more skilled, rather than just being a hoarder, can give you the

THE SOLAR STORM OF 1859

Known as the Carrington Event, a huge X-class solar flare hit the Earth in 1859. This coronal mass ejection was so powerful that the Northern Lights and Southern Lights were seen around the world and telegraph service was disrupted for weeks. A similar solar storm in 1989 caused over 6 million people in Quebec to lose their electricity. How does a flare do something like that? Solar flares and storms can affect modern technology with three types of emissions: magnetic, radio, and radiation. Magnetic emissions have the ability to overload electrical systems. Radio emissions interfere with communications. And the radiation is probably the worst of the bunch, causing planes to reroute and endangering satellites, spacecraft, and astronauts alike. In other words, it'll be a bad day to be outside, or flying in an airplane.

flexibility to make moves and potentially get out of harm's way. If you really want to cover your bases against death from above, take lessons from both camps.

PRESENT TENSE

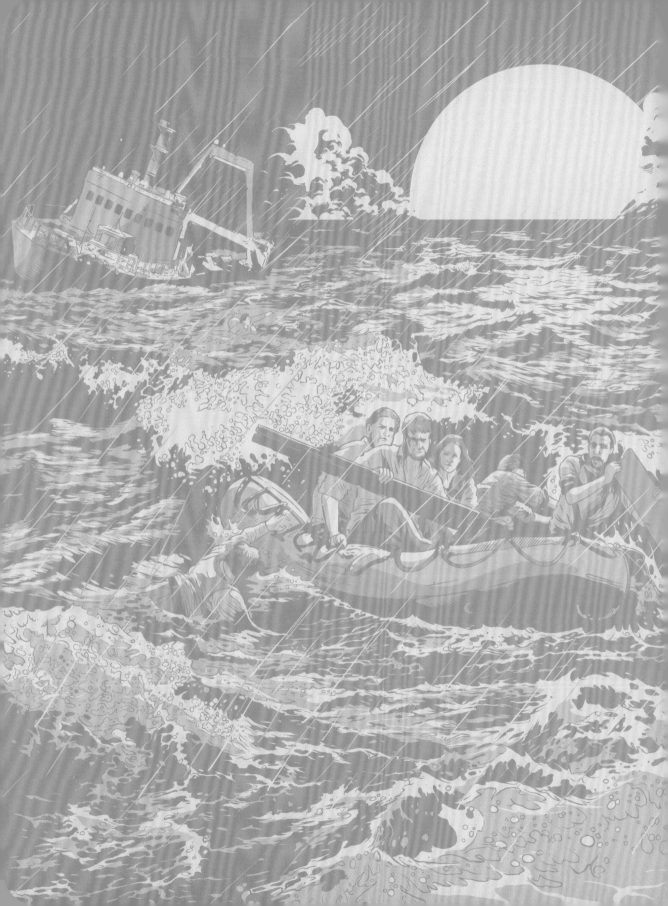

What's the biggest threat to us today? If you had a functional crystal ball (or the internet), you could look around and find out exactly what's going on in your local area and around the world, discovering the threats and emergencies that are relevant right now. In our second chapter, we'll take a look at the life-threatening events that are happening today and what you can do to boost your odds of survival. These may seem like the more mundane survival scenarios (like facing crime and storms, or getting lost in the wild), but commonplace events shouldn't make us complacent. Each one of these scenarios could take our lives and the lives of our loved ones, and for this reason we have packed this section with the survival information you'll need to help you navigate through these frightening emergencies. Despite the odds and against all expectations, you can survive with the right mindset, skills, and supplies. And who knows? You might even make it out in one piece.

LOST IN THE WILD

IS IT LIKELY TO HAPPEN?

It's rare, but no one is completely immune to this threat. The more times you venture out, and the further you go, the more likely you will get lost at some point.

HOW BAD COULD IT REALLY BE?

There is no "average" wilderness-survival scenario. Each is unique, and some can be quite dire. How badly lost and ill equipped are you? It matters—a lot!

CAN I IMPROVE MY ODDS?

The odds of being lost in the wild drop to zero if you never leave home, but with the right knowledge and gear, the odds of coming home safely improve dramatically.

MOST OF US ENJOY GOING FOR A HIKE, AT LEAST WHEN THE WEATHER AND COMPANIONSHIP ARE EXCELLENT AND YOU CAN FIND YOUR WAY BACK AGAIN. IT'S A DIFFERENT STORY WHEN THE WEATHER TAKES AN UNEXPECTED TURN AND WE FIND OURSELVES LOST IN THE WOODS.

*I*t can happen to any of us. Anybody, no matter how savvy, might miss a trail marker while on what started out as a simple little day hike, or perhaps get turned around while exploring off the beaten path (literally, in this case!). Even a familiar area can become bewildering or dangerous once the weather changes or perhaps if you haven't visited in a while and don't remember it quite as well as you'd thought.

All of which is to say that it's easier than you probably think to lose your way or become separated from your group during an outdoor excursion. You're even more likely to get lost in rough terrain, low lighting, bad weather, or any other conditions that hamper your ability to see where you are going or move through the environment.

And it's not your status as a lost hiker that gets you hurt or killed—not directly, anyway. After all, we've all been lost, maybe even panicked, and then found our way again. It's the problems that often go along with being lost that make the whole situation so serious. Getting lost means that you don't get to go home at the end of the day. Without access to your home or civilization, you may die of exposure or expire from thirst.

These tragic ends can be averted if you're able to procure shelter and water, though you may still starve to death over a long period of time (if food proves to be elusive). The average person can usually last only a few hours in cold conditions without shelter or proper clothing. If shelter can be made or found, that timeline bumps out to a couple of days before they croak from dehydration. If that lost hiker can find or create decent shelter and locate a water source, then they might last a few weeks even without access to food.

This all sounds grim, but here's the good news: Our ancestors survived in the wild, without all the high-tech resources that hikers carry today. With the right combination of skills and resources, we can survive being lost in the wild.

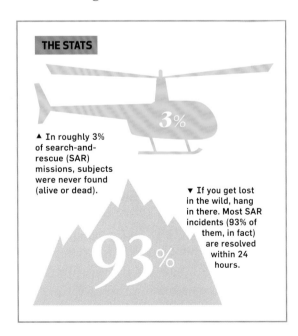

THE STATS

▲ In roughly 3% of search-and-rescue (SAR) missions, subjects were never found (alive or dead).

3%

▼ If you get lost in the wild, hang in there. Most SAR incidents (93% of them, in fact) are resolved within 24 hours.

93%

TAKE SHELTER Wilderness shelters aren't always tents or stick huts. Sometimes nature provides us with ready-made shelters that just need a few tweaks to become comfortable and warm. For someone lost in an old-growth forest, hollow trees and logs can become instant shelters (improved by filling them with insulating vegetation, like dead dry leaves). In a snowy area with large evergreen trees, the snow on the treetop will minimize the amount of snow beneath the branches. These tree wells can be insulated for better protection in wintry conditions. A vacant cave can also be a fine shelter, in any weather. Since underground temperatures are stable year-round, caves are cool in the summer and relatively warm in the winter; just make sure the cave is unoccupied first.

As mentioned already, we might last only a few hours in a cold-weather exposure event, but if shelter and water were available, the average person could last a month before they finally starve. With this sequence of threats clearly laid out, we can now understand our survival priorities! These are the things we need to tackle, and they're in the order we typically need to follow.

SET UP YOUR SHELTER Since exposure can kill us faster than dehydration, shelter becomes our top survival priority (unless we're in the rare situation in which first aid or defense are more urgently needed).

If you were smart enough to bring a tent, sleeping pad, and sleeping bag, you're all set. If not, maybe you were smart enough to bring a space blanket (a reflective Mylar blanket that packs down small but offers some warmth in cold weather). Lacking all of that, you'll have to make a shelter. When you assemble the right natural materials, you can construct a warm shelter from the resources that nature provides. After building a small, cozy frame from sticks and branches, you can cover the frame with a thick layer of vegetation (like leaves, grasses, or pine needles) to block the wind and rain. Complete your "nest" by filling the interior with multiple loads of fluffy vegetation to fend off the cold.

PROCURE SOME WATER This liquid resource can be found in many forms. Precipitation and waterways are the most common sources. None of it should be consumed "raw" if you have any way to disinfect it. Boiling the water for five minutes is an easy and effective disinfection method, though outdoor-recreation store products like filters and

disinfection tablets are also great things to carry in your kit.

BUILD A FIRE A campfire is one of our best friends in the wild. It boils our water and cooks our food. It provides warmth and light, and it even signals for help. Make sure you carry multiple fire-starting items on every trip into the wild. Things like lighters, matches, and spark rods are lightweight and cheap, and they can save your life.

FIND SOME FOOD With shelter, water, and fire supplied, you can improve your chances of survival by adding food to the equation. Food is always a lower priority in the short term, but long-term survival situations, food collection becomes much more important. If you don't know how to definitively identify local wild edible plants, focus on animal foods. If it's got feathers, fur, scales, or a shell, there's a good chance it's safe to make into a meal. The feather-and-fur crowd is the safest bet. When killed and thoroughly cooked, even small birds and mammals provide a decent amount of calories, and most are surprisingly tasty. Freshwater fish are another great food source, and most survival kits come with a little fishing gear as standard equipment. Worms, crickets, termites, and many other critters are safe for human consumption, too. Just cook them all thoroughly to kill parasites and pathogens. Don't eat leaves, nuts, or berries, unless you're 100-percent certain of their identity and edibility.

KEEP UP MORALE AND MENTAL HEALTH Isolation and stress can crush our spirits and cause a great deal of mental distress.

GEAR LIST

Before heading into the wild, pack a survival kit. The best way to improve your odds in a wilderness-survival situation is to have the right gear. Here's a minimum of what you should carry.

- ☐ Lighters, waterproof matches, and other fire makers, scattered throughout your equipment
- ☐ A metal cup, bowl, or pot to boil water for a safe and unlimited water supply
- ☐ Water-purification tablets and a container, to make water treatment easier than boiling
- ☐ A rugged, waterproof light source like a flashlight or headlamp
- ☐ A whistle to signal for help
- ☐ A signal mirror, to signal much further than the whistle
- ☐ An emergency shelter item like a space blanket or an emergency bivvy
- ☐ A high-quality knife and strong cordage, for dozens of multipurpose reasons
- ☐ A compass and map of the area
- ☐ First aid supplies to treat wounds and help you prevent infection
- ☐ An emergency food supply to give you energy and sleep warmer at night
- ☐ Fishing gear as a backup strategy for when the food runs out

In survival settings, both short- and long-term, it's vital to maintain a positive attitude, good morale, and a healthy mental state. Focus on positive things (like the fact that you're still alive) and work on productive tasks (to get a sense of control in a situation that is out of your control).

SIGNAL FOR HELP Plan ahead for your triumphant return to civilization, before you even know such a return will be in question. Before you head out on any outdoor trip, even a two-hour hike, someone responsible should know where you are going, what your route will be, and when you should return. This way, if you don't return to check in with them by the appointed time, your friend or family member can notify the authorities. And how can you help the golden-hearted SAR team who will come to look for you? You can signal for help. When your mobile phone is dead or somewhere else, you can broadcast your location with a bright fire in a prominent place. You could also use signaling equipment from your survival kit (like a whistle or a signal mirror). For aircraft, you could create huge words or symbols on the ground. Just make sure they are massive and have a high contrast value. Dark logs on white snow will be infinitely better than tan rocks on tan sand.

RESCUE YOURSELF Self-rescue might be your best chance, if you are lost and no one else knows where you are. IIf you have paid attention to direction as you headed into the wilderness area, and reversing course, you should be able to get back out. If you traveled north into the backcountry, heading south should bring you back. Failing that, you can try following a waterway downstream. There is often plenty of human activity along rivers and in coastal areas.

PREVENT DISASTER Avoid getting lost in the first place by taking a navigation class

T / F

MOSS GROWS ONLY ON A TREE'S NORTH SIDE

FALSE Pop culture like books, television shows, and movies just won't let go of this bogus survival tip: the erroneous idea that moss only grows on the north side of trees (and thus can help you find your bearings). In different environments, various moss species grow in a wide variety of places, including the south sides (and every other side) of trees. If you lost your compass and needed to find your way, a better bet would be celestial navigation. Both the sun and moon rise from the east and set toward the west. The exact position in the east and west will vary depending on the season and your latitude, but it's close enough to get you moving in the right direction. Learn to identify stars at night and use a solar compass at midday, to also help you get your bearings.

at your local outdoor-recreation supply store or survival school. Classes that teach map and compass skills will provide all the basics for navigation. You can also study navigation in written form. I give my highest recommendation to a book called *Essential Wilderness Navigation* by Craig Caudill and Tracy Trimble.

7 FEAR OF FLYING

Fear of flying (also known as *aviophobia* or *aerophobia*) is a legitimate anxiety disorder, and even though plane crashes and other aerial mishaps are exceedingly rare, many of us need more than an airplane cocktail to feel better about it. Therapy can help; the DIY variety can include breathing exercises and positive reinforcement. If you can associate happy memories and positive feelings with flight, and understand more of the safety measures that are in place on modern aircraft, your fears can be lessened.

Professional help is a better approach for those who suffer from crippling fears. For example, some sufferers are so frightened of flight and airplanes that they have a hard time even going to an airport to pick up loved ones, regardless of the fact that they are not expected to get on one of those big metal birds.

Wherever you are on the spectrum of fear and anxiety, there are some valid concerns to keep in mind: Fly reputable airlines, don't cause trouble, and keep your seat belt on even when the light's not lit. Each year in the United States, about sixty people are injured when planes hit clear air turbulence and they aren't wearing their seat belts.

2.5%

◄ This percentage of people have a clinical phobia of flying, in which they avoid flying completely or do it with significant distress.

▶ Roughly 40 percent of the population reports that they have some fear of flying.

40%

1/85,000

▲ If you went on a 500-mile flight every day for a year you would have only a 1-in-85,000 risk of dying in a crash.

IMPROVE YOUR ODDS

Do your homework before booking your next flight. Choose an airline with newer planes and a great safety rating. You may also feel better by picking a seating section that's historically safer than others. First-class and other seats in front of the plane, can take the brunt of the damage in nose-down air crashes. There are also circumstances that can affect the tail section. Mid-plane is statistically the safest area, and being closer to the emergency exits over the wings isn't a bad idea either. The worst seats on the plane (from a safety standpoint) are the window seats furthest from the exits.

BUSHCRAFT

IIIIIIIIIIIIIIIIIIIIIIIIIIIIIIIIIIIIIIIIIIIIIIIIIIIIIIIIIIIIIIIIIIIIIIIIIIIIIIIIIIIIIIIIIIIIIIIIIIIIIIIIIIIIIIIIIII

KNOW YOUR HISTORY

Our species has been surviving in the wild since the beginning—heck, at the very beginning, wild was all we had! And even though we've all come to enjoy the delights of civilization over the centuries, in times of crisis, we can still use these age-old skills to help us endure. History contains a surprising assortment of examples of this. People who have been marooned on islands have survived for years, using only the resources that nature provides. Other people who have intentionally fled into the wilderness have survived for decades without the support of the outside world. Whether you are responding to an emergency situation that is beyond your control or you are making a conscious decision to withdraw into the wild, you'll need some serious skills to last indefinitely. History shows us that a life in the wild will be harder than we imagine it to be, but it is possible. Our existence is living proof that humans can make it in the wilderness.

SET YOUR PRIORITIES

Begin by building a foundation in short term survival. You'll need shelter building skills, a working knowledge of water procurement, and the ability to make fire "on demand" to get you through the first week of life in the wild. To last longer, you'll need to add food procurement skills, cooking abilities and the know-how to preserve food. You may have to build this knowledge base one skill at a time, or you can learn them all by taking a survival class from a reputable school. Start with the basics and build upon that foundation. It's the safest way to relearn the skills of our ancestors, and it sure beats rediscovering them the hard way (on your own and in the wild).

TEST IT OUT

Most people don't buy a car without a test drive. Before you head off into the backcountry to act out your own version of a reality TV survival show, make sure that you have the necessary skills to survive. Start with some "survival weekend" campouts, testing your skills under a variety of conditions. I've told my students for years that they are getting a better class when the weather is rainy or otherwise more challenging than a nice sunny day. By learning and testing yourself under a wide range of conditions, you'll have a better idea of your capability and competency with each skill. You'll also find your weak spots.

BE HONEST WITH YOURSELF

Maybe you're great at friction fire, but you don't know your tree species. It's hard to replace your fire kit components when you don't have the skills of tree and plant identification. Honest testing allows you to find out what you really know, and what you don't know. With that information, you can better prepare yourself for the challenges to come!

ADVANCE YOUR SKILLS

Shelter, water and fire will be your main focus in the beginning of your stay in the

wilderness, but once those resources are secured, the long hard fight for calories can begin. You'll need every calorie gathering strategy that you can employ to make sure you'll have enough to eat. This means foraging for high calorie wild plant foods, trapping, fishing and hunting. If your life in the wild is intentional and well planned, you'll be smart to bring along durable traps, abundant fishing tackle and well-chosen hunting implements from the beginning. If your stay was "spur of the moment," then you'd need to know how to fabricate these supplies in the wild (and how to use them).

GET REAL ABOUT THE WORK AHEAD

Now here's your reality check. If you're heading into the wild because you're lazy and you think you'll avoid work with your wilderness lifestyle, think again. Your new day job is finding food, processing food, preserving food and storing food. That's a lot of hard work, and you still may go hungry at the end. There is a bright side, however. Enough of our ancestors pulled it off that we are here talking about it today. It can be done, with the right skills and determination.

WORK SMARTER

Don't do any work that can be avoided! That's right, you have my permission to conserve your strength. In its simplest sense, survival is all about calories. You should be constantly trying to limit your calorie losses during your wilderness stay, while simultaneously looking for opportunities to collect more calories. Now this doesn't mean you should avoid necessary work. For example, you may have to invest one thousand calories to build a shelter. Do it! You'll stay warm that evening (and each subsequent evening), and prevent the loss of thousands of calories each night (and a lot of shivering in the dark).

STAY WARM

Shelter is so incredibly important because the cold can be one of the most ruthless thieves of our body's stored calories. People who become lost on a frigid landscape often suffer a fast and shocking weight loss, and that will make you much less resilient to the struggles ahead. Even with warm bedding to sleep in and adequate clothing to wear, your body has to rewarm a lot of tissue with each breath you take. This rewarming happens through your body's efforts to ramp up your metabolism for heat. This burns a lot of calories. Be smart about your calorie expenditures, and you'll live to tell the tale.

IMPROVISE TOOLS AND WEAPONS

Humans have had to hunt animals for food, and defend themselves from predators both four- and two-legged, long before the advent of firearms or even bows. Harden a long, sharp-pointed stick by careful heating over a fire to make a simple spear for small game and fish. Knap a chunk of obsidian or chert into a knife; tie one to the split end of your stick for a better spear. Make cord from rawhide or vines, and tie stones to the ends to create bolas. The possibilities are as endless as your imagination.

IF ALL ELSE FAILS

If you're really struggling or you are in real danger from the environment or your circumstances, reset the experiment. You might be a little ashamed if your performance was poor, but it's better to be alive and embarrassed than to be a proud corpse. Leave the wild, wiser for the wear and tear. If you went into the wilderness to "find yourself" and things didn't work out, chalk it up as experience and find another adventure to pursue. You could also try again. Learn from your mistakes, and head back in the wild with more skills and more supplies. Maybe the second time will be the time you get it right.

STAY AFLOAT

IS IT LIKELY TO HAPPEN?

For those who never leave dry land, you have absolutely nothing to fear. For those who work, play, and commute over open water, there's always some risk.

HOW BAD COULD IT REALLY BE?

Drowning is the obvious threat; when we think about our ship going down. Just as likely are hazards like hypothermia in the water and injury during your escape.

CAN I IMPROVE MY ODDS?

There are plenty of things that you can do to avoid going down with the ship, and to survive on the open water, even with limited resources available to you.

SHIPWRECKS ARE THE SUBJECT OF SO MANY WORKS OF HISTORICAL FICTION—AS ARE RESCUES AT SEA, TRAGIC LOSSES, AND CASTAWAYS FROM ROBINSON CRUSOE TO TOM HANKS. BUT SURELY, MODERN PEOPLE DON'T NEED TO WORRY ABOUT SUCH AN ANTIQUATED FATE? NOT SO FAST.

*I*f we consider the fact that humans have been spread across the planet for ages, the evidence for watercraft in the remote past is inescapable. We've been sailing in various boats for thousands of years, and although our technology is leaps and bounds beyond that employed by our distant ancestors, we are still vulnerable to the threats that the very first mariners faced: losing our vessel and being claimed by the water.

Somewhere in the world every week, on average, two ships are lost due to some unforeseen and all-too-often-tragic event. And these numbers don't even include all of the smaller vessels and lesser fishing craft that are lost worldwide each day.

Some of these vessels fall prey to mechanical failures, but the fact is that a much larger number are lost due to bad weather. The good news is that large vessels (such as cruise ships, oil tankers, and cargo vessels) are suffering fewer losses today than they were just a few decades ago, but the bad news is that the same threats are still out there and none of them are going away. In fact, there are threats on the water that we've never had to face before.

Some of the largest vessels on the sea are now operating with crews as small as thirteen people. As automation spreads throughout all industries, overreliance on technology is leading to understaffed ships and fewer people looking out the windows as much as they once did, both of which are dangerous trends.

There are plenty of unfortunate events that can befall your ship, and an even larger number of variables. Your vessel could be sinking slowly in calm waters, or going down quickly in a storm. You could have a fire onboard or experience a major mechanical failure. Your vessel could even be on its side or upside down. These are just a few of the situations that can occur at sea, on large lakes, and in the world's large rivers. A myriad of variables will also have an impact on your situation.

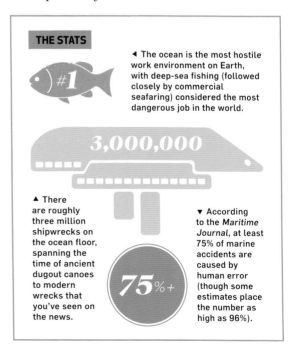

THE STATS

#1

◄ The ocean is the most hostile work environment on Earth, with deep-sea fishing (followed closely by commercial seafaring) considered the most dangerous job in the world.

3,000,000

▲ There are roughly three million shipwrecks on the ocean floor, spanning the time of ancient dugout canoes to modern wrecks that you've seen on the news.

▼ According to the *Maritime Journal*, at least 75% of marine accidents are caused by human error (though some estimates place the number as high as 96%).

75%+

PIRATES STILL ROAM THE HIGH SEAS

TRUE Avast, ye land lubbers! Take heed: The Golden Age of piracy has been over for more than two hundred years, and let's face it, Disney's version of friendly, eyeliner-wearing pirates never really existed at all. But that doesn't mean piracy isn't still a modern maritime hazard. There are more than a few places where pirates and piracy remain alive and well. Globally, piracy instances are down about 50 percent from their 2010 peak (over 400 ships were attacked that year), but there were still over 200 attacks in 2018. If those numbers don't dispel your fantasies, you can forget about the tricorn hats, cutlasses, peg legs, and parrots. Today's pirates are usually gun-wielding thugs who take vessels hostage for ransom (among other international crimes). Or, more tragically, they ply their dastardly trade in waterways where unarmed refugees are attempting to escape strife in their homelands. So, what can you do to prevent your vessel from being boarded by these modern-day scalawags? Learn about the global hot spots for this criminal activity, and avoid those waters. If boarded, prepare to fight for your life, as it will mean little to them.

So, what factors do you need to weigh when pondering your level of risk?

Some things are within your control and some are at the mercy of fate. Factors such as the size of your vessel and how well maintained it is—particularly, the safety features such as life vests, flares, and the like—are things you can get a handle on to improve your odds.

Particularly when it comes to safety, this is no time or place to cheap out. Inspect your vessel carefully and be sure any and all safety equipment is complete, up-to-date, and in good repair. If you're on a vessel that's not your own, don't hesitate to ask about safety matters. Any skipper who gets offended at such questions is not someone you want to be sailing with anyway.

As to the factors that are out of your control, your proximity to land when you hit trouble afloat, the type of threat your vessel faces, and the extent of the damage it sustains will all play a role in your survival. There's not much you can do when your vessel explodes with no warning, but there's plenty you can do when you're sailing in a well-stocked yacht on the lake with a slow leak. First on your agenda is calling for help. Using the vessel's radio, send out a "Mayday" call, and relay all the details you can provide when you get a response.

Provide the vessel's name, your current location, and the nature of the emergency, and you've made the best move to ensure your survival. If no one knows there's a problem or where you are suffering distress, no one will head your way to help. If the vessel is afloat, stay with it. If it's heading under the waves, blow up the life raft and put it to use.

So, what do you need to know in order to communicate that you're in distress on the high seas (or stormy lake)?

MAKE THE CALL When your vessel is in distress, use the VHF radio on channel 16. The correct phrase is "MAYDAY! MAYDAY! MAYDAY! Coast Guard, this is (your vessel name)." Wait for their reply (or anyone's reply), and provide your location and the type of distress.

USE YOUR BEACON If your vessel has an EPIRB system onboard, use it. This stands for "emergency position-indicating radio beacon," and it notifies rescuers via a global satellite system. Just push the button—the device does the rest.

POP SMOKE Both orange smoke and orange dye markers in the water are both internationally recognized signals for help. The smoke can be seen from other vessels and aircraft, while dye in the water is generally visible only from the air.

FIRE A FLARE Red flares are another globally known signal for distress.

RUN UP A FLAG One of the best-known distress flags looks a bit like an exclamation point. It's a black square and ball on an orange background. Run this up the mast when your vessel is in trouble. Hoisting the semaphore flags for "November" and "Charlie" will also serve.

HONK YOUR HORN The continuous use of your foghorn is a simple signal for an emergency.

DISTRESS SIGNALS

Need to call for help on the high seas and your main choices are all unavailable? You have even more options available on board. Start looking around your craft!

FLAMES ON A VESSEL A ship on fire, belching orange flames and black smoke, will be an obvious sign of trouble.

RED STAR SHELL Similar to the light shed by a flare, this rocket's red glare is sure to get attention quickly.

GUNFIRE AT ONE-MINUTE INTERVALS If you have a firearm and can afford to spend the ammo, shoot a round skyward every sixty seconds.

SOS Sound a horn or other noisemaker, or use a bright light to send a simple signal of three short, three long, and three short calls or flashes.

ORANGE FLAG AND BLACK BALL No flags? Try a 3D version: Tie a square of orange fabric and a black rubber ball to the mast!

WAVING ARMS Put your arms up high and wave them in a big Y shape at passing craft!

RADIOTELEGRAPH ALARM Sound out an SOS by radio instead of signal by light.

RADIOPHONE ALARM Dial for help or call mayday on a radio cellular phone.

STAYING AFLOAT When a raft or dinghy goes under, your problems on the water get a lot worse, for more than one reason. Not only will larger vessels have more debris in the water around them, you're also more at risk from physical injury trying to get off the vessel. (As the craft moves unpredictably, the passengers, crew, and objects can crash into each other.) Furthermore, larger vessels also pose the risk of water cavitation. This is a hydrodynamic effect that can happen when a large sinking object puts enough bubbles in the water that the water becomes less buoyant. It's not pulling victims downward, but it is making it harder to float. If you have to jump off a fast-sinking large ship, swim away from the bubbling water as quickly as you can, so you don't go down with the ship.

DON'T DROWN The most obvious threat in a sinking-ship scenario is drowning, and it doesn't take much water in the lungs to do it. If you find yourself in such a situation (or even rough seas), put on your personal flotation device (aka PFD, or life jacket). If you do end up in the water, you can reduce your risk of drowning by doing your best to keep calm. A panicked state makes you more of a hazard to yourself, and to anyone who would try to rescue you. If you're in the water without a PFD, try to improvise flotation: Tie off the cuffs or sleeves of wet clothing, flop it out of the water to fill it with air, and back down to you to help keep afloat. There will likely be floating trash in the water around you if your vessel goes down, and this can also be added to your clothing for enhanced flotation.

FIGHT HYPOTHERMIA Water is one of the best conductors of heat, and if we end up in the water, it can easily strip us of the warmth we need to stay alive. Even warmer waters aren't safe, since you can die of hypothermia in 80°F water (it just takes a week to do it). In colder waters, hypothermia can happen in hours or even minutes. If you were able to put on a PFD before or after you went into the water, you won't have to tread water to stay afloat. This allows you to curl up in a ball (in what is called HELP, or Heat Escape Lessening Posture) to minimize heat loss. Often, you can reduce your exposure by crossing your feet and bending your knees. Fold up your arms, hold your hands under your armpits, and stay curled up while the PFD keeps you on the right side of the water.

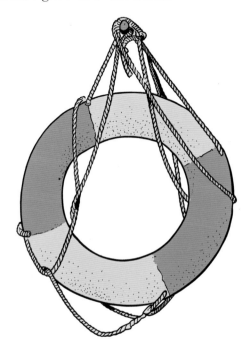

SURVIVAL ON THE OPEN WATER

The oceans are the largest wilderness area in the world, and despite there being water everywhere, you're essentially in a desert—there's virtually nothing to eat or drink, and the environment can be exceedingly hostile. When things go wrong, they go really wrong, and your life raft will be the only shelter you'll have in this wild landscape. Depending on your unique circumstances, your degree of safety will vary by the degree of protection from the elements. Here's a simple breakdown of your lines of defense.

BOAT If your yacht was towing a smaller boat, or if you were aboard a cruise ship that had lifeboats, this vessel can become your refuge. People have survived for months in these small craft, even in the open ocean. José Salvador Alvarenga holds the world record for the longest solo survival at sea, adrift for 438 days in the Pacific and floating over 6,700 miles.

LIFE RAFT A small, inflatable raft doesn't really offer the kind of room or insulation you'd find on a lifeboat, and there's only a single thin layer of rubber between you and the water. Still, it can keep you afloat for months, and most life rafts also carry an integrated survival kit.

LIFE VEST Your PFD is a true lifesaver. Make sure you have one for each passenger and crew member on every vessel. Your survival will depend on the water temperature and any hazards present in the water, but still, you might last up to a week floating in just a PFD in the warmest waters.

GOOD/BAD IDEA

DRINKING SALT WATER For those stuck on a life raft, one of the most important (yet simple) survival tips is to avoid drinking salt water. It's a tempting beverage, since you are surrounded by it, but seawater is roughly 3 percent salt by volume. This is enough sodium to disrupt the electrolytes in your brain, causing survivors to make insane decisions (like jumping out of a raft in shark-infested waters or trying to swim to shore with no land in sight). This high level of salt also dehydrates your cells, as your body struggles to process the excessive amount of sodium. Your best bet for this situation is to collect rainwater and ration it. Rainfall provides a source of fresh water for drinking, and it can be stored in bags, bottles or any other containers you can improvise from the available materials or floating trash.

IMPROVISED FLOTATION You can place floating debris in your clothing or even use your own clothing (such as your pants) as a flotation device. Be creative.

SURVIVAL WITH NOTHING How long can you survive without any flotation or protection from the water? This will depend on the water temperature and your skills in swimming, treading water, and floating on your back. You might last a few hours or even a day, but you'll fall asleep sometime, and it's fairly impossible to sleep and tread water at the same time.

THE VERSATILE COCONUT Maybe you didn't find a Wilson volleyball on the beach to turn into your new best buddy. That's okay. In tropical climates, the humble coconut can fill the gap, and there's so much you can do with it! Green coconuts are a good source of water, holding about 12 ounces of liquid each. Just try not to drink too much: More than a few per day can cause diarrhea, robbing you of the water you gained. Mature brown coconuts provide about 500 calories each, due to the high fat content. The oily meat of these fuzzy brown orbs is high in potassium and many other minerals. It can be eaten raw, grated and pressed to make coconut milk, or diced up and cooked. This food source can also be used as trap bait. Even old dried coconut husks are useful, as a firewood alternative and a source of fiber for tinder and rope.

LIVE ON A LIFE RAFT You've managed to survive the shipwreck, but now how do you make the best of your time aboard a life raft? There are plenty of stories from the past, along with lots of even more recent instances of oceanic survival. Some survivors—such as Steven Callahan, who was afloat in the Atlantic for seventy-six days in 1981—were able to survive by collecting rainwater and eating raw fish. Others have sustained themselves by catching seabirds and turtles, and eating them raw (after all, there's no way to start a cook fire aboard a lifeboat); water supplies have been supplemented by drinking the blood from such catches. To snag any live animal from within the confines of your life raft, you'll have to be fast—and we mean lightning fast. You'll also have to learn how to patch damage in your vessel, prevent sunburn and dehydration, and maintain your sanity. Holes and leaks in rafts have been patched with crafty sewing skills. Sunburn has been prevented by wearing clothing, even in the highest heat of midday. Sanity has been preserved by everything from singing to journaling to praying. The best oceanic survivors have spoken about letting go of any expectation of being rescued, and instead accepting that your raft life is your whole life now.

SURVIVE ON A SANDBAR Hey, little buddy, your three-hour tour didn't turn out so well! So, how can you survive for longer than three hours when you're stuck on a sandbar out in the middle of nowhere? Rationing may give you the edge you need. The act of rationing is a very useful practice, and it can be defined as creating a fixed allowance of provisions, especially if you're in the middle of a shortage. It's essentially at the intersection of planning and self-control. Get started with your rationing by deciding how long you want to spread out your resources, then determine how much you have and how much to use (by yourself or for your group). Work up a plan for use and stick to it. In this scenario, you could ration fresh water, food, sunblock, or any other resource that you require. It's also a helpful strategy to anchor your lifeboat or liferaft so it can't get away from your sandbar. You definitely can't afford to have it drift away on a high tide.

SIGNAL FOR HELP

Effectively signaling for help is one of your best strategies for getting rescued. Based on your available resources, you can employ various signal methods with the resources on a craft or on an island. If you're expecting a quick rescue response, you ,ay not to get too resourceful. However, if the visibility is poor, know that your life raft (and maybe even your PFD) should have a strobe beacon attached. This flashing light can lead rescuers right to your location.

LIGHT IT UP As in so many survival situations, fire is your friend. If you've got the fuel to space, know that three fires in a row on a beach is an internationally recognized signal for help. Make them as big and bright as you can, and space them an equal distance from one another. You could also use a bright flashlight to flash an SOS message to a vessel or even a low-flying slow aircraft (such as a helicopter). An SOS can be done with three short, three long, and three short flashes. Time the flashes carefully so that they clearly show a pattern—otherwise, they may appear to be random flashes of light.

RESERVE A SATELLITE Since there's a marked shortage of cell phone towers out on the open sea, your mobile phone won't be of much help to you here. It may be wise to consider bringing a satellite phone along for emergencies. Plan ahead even further by getting local emergency numbers before you head out (like that of the nearest US Coast Guard station) and choosing a more rugged satellite phone model—one that a stray splash of ocean water won't ruin.

Building a raft won't be the best survival strategy for every situation, but it's a great skill you should know, just in case.

STEP 1 Test the local materials—logs, bamboo, and driftwood—to determine which pieces are the most buoyant (and sturdy), then collect a large pile of the most suitable raft material.

STEP 2 Gather all the cord and rope you can scavenge. If none is available, test any of the local vines and long roots you can find for strength (and flexibility—all the toughness in the world won't help if you can't tie them into knots). It's usually best to allow these natural materials to dry for a few days before using so that your knots and lashings stay tight.

STEP 3 Begin by lashing one log next to another, and follow up with more. After that, begin adding crosspieces and diagonal pieces for structural integrity. Don't be afraid to overbuild your raft so that it doesn't underperform. If it breaks up after the first big wave, you're in trouble. You'll also need to create a paddle, which can double as a rudder.

STEP 4 Build a shelter on your raft, and stock up with as much fishing tackle, food, water, and any other necessary supplies as you can amass. Say your prayers and push out into open water.

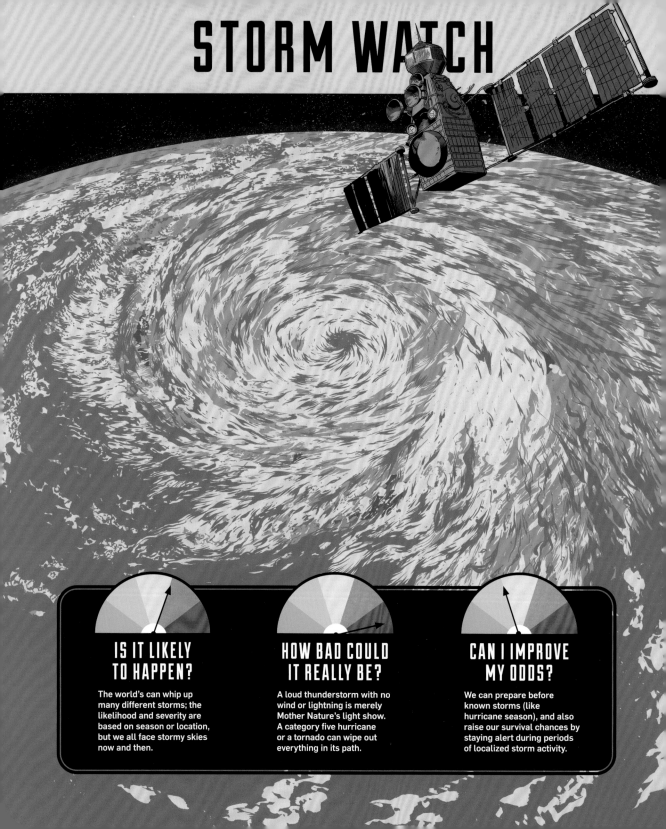

STORM WATCH

IS IT LIKELY TO HAPPEN?

The world's can whip up many different storms; the likelihood and severity are based on season or location, but we all face stormy skies now and then.

HOW BAD COULD IT REALLY BE?

A loud thunderstorm with no wind or lightning is merely Mother Nature's light show. A category five hurricane or a tornado can wipe out everything in its path.

CAN I IMPROVE MY ODDS?

We can prepare before known storms (like hurricane season), and also raise our survival chances by staying alert during periods of localized storm activity.

LIKE A SCENE OF BIBLICAL WRATH AND JUDGEMENT, A STORM CAN SWEEP THE LAND WITH DESTRUCTIVE WINDS, TORRENTIAL RAIN AND HAIL, AND DEADLY LIGHTNING STRIKES. NO PLACE IS OUTSIDE THE REACH OF THE ELEMENTS, AND YOU ARE SAFE ONLY WHEN YOU ARE SHELTERED.

Children and pets alike are honest in their fear of the elements—crashing thunder, glaring lightning and high roaring winds, along with storms of rain, snow, or hail. They cower, shiver, and hide while we adults have to put on a brave face and try to act like it's just business as usual. But since they're taking shelter under the kitchen table, aren't the pets and kids actually the smart ones?

KNOW YOUR ENEMY Storms come in many shapes, sizes, and seasons, but they all have some simple but important things in common. First off, they can all be potentially deadly. From thunderstorms and tornadoes that sweep through local areas to massive hurricanes covering an area the size of a small nation, these storms have an arsenal of deadly weapons at their disposal. Driving rain and icy hailstones pour down from overhead and contribute to flooding, while powerful gusts of wind buffet people and objects about, and lightning strikes can both knock out power stations and start fires.

A CLEAR AND PRESENT DANGER The other issue to consider with storms is how frequently they can occur. Bad weather is nothing new at all, really; there are powerful weather events constantly occurring across the globe, but this does not make any of them any less dangerous, and we should still consider these windstorms, tornadoes, and hurricanes some of the biggest threats.

Storms are a menace that our species has faced since the dawn of history, and unless some scientist creates a successful weather-control machine (a highly unlikely scenario), we're likely to be facing this rogue's gallery of natural foes until the end of time. We know they are coming, so we seriously owe it to our loved ones—as well as ourselves—to be prepared.

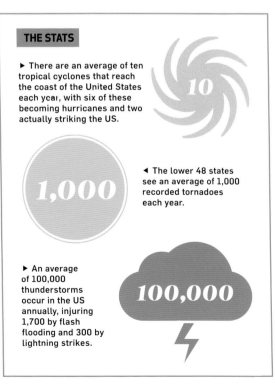

THE STATS

▶ There are an average of ten tropical cyclones that reach the coast of the United States each year, with six of these becoming hurricanes and two actually striking the US.

10

◀ The lower 48 states see an average of 1,000 recorded tornadoes each year.

1,000

▶ An average of 100,000 thunderstorms occur in the US annually, injuring 1,700 by flash flooding and 300 by lightning strikes.

100,000

UNDERSTAND THE CORIOLIS EFFECT

Flow patterns ranging from gentle trade winds to destructive weather events such as hurricanes are all examples of the Coriolis effect. To understand this force, think about the shape of the Earth and the way that it moves. Our planet moves fastest at the equator, where it is trucking along at nearly 1,000 miles per hour (1,600 km/h). Near the poles, however, the Earth creeps at a sluggish pace of 0.00005 miles (0.00008 km) per hour. Now, consider air movement. When warm air rises from equatorial areas, it naturally flows toward the poles. As the Earth spins, air and moisture are deflected to the right in the northern hemisphere, and to the left below the equator. These forces create trade winds, and they also create storms that rotate counterclockwise in the northern hemisphere ,and weather systems that rotate clockwise in the southern hemisphere.

70 deaths by flash flooding, and an average of 31 deaths from wind damage. Check local weather forecasts and watch the horizon for dark skies. At the first rumble of thunder (or before), stay sheltered until the storm is gone for 30 minutes (to avoid lightning on the back edge of the weather front).

TORNADOES Twisters happen everwhere except Antarctica, but North America has the most. Large, central flatlands and intersecting weather patterns mean roughly 1,000 tornadoes happen in the US yearly, causing about 1,500 injuries and 80 deaths. As with other storms, check local weather reports; seek shelter if warning is given.

HURRICANES These massive storms cause an average of 60 injuries and 17 deaths in the US yearly; worldwide losses are much higher. Prepare for hurricanes by keeping a full tank of gas in your vehicle and some basic emergency supplies in your home. Be ready to hunker down for a few days or to evacuate with your family and pets should evacuation orders be given.

THUNDERSTORMS There are about 100,000 thunderstorms, thunderstorms, our most frequent storm type, yearly in the United States, causing about 1,700 injuries and

SHELTER IN PLACE The storm has hit, but what should you do? In your home (or at some other location), pick the safest and sturdiest spot you can get to quickly and stay there. If you're in a house with a basement, that's likely to be your safest spot (unless flooding is an issue). Head down there and crawl under some kind of sturdy protection. This could be a heavy table, a work bench, a mattress, or whatever. Stay keenly aware of the position of heavy objects (like refrigerators, waterbeds, pianos, and the like) on the floor above the basement, and don't hang out under those spots. If you're in a building with no basement or sublevels, get to a bathroom, closet, or windowless room—ideally, one on the lowest floor. Failing that, find an interior hallway with no windows. If you're sheltering from a tornado, jumping into a bathtub may offer partial protection, but cover up with some sort of thick padding like a mattress or a pile of clothing, to cushion you from falling debris. In any structure, don't stay near windows or sliding glass doors. These can shatter and cause dangerous lacerations as the broken glass shards are driven by the wind.

SURVIVE IN THE OPEN Getting caught out in the open during a tornado may not be the death sentence that it seems. If a twister touches down in the open outdoors—and you see no sturdy shelter within running distance—lie face-down flat in the lowest area possible nearby. Protect the back of your head and neck with your arms and any extra clothing you may have. Don't try to hold onto trees, or stay near them or other objects. They may be blown onto you, or

OPEN WINDOWS IN A STORM CAN SAVE YOU

FALSE You may have heard that opening a window during a tornado or other storm can help equalize air pressure and prevent other windows from shattering. This isn't true; it can actually cause more structural damage. The average tornado is too powerful and the moving air is too quick to "equalize" with the pressure inside a house. By leaving one or more windows (or exterior doors) open, you're actually helping the force of a tornado to push upward on the roof from the inside. Coupled with gusts of wind outside, the force of the twister is even more likely to tear the top off of your dwelling. It's also important to point out two other issues with this old wives' tale: First, if you're close to a tornado, it can open the windows by itself (smashing them with debris). Second, and more importantly, don't waste your time with windows. Head straight for the safest room in the house and wait out the storm.

you may be scooped up and hurled at the objects during the tornado. If you're caught in the open during a hurricane, head for higher ground to avoid flooding, and find any structure that can block the wind.

HOW TORNADOES FORM

It may seem sometimes as if these powerful and deadly storms come out of nowhere—and when a funnel cloud suddenly stabs down to the ground, it's easy to believe that. However, a lot of complex forces are at work, and the conditions must be just right, when a tornado takes shape.

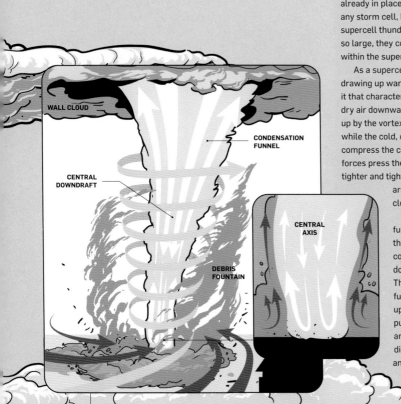

IN THE HEART OF THE STORM

Tornadoes only form when there is a powerful thunderstorm already in place. Every tornado gets its start from not just any storm cell, but a an extremely powerful system: a supercell thunderstorm. These massive storm systems are so large, they contain a vortex—a whirling column of air within the supercell.

As a supercell grows larger, the vortex expands and tilts, drawing up warm, humid air from below the storm—giving it that characteristic widening crown—and expelling cold, dry air downward at the same time. The moisture pulled up by the vortex condenses into clouds within the updraft, while the cold, dry downdrafts cascading down the vortex compress the cloud mass from the inside. These competing forces press the cloud into a spiralling form, forcing it into a tighter and tighter spin. Just like a figure skater pulling their arms in and rising up on one toe in a spin, the cloud mass increases in density and speed.

As this tightly-compressed, madly-spinning funnel cloud emerges from the underside of the supercell (known as a wall cloud), the cold downdrafts force it further and further downward, until it finally touches the ground. This is when a tornado is truly born. The funnel cloud's central axis links all the way up through the supercell and into the vortex, pulled along by its parent storm and ripping up anything below it in a fountain of debris—finally dissipating only when the storm has lessened and the vortex has weakened.

AVOIDING ELECTRICAL DISCHARGES

Fully enclosed buildings provide shelter from the wind and blowing debris, and offer the best protection against and one of the worst weapons of severe weather: lightning. There are an average of 300 injuries and 55 fatalities from lightning strikes in the United States each year; this threat is virtually eliminated by sheltering in sturdy buildings. Their electrical wiring and any metal piping offer a grounding effect in the event of a lightning strike to the structure, although there is a drawback: You should still stay away from any conductive items such as electrical switches, outlets, or wiring; corded telephones and lamps; and plumbing pipes and fixtures during the storm. Continue to avoid these items for 30 minutes after the storm to allow any lingering static charge from the lightning to dissipate.

DEAL WITH A POWER LOSS

During and after the storm, loss of electricity is a real possibility. Fortunately, there are plenty of workarounds that can help you provide for your needs. While sheltering indoors, one of the first things you'll want is lighting; even in daytime, you'll need indoor lighting as the dark storm clouds block the sun.

Candles are a traditional choice, but they do present a fire hazard (especially if you have any pets or small children that might knock them over). The dark won't seem so oppressive if you have battery-powered lighting options. Flashlights, headlamps, and camping lanterns are all great choices. If you happen to have a backup generator to provide power for light and heating or fans, so much the better, as long as you can run one without causing any fires or venting exhaust fumes in an enclosed space.

Power for smaller devices can also be provided by portable battery banks, and if you have the kind that have solar panels built into their sides, these can be easily recharged on their own with a little time in the sunlight.

EAT UP You'll also need to feed yourself and your family during the outage. It's usually best to eat the most perishable food first. This includes the food in your refrigerator and freezer. Enjoy the ice cream while it lasts, and when the storm has passed, you can cook anything from frozen pizza to meat and veggies on an outdoor propane grill to keep down the risk of fire.

SNUGGLE UP Likewise, if you need to keep warm, stick with blankets or electric heaters, and stay in the smallest rooms in your home. It might be tempting to use your grill to heat the room, but you run the risk of a carbon monoxide buildup.

While you're waiting for the power to be restored, turn off any wall switches, and unplug any of your expensive or sensitive electric equipment. An electrical surge from returning power could damage devices such as computers, televisions, and other appliances and delicate electronics, as well as potentially starting electrical fires in any damaged equipment if the surge is strong enough.

ONCE THE STORM HAS PASSED

Once all the drama is over, it's time to start the inevitable cleanup.

SURVEY THE DAMAGE If you happen to be knowledgeable enough about modern home construction, give your home a thorough checkup after a severe storm, well before you worry about cleaning up the yard or anything else. You'll need to make sure that your home is safe to occupy, and that there are no gas leaks, sewer leaks, electrical issues, structural damage, or other problems that could impact your health and safety. Check attics, basements, and crawlspaces for any signs of damage to your home's structure. While you're under the house, be sure to check for any leaks in pipes or signs of water. If you have gas heaters or appliances, sniff around for the rotten-egg smell that is added to liquefied petroleum and butane (since these gases naturally have no odor). And if in doubt, hire a professional (like a home inspector) to check out your dwelling.

BEWARE OF DOWNED POWER LINES Downed power lines are a serious hazard in the aftermath of many types of storms. Even if they're on the ground, lethal amounts of electricity can still be flowing through the lines, ready to turn storm survivors into ironic secondhand casualties. Make sure you stay far away from any utility lines on the ground. If you suspect that any utilities are damaged, notify the local authorities and the utility provider.

BE A GREAT NEIGHBOR Now that the storm is over, you have an excellent opportunity

---

ROLL THE DICE

STORM-DAMAGE INSURANCE CLAIMS If you're a homeowner wondering who will help you recover after a severe storm, look no further than the company that you've been paying hefty sums of money to since the day you moved in—that's your homeowner's insurance company. Whether your home or property was damaged by hail, thunderstorm, blizzard, tornado, or hurricane, these companies are obligated to help you. Reach out to your insurance agent as soon as you can (you probably won't be the only one calling, and you'll want to be at the top of the list). Your agent will be able to help you determine what damages are covered by your insurance plan (and what isn't covered). To assist your claim, take plenty of photos to document structural damage and destroyed property. Always take these pictures (lots of them, and taken from different angles) before you start any cleanup. The more damage you can prove, the bigger the check will be.

---

to help others out while they clean up the neighborhood and deal with the aftermath of the storm. Just make sure that you're wearing protective clothing, gloves, dust masks, and goggles as you clean up home debris, and be very careful when cutting up fallen trees. Bent or partially broken tree trunks and branches are some of the most dangerous wood to cut into, as they can suddenly spring up with powerful (and potentially deadly) force when cut.

WALL OF WATER

IS IT LIKELY TO HAPPEN?

Flooding can be an annual event or a sporadic disaster. Even less predictable, tsunamis can strike after an earthquake (or other event), unleashing a deadly wave.

HOW BAD COULD IT REALLY BE?

Flooding is very dangerous when you're in the water's path and unable to flee, and those farther away can still be impacted by infrastructure damage.

CAN I IMPROVE MY ODDS?

You can't stop a flood or a tidal wave, but you can stay alert to the weather, know the signs of danger, and hopefully react quickly enough to get out safely.

SINCE THE DAYS OF NOAH, THE IDEA OF A WATERY GRAVE HAS HAUNTED US. EVEN THOUGH WE HAVE ACCESS TO SOPHISTICATED WEATHER REPORTS AND SEISMIC EQUIPMENT, WE ARE STILL AT RISK FROM THIS AGE-OLD MENACE AT THE SHORE—AND IN THE MOUNTAINS AND DESERTS.

The word *tsunami* is Japanese for "harbor wave," though tsunamis are known in scientific circles as seismic sea waves, and they imperil areas far beyond the Pacific Rim. Smaller tsunami waves may be only a few feet high, but they can reach far inland at great speeds, creating massive amounts of damage. The largest tsunamis can measure more than 100 feet (30 m) in height, and can travel up to 500 miles per hour (800 km/h).

Whatever you call them, these massive waves are generated when some external force suddenly causes a huge volume of water to be displaced.

The most common way for a killer tsunami to be triggered is a scenario in which a powerful earthquake hits in an area where the seafloor's shaking can move significant amounts of seawater. However, these waves can also happen in large lakes. They can be caused by volcanoes, landslides, asteroid impacts, and even the detonation of a nuclear weapon under the water.

It's important to know that when this displaced water hits land, the first wave is not always the strongest. It's common for successive waves to increase in size and strength. While a considerable amount of damage is dealt by the initial impact of the high-speed wall of water travelling inland, a secondary hazard comes into play as the wave grabs debris, which can strike survivors in the water.

Of course, tsunamis and other killer waves are just one of the more dramatic ways that water can kill. The fact is, far more lives are lost, and more property is damaged, through flooding. In some parts of the world, catastrophic floods are an annual danger, part of the landscape of existence. In others, floods can happen with very little warning. River flooding has been one of the deadliest natural disasters throughout history.

In any form, a wall of water can be a dangerous adversary—especially when it catches us by surprise.

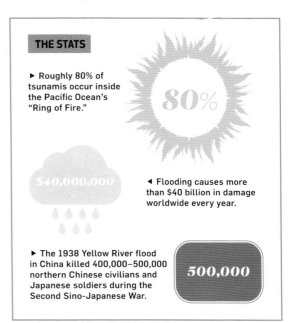

THE STATS

▶ Roughly 80% of tsunamis occur inside the Pacific Ocean's "Ring of Fire."

80%

$40,000,000

◀ Flooding causes more than $40 billion in damage worldwide every year.

▶ The 1938 Yellow River flood in China killed 400,000–500,000 northern Chinese civilians and Japanese soldiers during the Second Sino-Japanese War.

500,000

DON'T LOOK One of the strangest forces of nature, tsunamis seem to defy physics with their ability to retain momentum. These rushing pulses of water can travel across an entire ocean with very little loss of energy. They can't do this feat, however, without leaving clues that scientists can read. By calculating the time and strength of an earthquake event, the depth of the water, and the relevant distances, scientists are able to make accurate estimates of tsunami timing and strength. So, when the emergency call goes out for a pending tsunami, pay attention. Your best bet is to head for the hills, seeking safety on higher ground. This is direct conflict with our natural curiosity; many who are lost in tsunami events are those who rush to the shore to see the retreating water and gawk at the scene. These are often the ones who drown (or are never seen again). Curiosity will make you a victim, while caution will give you a better chance at being a survivor.

While these deadly deluges can strike with very little warning, awareness of the signs, and what to do, can literally mean the difference between life and death.

TSUNAMI SIGNALS Disasters like these don't happen in a vacuum. There are usually some warning signs you can observe before a tsunami arrives. For starters, any earthquake in a coastal region should send you hurrying inland. You don't always see tsunamis accompanying earthquakes (thankfully), but there is a direct relationship between the two. You might also notice a change in animal behavior. Many animals are more sensitive to the Earth's vibrations and air pressure changes than humans. The most obvious warning sign of all is receding water. When a drawback trough causes coastal waters to recede, exposing normally submerged areas, a tsunami is very likely to follow. If you spot a drawback, you have less than five minutes before the harbor wave hits. Do not dawdle.

GET TO SAFETY Knowing the risks is the first step to staying safe. In the United States, Hawaii, Alaska, Washington, Oregon, and California have the greatest risk of tsunami. Hawaii, in particular, is struck by one small tsunami every year and a major one every seven years. The largest recorded Hawaiian tsunami impacted the coast of the Big Island in 1946, as 30-foot (9-m) waves struck, traveling at an estimated 500 miles (800 km) per hour. When you hear a tsunami warning, or see any signs that cause concern, head upward and inland as fast as you can. Make your way to an elevated spot and stay there until the "all clear" is given. At worst, you look like Chicken Little when you're caught fleeing from nothing. But on the right day, your caution keeps you alive. When fleeing to higher ground isn't an option (you're in an area without hills or tall buildings), don't try to "swim" your way out of a tsunami wave. Instead, grab onto a floating object and drift with the current. Save your strength so you can climb out of the water when you have a chance to do so.

Victor Israelsson

A preteen tourist tossed by a massive tsunami

On December 26, 2004, a magnitude 9.3 earthquake in the Indian Ocean created a series of massive tsunamis. This was the second most powerful earthquake in modern times, and during the 15 minutes of intense shaking, the quake released energy comparable to the detonation of 23,000 atomic bombs. In the hours that followed, more than a dozen countries were struck by a series of huge and deadly waves, leaving the final death toll above 230,000 (and it may have been as high as 283,000).

Despite all the horrific losses, this event leaves us with some remarkable tales of people who survived, using both tenacity and luck. One of these unlikely survivors is Victor Israelsson. At the time, Victor was 12 years old and vacationing with his family in Thailand. Victor recalled: "When I looked out at the horizon, it was like the ocean was pulling back, sucking itself in. Everyone was just on the beach with their video cameras." Then he saw something that looked like "very low-sitting clouds coming towards us."

But it wasn't a low cloud coming toward the beach–it was a tsunami. By the time Victor and his family realized their peril, it was too late to flee. When the wave hit, the family was separated and Victor was struck by debris. He said, "When people ask me how it felt, I just say, 'Imagine being thrown into a washing machine and someone pressing 'On' for ten or fifteen minutes.'"

Victor finally got to higher ground with other survivors, but he was the only one of his family to survive.

MAP IT OUT How can you tell if your home is in the path of a potential flood? This is a great question, as it's not always obvious. If your house is in a hole beside a mighty river, you've got problems, but these aren't the only places that flood. The US has more than a dozen flood-zone classifications which are ranked by FEMA (the Federal Emergency Management Agency). These zones can be seen on special maps that estimate the risk of flooding in each area. By visiting FEMA's Map Service Center website and typing in your address, you'll find out if your property is in a flood zone, and what kind of risk you face. For those with larger properties, keep in mind that the FEMA map may show your lot being in the flood zone, but your actual house site may be above the zone. For more clarification, check with your local authorities or tax record database to find out more about your property's flood risk. You can also check with your home-insurance agent.

A tsunami isn't the only event that could leave you surrounded by floodwaters. The storm surge from a hurricane can send huge volumes of water over low-lying areas and up rivers. A quick spring thaw in icy highlands or a rapid snowmelt can cause seasonal river overspills. Don't forget about the failure of human-made structures. Broken dams, burst dikes, and ruptured levees can all send water rushing into places that aren't typically flooded. Even heavy rains can lead to flooding when you're in the wrong place at the wrong time. Always be aware of your flood risk, at home and in your travels, and get to higher ground if you suspect a problem.

DO THE RIGHT THING Some floods are slow moving and predictable, allowing you plenty of time to escape the area. Other types of flooding are fast, violent, and hard to predict. Flash floods happen quickly, due to heavy rainfall in upland or canyon areas. They also occur with the sudden release of water from an ice-jammed river or the failure of a dam or levee. Nearly 100 people die in floods each year in the US, and the majority of these cases involve vehicles that were driven into floodwaters (usually water crossing a road and at nighttime). It takes only 2 feet (0.6 m) of fast-moving water to wash a vehicle right off the road, and it takes just 6 inches (15 cm) of swift water to knock down a person. Your best bet in the event of flooding is to evacuate before it hits. And if you do get caught somewhere and floodwaters are blocking the road, don't try to drive them. Turn around and go somewhere else.

PROTECT YOUR PROPERTY Traditional sandbags are a fine way to safeguard your home or business, but these aren't the only option anymore. The old style of sandbags can weigh upward of 40 pounds, and their porous nature causes them to hold on to floodwater (which can contain sewage and other filth). Modern versions are lighter, thanks to their white granular filling of polyacrylamide (a substance that binds together when wet). Another contemporary option is water-filled barriers, though these cannot be stacked like true sandbags. To fill and build with traditional bags, have a helper hold the bag open and fill it slightly more than halfway. Don't tie the bag shut—just fold it over for a better fit in your wall. Start your sandbag structure by laying the bags end to end, and then make subsequent courses with overlapping gaps (like laying bricks). Go taller than you expect the flood to reach; make a wider base for taller walls.

IT JUST MIGHT WORK If you're caught in a flood trying to protect your home or some other property without any proper sandbags, there are some other materials that can work as sandbag filler and containers that can be substituted for the sandbags themselves. If you're an avid gardener, you might already have some materials on hand that are ready to use. Plastic bags full of dirt, heavy mulch, pebbles, or other garden materials can be used as sandbags right away. Lighter materials (like dry potting soil or lightweight mulch) can be weighed down by pouring water in the bags.

You can also get good results with pillowcases filled with dirt or sand, or double-thick trash bags filled with the same. Get creative. Use an old sheet and some zip ties to make sandbags from kitty litter, or steal the sand from your kid's sandbox and roll it up inside a tarp.

SANDBAG TIPS

If you're making a sandbag wall, use these tricks to make your wall more effective.

LEAVE SOME ROOM Don't build a sandbag wall tight against any building. The pressure of the water can actually damage the structure. Leave a gap so that the sandbag wall can shift a little. This also gives you room to move behind the wall (very useful, if you need to build the wall higher).

ADD SOME PLASTIC A loose layer of plastic sheeting or a waterproof tarp can conform to the shape of a sandbag wall and add extra water resistance. Leave it loose, as tight plastic may rip under pressure.

ALLOW ENOUGH TIME AND MATERIALS It takes quite a bit of sand to make sandbags, and quite a few sandbags to make a wall. You'll need sixty average sized sandbags to make a wall 1 foot tall and 10 feet long. This will not only take sixty empty bags, but also nearly a cubic yard of sand to fill them. If the average person needs 3 minutes to fill and place a sandbag, so you'll need 3 hours for one person to build the wall in question. Sandbagging isn't a practice you postpone. If you're doing it, get an early start.

BURSTING INTO FLAMES

IS IT LIKELY
TO HAPPEN?

In the US alone, fires kill
thousands and cause billions
of dollars in damage yearly.
Fires can strike anywhere; if
you're in a dry climate, a fire
is likely to affect you one day.

HOW BAD COULD
IT REALLY BE?

Fire dangers run from minor
injuries to disfiguring burns
and death. It all depends
on the particular fire you're
facing, and your options for
escape and defense.

CAN I IMPROVE
MY ODDS?

Smoke alarms and carbon
monoxide detectors are
great for improving the
outcome of a fire; plenty
more tools and techniques
can help you beat the odds.

FIRE HAS ALWAYS BEEN AN ELEMENT WITH A DUAL NATURE—FRIEND AND FOE. EATING AND BREATHING LIKE A LIVING CREATURE, IT HAS BEEN USED AS A TOOL OF CIVILIZATION AND TECHNOLOGY THAT HAS ALSO DESTROYED COUNTLESS LIVES OVER THE SPAN OF HUMAN EXISTENCE.

To lay the foundation for this section, it's important to understand what a fire really is and what it does. After all, we have so many associations with fire, from the spiritual to the mythological to the survival-oriented that it's easy to lose sight of it as a simple natural phenomenon.

From a scientific perspective, fire is a chemical reaction. Neither good nor evil, it's just a form of very rapid oxidation that releases energy. This happens when the correct combination of heat, fuel, and oxygen come together—which means that we can also kill that fire by taking away enough of any of those three requirements.

As someone who spends a fair amount of time thinking about fire, I find it interesting that the heat-fuel-oxygen trifecta isn't the only set of "threes" involving fire. Another important one concerns fire extinguishers.

Extinguishers are a diverse range of tools for fire suppression, with many different kinds on the market. And yet, despite this seemingly wide range of options, they can be divided into three different categories: dry, wet, and gaseous.

Dry chemical extinguishers work by spraying a chemical powder (typically, monoammonium phosphate), which blankets the fire and snuffs it out.

Wet extinguishers may simply spray water, or something more specialized such as a fire-suppressing foam.

And finally, gaseous extinguishers may employ carbon dioxide, halon, or other gases to suffocate the flames.

As a final point of curiosity, the trinity theme continues yet further, into the degrees of burn injuries on skin: After a close encounter with fire (or anything heated by a fire), superficial burn injuries are classified in three stages of severity.

First-degree burns are red and painful, but also relatively shallow. Second-degree burns are worse, often with blistering on the outer layer of skin and damage to underlying skin layers. Finally, third-degree burns are the worst of the lot, damaging the full skin thickness.

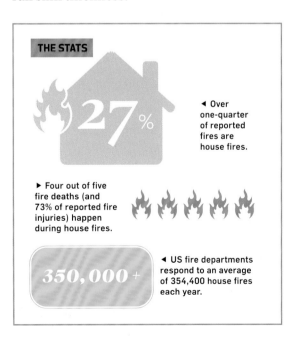

THE STATS

27%

◄ Over one-quarter of reported fires are house fires.

► Four out of five fire deaths (and 73% of reported fire injuries) happen during house fires.

350,000 +

◄ US fire departments respond to an average of 354,400 house fires each year.

WHAT OXIDIZERS CAN FEED A FIRE?

Oxygen isn't the only oxidizer that can feed a fire. Pool chemicals such as chlorine are some of the most reactive oxidizers in homes, readily energizing fires and releasing toxic fumes. For these reasons, pool chemicals should be stored in an outdoor shed, not in the home. Sodium nitrate, a preservative used in curing bacon, ham, sausage, and other meats can also burn and create toxic fumes. Concentrated hydrogen peroxide speeds up the burning of flammable materials. Nitric acid, found in metal polish and fertilizer, can enhance a fire and irritate mucous membranes (like the lining of your nose, mouth, and throat). These are just a few of the troublemakers around us, so read all labels and know the product hazards. Keep all household chemicals in tightly sealed containers and stored separately from other chemicals.

FOCUS ON FIRE PREVENTION The best way to fight fire is to prevent it from starting. Most of us know that we should keep matches away from children, but that's not how most fires start. The majority of house fires are started by cooking mishaps, followed by heating equipment, electrical fires, smoking, and candle accidents. With this in mind, do your best to fireproof your home. In the kitchen, keep flammable materials like kitchen towels and paper away from stoves. Replace gas appliances if they begin to show faults, particularly failing pilot lights. For your heating system, have a professional do a periodic inspection and cleaning. You can also check your home for overloaded electrical outlets and power strips. Speaking of electronics, smoke alarms are the best gadgets to prevent fire injuries and save lives in your home. Make sure you have a functional smoke alarm in every area of the home. These affordable devices should be mounted high on the wall or on the ceiling in the kitchen, the basement, and every bedroom. Replace batteries annually, and replace the units themselves every decade. Not convinced? More than 60 percent of house fire deaths happen in dwellings without working smoke alarms.

STOP A SMALL FIRE When fire prevention fails, there may be a chance to stop the fire before it grows. Grease fires, one of the top kitchen threats, can be stopped by dropping a tight-fitting lid on the vessel, or by pouring baking soda on the fire. Never use water or flour—these will only result in an explosive fireball. If the fire is

bigger than a flaming pan of bacon, use a fire extinguisher rated for kitchen fires (one should be readily available in every kitchen). First, though, call 911 and provide the operator with your clearly spoken address and the word *fire*.

CHOOSE THE RIGHT ONE Fire extinguishers are rated by class, each for a different type of fire. Hedge your bets with an option labeled with more than one class, like AB, BC, or ABC. The wrong extinguisher may not save the day, but the right one can snuff out the flames (when used quickly and correctly).

CLASS A For fires fed by solid materials such as paper, plastics, cloth, wood, and rubber.

CLASS B Stops flammable liquid fires caused by igniting grease, oil, gasoline, or oil-based paints.

CLASS C Used to put out fires involving electrical equipment.

CLASS D Extinguishes fires fueled by flammable elements such as magnesium or sodium.

CLASS K Puts out fires involving animal or vegetable oils or other cooking materials.

USE IT CORRECTLY Fire extinguishers are generally user-friendly, but you should get familiar with one long before you need to use it. Check the gauge on your extinguisher seasonally to ensure the pressure needle is in the green area, and you'll want to keep the extinguisher accessible. Most extinguishers operate best with the PASS technique:

SPONTANEOUS HUMAN COMBUSTION HAPPENS

FALSE Stories of people bursting into flames without any external source of ignition have been around for centuries. Science, on the other hand, is not so sure. Most cases seem to involve people who passed out from drugs or alcohol, while smoking cigarettes. As their clothing and surrounding fabrics began to burn, the body fat near their skin melted and flowed into the fabric, creating an effect similar to the wick on an oil lamp or candle. The damage looks unusual— sometimes the hands and feet fall off (they're low-fat body parts), remaining unburnt outside of a pile of foul ashes—but there's nothing mysterious going on. These unfortunate souls simply lit themselves on fire, with grisly results.

P — Pull the safety pin on the extinguisher handle (you'll need to break a seal to do this).

A — Aim the extinguisher nozzle at the base of the fire—not above or at the flames.

S — Squeeze the handle.

S — Sweep the nozzle back and forth, spraying side to side across the base of the fire. Keep spraying until the fire is out.

HEAL MINOR BURNS Small burns are a common injury in all types of survival scenarios. In the event that you're on your own without medical supplies, there is a globally available lawn weed that can help. It's called plantain (scientific name *Plantago major*) and this low-growing weed is found in lawns worldwide. This annual herbaceous plant has parallel veins and smooth-edged simple leaves that grow in a circular arrangement. The leaves and seeds are edible, but the fresh leaves can also be crushed into a paste and applied to most wounds (including burns). As the juice soaks into your skin, tannic acid reduces swelling, and a compound called allantoin increases the water content of the extracellular matrix of the skin. This activity enhances the flaking and peeling of upper layers of dead skin cells. It also promotes cell proliferation and wound healing underneath—not bad for a weed that everyone tries to eradicate!

GET OUT OF HARM'S WAY

In many cases, the wimpy squirt of a small fire extinguisher just isn't going to cut it. Even a full-size extinguisher likely won't be enough, and you should never push your luck. (You know that by now, right?) In fact, unless you have the gear, training, and backup of your local firefighters (unlikely), you won't be able to withstand the heat and smoke of a majorly engaged structure fire.

Whether you're in a single-family house or a *Towering Inferno*-type high-rise, your best chance of beating the odds in a structure fire is to escape from that structure. This works best when you have a predetermined escape plan. A good plan has the following components:

- Pick an official meeting spot for your family to find one another in an emergency.
- Pick one family member who is supposed to go to a neighbor's house to call for help.
- Build a plan with multiple escape possibilities from every room of the home, if possible.
- Agree to never enter a burning home for any reason; allow the firefighters to do their jobs.
- Practice low crawling to get out of the house, stop-drop-and-roll, and escaping in the dark.
- Consider purchasing an escape ladder for multistory homes without a fire escape, and smoke escape hoods for high-rises and larger buildings. These hoods are see-through, high-temperature-tolerant plastic bags with a built-in ionic air filter, saving wearers from smoke inhalation and allowing them to see through eye-stinging smoke. Keep adult-size hoods ready on the nightstands of adults and teens. Parents of younger children can keep the smaller child-size hoods with theirs, to keep the kids from playing with their hoods or moving them. In the event of a fire, adults hood up first, then help the children, then flee to safety as quickly as possible.

6 TIGHT SPACES (CLAUSTROPHOBIA)

Finding yourself nervous about climbing into an MRI machine? Or feeling anxious about a ride in a cramped elevator? Or maybe you peered down the opening of that enclosed tube slide at the waterpark and refused to take the ride, even after your friends jumped in and splashed down safely into the pool at the end? You might be claustrophobic.

Derived from the Latin word claustrum, meaning "shut-in place", claustrophobia can be set off by a variety of stimuli such as being in a windowless room or one that locks from the outside; being in an elevator or small vehicle; or wearing too-tight clothing (especially if it's tight around the wearer's neck). Even thinking too much about such conditions can trigger an anxious response in the person suffering from claustrophobia, leading to panic attacks, including a sensation of tightness in the chest or a choking sensation in the throat. This fear may be based in trauma related to confined spaces, or from issues in the amygdala—the structure in the brain responsible for regulating fight-or-flight responses. It may also be a "prepared phobia" wherein the victim is genetically predisposed to end up with an excessive, irrational fear of a potentially harmful stimulus or situation.

15.23 miles (23.68 km)

◄ The length of Norway's Lærdal Tunnel, the longest in the world; it includes three turn-around areas with lighting meant to ease claustrophobia.

▼ Up to 60 percent of the events that are feared by claustrophobics never actually occur.

60%

13%

▲ An NIH study on claustrophobia showed 13 percent of patients who had an MRI report having panic attacks during the scan.

IMPROVE YOUR ODDS

Claustrophobia is not necessarily a fear of the tight space itself, but of what could happen as a result of being in that space. It is treated in a variety of ways, primarily through cognitive therapy, in which the patient is taught to modify their own thinking about their fears. Exposure therapy is also highly effective, when the patient is subjected to gradually more intense stimuli, such as starting with a small room and finishing with an MRI machine; such treatments have proven to reduce anxiety by up to 75 percent. Anti-anxiety medication and relaxation techniques are useful in reducing anxiety during exposure.

DON'T DRIVE THROUGH A RAGING FIRE

In October of 1991, the massive Oakland Hills firestorm swept through California. Starting as a grass fire, it reignited the next day. Windblown flames ate through apartment complexes, subdivisions, and streets full of homes, blowing sparks across highways and an eight-lane freeway. The fire was finally contained after the wind slowed, but it still killed 25 people and injured 150. All told, the fire caused $1.5 billion in damage and destroyed 3,791 homes. Timely evacuations saved thousands of lives, but some tried to drive through the flames. Many have died while doing so, as their cars were easily swallowed up, their paths were blocked, or they simply ran out of gas. Evacuate well before a fire reaches your area. When that's not possible, drive to the other side of a large body of water to get away from the fire's path.

DEAL WITH A WILDFIRE They start in many ways; a mix of drought and heat can set the stage. Add in a carelessly tossed cigarette, a lightning strike, an accident, or some good old-fashioned malice, and you've got a fire for the record books. Wildfires can occur in many outdoor environments—prairies and dry deserts are obvious settings, but dry forests are also a likely location. Some of this is seasonal; for example, regions that have a dry season or a windy month are likely seasonal hot spots for fires. Other

areas can create the ideal conditions for a wildfire on a more sporadic basis. Whatever the conditions, the same rules for escape will apply: Flee to an area with a break in the fuel, which will likely be a break in the fire as well. Also, pay attention to the wind; the most dangerous place is uphill and downwind from the flames. If the wind is blowing toward the fire from your position, run into the wind (and away from the fire). When the wind is behind the fire, blowing toward you, take a path perpendicular to the wind. Move fast; the fire will come at you quickly. Get into a river, lake, or other body of water, if possible. Submerge as much of yourself as you can, and use a wet piece of cloth over your face as a heat shield and smoke filter. You can also try to get under a road if you can squeeze into a culvert or drainpipe. Avoid brushy canyons and other natural chimneys as shelter locations; their natural wind patterns can draw fire in and trap you.

FLEE THE SCENE Refineries, power plants, chemical storage tanks, and other facilities on the modern landscape are not immune to disaster. In the event of an industrial fire, there's more to fear than flames: Burning hazardous materials can produce toxic— even radioactive—smoke. In the rare event of an industrial fire near you, it may make better sense to shelter in place. Stay in your home or business, taping up windows, doors, and other points where air can enter the structure. If the roads are open, you can also hit the trail. Figure out which way the wind is blowing (with online meteorological information, or the old-fashioned way—by looking at the clouds), and head upwind and away from the disaster.

KILL YOUR CAMPFIRE Since the 1940s, Smokey Bear has been telling us that we can prevent forest fires, and it's absolutely true. When your campfire is no longer needed, it's very important to extinguish the fire properly and completely so it doesn't turn into a wildfire after you hit the trail. The most effective way is drowning the fire with plenty of water, and it also helps to let your fire burn down to ashes. Reducing fuel volume before putting out the fire means you won't have to worry about drenching a heap of burning wood. When it's time to end your fire, separate the remaining fuel by moving the wood apart (but still keeping it within the fire pit or ring). You can also spread out the ash and charcoal; dispersing the materials makes them much easier to extinguish. Then start sprinkling water over the hot materials, using any available container. You don't have to waste your clean drinking water or dirty up your water bottle with raw water. Use a pot, a pan, or even a hat made from thick fabric to scoop raw water from a local waterway. Once the fuel, charcoal, and ashes are wet, use a stick to stir the materials together and apply more water if you see red embers. For areas with duff and other fire-hazardous soil types, you can also use your stirring stick to poke holes into the ground inside the fire pit and dump on more water. These holes funnel water down into the dry organic soil material, which may be smoldering below the surface. When water is too scarce to spend any of it on fire control, you'll have two other primary options for fire-extinguishing: The first option is to burn the fire down completely. When only ashes remain and they are cool to the touch, your fire is dead. If this isn't an

T / F

SUCKED UP BY A FIREFIGHTING PLANE

FALSE It's a grim form of entertainment, but we seem to be endlessly fascinated by stories that involve shocking imagery, bitter irony, and dumb ways to die. point: Since the 1980s, there's been an urban legend about swimmers being scooped up by firefighting aircraft and deposited over a wildfire. Some versions of the tale titillate the reader with details, describing a burnt corpse being dressed in a wetsuit with flippers, face mask, and air tank. Other versions leave our poor swimmer or diver perched in a high treetop, sometimes alive, but, more commonly, burnt to a crisp. While it is true that fish are occasionally slurped up and then dropped on forest fires, it's simply impossible for these aircraft to scoop up a whole person. Even the largest water reservoirs on firefighting aircraft are filled through openings that are way too small to suck up a person.

option, you can also bury the fire with dirt, though this won't put it out quickly. (Embers may stay alive for hours under a dirt pile.) However you choose to kill your campfire, don't leave the area until you're sure the fire is completely dead.

TEN SURVIVAL USES FOR FIRE

1 **LIGHT** In the sections you've just read on wildfires and house fires, it would be easy to get the impression that fire is humanity's natural sworn enemy—and, indeed, it can be a formidable and deadly foe. But that isn't always the case. Indeed, fire can provide tons of benefits to those who are sufficiently self-reliant (and safety minded!). We'll look at a number of those things here—but few of them are as essential and irreplaceable as light. After all, you can always add more layers of clothing to warm up, so while fire is incredibly useful for warmth, this may not be its most valuable asset. But if you can't see in the darkness, a bad emergency situation can easily get a whole lot worse. Whether we're talking about the fire you make in your campsite, a candle in a lantern, or a homemade torch, fire can provide both static and mobile light sources.

2 **WARMTH** After light, warmth is the next most important way that we use fire. The warm glow of a flame can be simply a source of comfort, or it may be more vital to life and health. The warmth of a campfire can prevent hypothermia, or if it's too late for that and a member of your group is dangerously cold, the fire can also help you treat it. Elevate the affected person's body temperature by placing warm stones under their armpits to restore their proper body core temperature, and provide sips of warm beverages (if the victim is awake). And if you're looking for the best night's sleep you've ever had on a winter campout, heat up a stone near the fire until it's around 150 °F (66 °C), wrap it in insulating cloth and place it in your sleeping bag. You're welcome!

3 **DISINFECTING WATER** In my experience, disinfecting water is the third most useful application of fire. By boiling water for five to ten minutes (in any kind of fireproof vessel), you can kill the various pathogens that would sicken you or, worse, turn you into a mobile parasite farm. A metal pot is the modern default for a durable boiling vessel, but even cast-off garbage will work well. Set a water-filled beer bottle or soda can on the edge of a fire. The water will soon boil and provide you with a safe drink.

4 **COOKING** I doubt our species would have ever gotten the hang of cooking without the magic of fire. Seriously, there aren't many options for cooking and killing pathogens without fire. You might be able to cook some meat on a long stick over a lava flow (though it is not recommended), or boil up a sulfurous stew in a hot spring, but neither of these land features are common (nor are they appetizing heat sources). With fire, however, you can boil, bake, roast, fry, and perform many other tasty cooking operations. In fact, many food historians agree that we ate before we tamed fire, but we never had cuisine until we started cooking.

5 **SIGNALING** The light and smoke from fire have been used as signals for millennia, but before you spark up a fire, there are several things to consider. First, the fire should be in a very visible place, with as little as possible blocking it from view, so that both the smoke and the firelight can be seen from above and at a distance. Second, the fire should be located somewhere it won't get away from you. Third, don't build a fire so large that you can't put it out. Speaking of visibility, consider contrast. On a cloudy or foggy day, no one will notice white smoke. Throw plastic, motor oil, brake fluid, or other petroleum substances in the fire to produce much more noticeable black smoke.

While shelter should always be your first priority, when it becomes clear you may be spending more time in the wilderness than expected, fire is a close second. But even when sheltering in place at home, you'll find that this elemental force can aid your survival in many ways.

6 **MODIFYING MATERIALS** Fire has a secret power: It can transform materials and change their qualities. Not only can a fire turn dried clay into ceramics, it can fire-harden materials like wood, antler, and bone. All you have to do is toast the item over the fire, just above the flames. Bone is ready as soon as it starts to turn tan. Wood and antler, similarly, should be turned over the fire until they start to look a little toasted in color. Fire can also be used to alter stone for sharper arrowheads and knives. This can be done by burying large stone flakes under a hot fire. As the stone heats, it becomes more glasslike and will break with a sharper edge.

7 **REPELLING ANIMALS** Fire can work well for driving off dangerous animals, but lions, tigers, and bears aren't the only creatures it can repel. Burn a smoky fire, and the smoke will work as a natural insect repellent. Make the smoke portable by burning cattail seed heads: The cattail is a tall, grasslike plant that favors sunny swamps and open wetlands. Collect some of its iconic brown seed heads and apply an open flame to one end so that it starts to smolder. Aim the glowing end into the wind, and enjoy the reduced insect population as the unpleasant-to-bugs smoke wafts around you.

8 **WOODWORKING** While of course your results won't be as precise as if you'd had access to the proper metal-cutting tool, fire can be used for woodworking via controlled burning. This ancient process shapes wood by slowly burning it. It's time consuming, but easy enough to do. Place some burning coals on the wooden item you intend to burn, then let them eat away at the wood. Once some charcoal has been produced on the item's surface, you can remove the coals, scrape away the charcoal, and place more coals on the same spot. Repeat this burn-and-scrape activity until you have excavated the necessary wood, and use the technique to make wooden bowls, platters, spoons, and even canoes.

9 **DESTRUCTION** Yes, fire destroys things, as we have clearly seen over and over again throughout history, but sometimes this destruction serves a constructive purpose. We've already mentioned that fire can kill the pathogens in our drinking water and food, so that's a positive use for fire's destructive side, but fire can also allow us to dispose of unwanted or harmful things. For example, fire could be used to burn garbage in a grid-down scenario or burn dirty materials in a pandemic setting. And have you ever considered what a bonfire really means? The word comes from the Middle English word bonefire, or literally, "a fire of bones." Guess what that's all about.

10 **MEDICAL AID** The irony shouldn't be lost on us, that such a harmful element can also heal, but fire has long been used in association with therapeutic practices. A fire can brew medicinal teas, and be used to create ointments, salves, and poultices. Fire can be put to use not only to prepare medicinal herbs and the like, but to sterilize blades, tweezers, or other medical tools. The fire can also heat up a metal object for cauterization, which dates back to ancient Greece, and it was used more for the control of heavy bleeding, rather than the prevention of infection, as we assume today. Even some of the things that fire produces, like charcoal, have a healing benefit. Ingested in small amounts, charcoal can absorb excess acid and even toxins in the stomach and gastrointestinal tract.

PERSONAL SAFETY

IS IT LIKELY TO HAPPEN?

Criminals target everyone; you may end up as collateral damage at some point. Even a hermit in a cabin may get mail stolen or his photo used to catfish hipsters.

HOW BAD COULD IT REALLY BE?

We're including everything from being short-changed to, well, mass murder. Possible crimes are as diverse as the people who can potentially commit them.

CAN I IMPROVE MY ODDS?

The answer is, "It depends." That said, deterring many criminals can be surprisingly easy. On the other hand, some are stopped only by extreme measures.

THE FIRST PROPERTY CRIME PROBABLY HAPPENED IN PREHISTORIC TIMES, WHEN A COVETOUS CAVEMAN COULDN'T RESIST SWIPING ANOTHER'S SLICK NEW SPEAR. DESPITE OUR ADVANCEMENT SINCE THOSE TIMES, WE STILL CONTINUE TO FACE THE SAME OLD PROBLEMS.

We live in a society—a construction of ideas, guidelines, and laws—and the boundaries of society are what have helped us create and maintain peace and prosperity for a very long time. One of the world's oldest surviving sets of laws is known as the Code of Hammurabi, which is dated to around 1754 BCE.

CRIME AND PUNISHMENT While it's main focus is on business matters, such as contracts and payments, the Code also deals with personal matters such as dispensing of inheritance; the code likewise spells out a list of various acts that we would consider "criminal" behavior in modern society—as well as providing a list of fitting punishments drafted to match those crimes. It's not just the Judeo-Christian Bible that mentions the words "an eye for an eye" in regard to justice; such a concept is also found written within the Code of Hammurabi.

MODERN MEAN STREETS These days, our laws are too numerous and complex to fit onto a single stone pillar erected in the town square, and as human society has expanded and each culture has developed differently in each region, our various laws also have grown to differ greatly from place to place. Even the most venerable and wise judge can't memorize them all, but

unfortunately for some, ignorance of the rules is still no excuse for breaking them.

BEWARE OF PREDATORS Most people tend to have an internal moral compass that helps keep them on the right side of the law. However, there will always be a segment of the population that is willing to embrace the dark side, whether out of a desire for personal gain or a sense of cruelty, or because they simply lack the internal compass that others rely upon. These are the kinds of people that we need to defend against, and the information in these following pages can help.

THE STATS

▼ There are roughly two murders per minute in the United States.

▲ Five property crimes (like burglary and theft) occur for every violent crime in the US

$280,000,000,000

▲ The estimated annual cost of the US criminal justice system, including police, the court system, and prisons.

SELF-DEFENSE You were aware of the threat and you tried to flee, but to no avail. You're cornered by the bad guy, and now it's time to act. While it doesn't take a martial arts master to figure out how to defend yourself with an icepick for a weapon or a trash can lid for a shield, it's better to have a planned response to the threat of personal attack (than to try to grab random objects for defense). Find out which weapons are legal to carry in your area, train with those weapons on a regular basis, and make sure you have them with you every day. When the time comes to put your skills to work, fight your way out of the situation with sheer savagery and violence of action. Most criminals want a compliant victim, so do your best not to be that.

WATCHING FOR POTENTIAL DANGER

The best tool in your kit for the prevention of crime is your awareness. When we walk through life with our nose in our phone and our ears plugged with music, we are at the mercy of those who would treat us like prey. Be conscious of your surroundings at all times, and aware of the situations around you. Situational awareness is the ability to pay attention to details and process the information; you can use this information to identify threats and create plans to handle the threats or avoid them. We can all take steps to develop a more alert mental state. Enhance your own natural powers of observation with these three simple acts.

ELIMINATE DISTRACTIONS Playing games or chatting on your cell phone, reading a book, or listening to music through headphones may seem harmless enough, but they ruin your situational awareness.

LOOK AT PEOPLE Don't make eye contact with strangers (who may perceive your stare as a threat), but pay attention to body language and actions of people around you.

WATCH YOUR SURROUNDINGS No matter your location, pay attention to the lay of the land. Understand where you are, where you are going, and which way to go if you must backtrack, and assess any possible dangers.

FILING A POLICE REPORT

If you are a victim of or witness to a crime, you can report the incident to local law enforcement. The old-fashioned way is in person: Bring your ID and any photos or video. Give all the details you can, and get a copy of the report. You can also use the website of the local police department. Less common, but still possible, is to call the nonemergency line; provide as much detail as you can, get the report number, and request a full copy for your records. File your report as soon as you can; you never know when you can help crack a case.

COMBATING CYBERCRIME

It seems like data breaches and other hacks threaten our private information, our life savings, and even our safety on a daily basis. When enough is enough, you can always choose to pull the plug on our computer-centric lifestyle (see the sidebar on this page)—alternatively, instead of rejecting technology, we can put more of it to work.

Since anyone who does business or interacts with anyone at all through the internet could become a victim, it's important for all of us to take cybercrime seriously. There are many systems in place that prevent cybercrime each day; one of the most common is two-factor authentication (2FA), one of the simplest forms of extra security. A great example is your debit card: In order to take your money out of an ATM, you need a bank card (something that you possess) and the correct PIN (something that you know).

Three-factor authentication (3FA) goes a step further, requiring biometric data—a retina scan, a fingerprint, facial recognition, voice recognition, analysis of our gait or stride, even something more unusual about our physical makeup such as the geometry of our earlobes. 3FA can help us to preserve what we have, and paid identity-protection services can help us protect who we are. Along with multiple layers of security such as 2FA and 3FA, some systems even offer a onetime access code or a yes/no confirmation; such methods are either usable only once each or are sent to us to use as confirmation through our email or texted to our phone numbers by mobile phone, so be sure no other individual has access to that account or device.

It's a complicated world out there, and it's our responsibility to keep up with the changing technology we have available. It might sometimes be tedious, but so are locks on doors and combinations on bank vaults—and all of these are part of systems that guard against identity theft, banking fraud, and stolen information.

THE ODDS

As the population increases and times get tough, crime is on the rise. An average of 15 percent of American adults are victimized

CRIME TYPE	UNIFORM CRIME REPORTING RATE (per 1,000 US residents, 2017)	DESCRIPTION
SEXUAL ASSAULT	0.4	THIS FORM OF ASSAULT TYPICALLY INVOLVES SEXUAL INTERCOURSE OR OTHER FORMS OF SEXUAL PENETRATION, PERFORMED WITHOUT CONSENT.
BURGLARY	4.3	THE FBI DEFINES BURGLARY AS THE UNLAWFUL ENTRY OR ATTEMPTED ENTRY OF A STRUCTURE TO COMMIT A FELONY OR THEFT.
VEHICLE THEFT	2.4	SOMEONE IS DRIVING AWAY IN YOUR CAR AND IT'S NOT YOU. YOU'RE NOW THE VICTIM OF GRAND THEFT AUTO!
ROBBERY	1.0	WHEN THEFT AND VIOLENCE MIX, THIS IS KNOWN AS ROBBERY.
MURDER	0.1	SOMEBODY HAS PERISHED.

by some sort of crime each year. If that isn't alarming enough, violent crime tripled between 2016 and 2019, rising from 1% to 3%.

To defend yourself, understand the threat, laws, and locations to avoid. If you live in a high-crime area, it might be time to move.

DETAILS	NOTES	ONE THING TO REMEMBER
Sexual assault is often carried out by physical force, coercion, abuse of authority, or against someone unconscious, incapacitated, intellectually impaired, or below legal age of consent.	Same-sex prison rapes are likely to be the most common form of this crime; the true numbers are unclear as actual incidents are underreported.	It's not just pretty young women who are victimized in this way. All types of people in all age groups are traumatized by this crime.
When a person forcibly enters a residence or certain other structures (such as a garage or shed), with the intent to steal and no legal right to be there, they are a burglar.	The 2020 coronavirus pandemic has caused burglaries to spike throughout the world, as desperate people look upon shuttered businesses as easy targets.	Most burglaries are quick, and occur in broad daylight. Keep your doors and accessible windows locked, even in daytime.
If you take a car from the owner's immediate presence and against the owner's will using force or fear, that is a carjacking—an even more serious offence than car theft.	The United States leads the world in vehicle theft, with a staggering 721,053 vehicles stolen in 2012.	Lock your vehicle doors when you drive, and keep your vehicle locked in your driveway as well. Don't let yourself become an easy target.
Robbery involves the threat of violence or use of force to steal property, and is classified as a violent crime.	Bank robbery is the most iconic form, but muggings are much more common. Brandishing a weapon is considered armed robbery.	This is much different from personal theft, which includes attempted or completed purse-snatching or pickpocketing. Robbery adds an element of physical harm.
One of the worst of all crimes, and it's hardly rare. In 2018, 15,498 murders were committed in the US alone.	Tijuana, Mexico, is ranked number one in global murder rates.	Don't go to Tijuana—or any other global murder hot spot.

TOP TEN SELF-DEFENSE TIPS

1 **HEADBUTT** The best way to win every fight you get in is to never get in one. That can be possible if you have a defensive mindset and maintain awareness of your surroundings. If you observe carefully, look for nonverbal indicators, get a sense of the crowd, control your space, and plan your transitional movements, you'll stay safer than someone with their head buried in their phone. That said, sometimes a fight is inevitable and you're taken by surprise. If you're grabbed from behind, drive the back of your skull into your assailant's face with all the speed and force you can muster. The dense occipital "bun" on the back of your skull is more robust than the delicate bones in the face. If you have to deliver such a strike from the front, aim for the bridge of the target's nose, using the part of your head around where your hairline is located.

2 **THROAT PUNCH** A hard, fast, well-aimed punch to the throat can end a fight—and from an anatomical standpoint, this strike does make a lot of sense. When you flip on a nature show on TV, you'll see predators often start their attacks on the hindquarters of the prey—but as soon as they can reposition, they will go for the throat. On most creatures, the throat is a vulnerable area, and this is especially true of thin-skinned humans. One swift, strong strike to the throat can leave your opponent breathless, in pain, and very distracted. If you're worried that you won't pack enough punch with a fist, make that strike a chop with your wrist. Alternatively, if you're at the right angle, you can also use your forearm or your elbow (see the next entry for more detail).

3 **ELBOW TO THE FACE** Why use your hand (and the twenty-seven fragile bones in each one) when you can use a body part that is a natural weapon? Your elbow is composed of large, resilient bones, and elbow strikes are a staple in many martial arts systems, like Thailand's muay Thai and Israel's krav maga. Even a kid or granny can do them. For a horizontal strike, bend your striking arm, then swing it parallel to the floor and into your opponent's face. You can hit with your forearm (to bludgeon someone) or make contact with the point of your elbow (an even harder hit that can actually cut their skin). Keep your other hand up to block, since you will certainly be in close for this strike.

4 **UPWARD STRIKE TO THE NOSE** No creature likes getting hit in the nose. This is a documented tactic for driving off predators such as polar bears and sharks, so it should come as no surprise that a nose strike could leave your attacker stunned (and dealing with impaired vision due to the involuntary flood of tears). One of the better nose strikes is an upward, heel-palm strike to the schnozz. With your hand flexed backward and your fingers pointed upward, thrust the heel of your hand upward toward your opponent's nose. Aim your attack so that the lower edge of your palm strikes the nose, since this part of the hand is in line with the forearm bones, and bears the most weight.

5 **HAMMER FIST TO THE HEAD** For the untrained defender, punching the bad guy in the face with your fist may hurt you just as much as it will hurt them, and if your hand is broken during the strike, you may have lost right there. One better option can be a hammer-fist strike. This combative technique is a natural movement in which your fist comes down or out, as if you were stabbing your foe with an ice pick. Contact is made not with your knuckles, but with the side

Law enforcement officers and self-defense experts will tell you that your best defense is always to get out of a bad situation before you need to use any of these techniques, and I heartily concur. That said, if someone is attacking you, you'll want to know some measures to take for yourself.

of your fist (the one without the thumb). Twist away from your foe to load energy, then rotate back while engaging your body weight, and strike. Hit their head, and target the back of their head, if possible.

6 **KNEE TO THE GUT** Like the elbow, the knee is one of the body's natural weapons, and a well-delivered strike can convey a significant amount of force. Since most people can't bring their knees too high, this strike is often used against the lower half of an opponent's body. To deliver the blow, pop your foot off the ground with a quick, springy movement, lifting your knee toward the targeted body part on your attacker (like their gut or, better yet, their groin). Drive your hips forward as the knee connects, and some of your body weight will be added to the impact. Bonus points if they throw up after the strike.

7 **GROIN KICK** It's dirty fighting, but a hard kick to the undercarriage will jolt your attacker, and it can open them up for additional strikes. They may not be down for the count, as drugs, alcohol, and adrenalin can dull the pain, but it's worth trying. The groin is a very tender, nerve-rich area on any creature—man, woman, or beast. So even if you're dealing with a female assailant, you can go for a kick to the junk. To avoid injuring your toes and hampering your effectiveness for the rest of the fight, strike with your toes a little past the groin, so that your shin bones or the top of your foot makes contact instead.

8 **STOMP KICK TO THE KNEE** The stomp kick is a very natural and powerful strike, taking advantage your strongest muscles (your thighs and buttocks), as well as gravity. When used in conjunction with your body weight, the stomp kick is devastating, and we all already know how to do it. Imagine stomping on something. That's the technique. Raise your knee and then drop your foot hard onto the target (while simultaneously adding your body weight). A stomp kick to the front of an assailant's knee will hyperextend the knee and cause major damage. Similarly, a stomp kick to the side of the knee will buckle the leg and damage the joint.

9 **INSTEP STOMP** Now that you know how to perform a stomp kick, you can apply it in many ways. For those with limited mobility or those who may not be able to make a strong kick to an attacker's knee, consider the instep stomp. The instep is the middle of the foot, and it is filled with a number of small and thin bones, plenty of tendons, and countless nerves. Whether your foe is facing you or has grabbed you from behind, a heavy stomp to their instep can break bones and dislocate joints, potentially taking your opponent off their feet. If your foe can't stand, they also can't chase you or fight effectively.

10 **EYE WASH** During the stress of a real fight, you may stab too hard with the tense fingers of a traditional eye gouge (or you may miss and strike their skull with your fingers). The "eye wash" is a user-friendly version of the dirty fighting tactic of eye gouging, and it is modified to keep you from injuring yourself. Rather than poking someone in the eye with rigid fingers (a la The Three Stooges), simply "wash" your relaxed fingers across their eyes in a sweeping motion. The eye wash will keep you from jamming your fingers (disabling your own hand), and it is a surprising and painful attack. After all, if they can't see you, they can't fight anymore.

CRIME BREAKDOWN

CRIMES BY GENDER OF CRIMINAL*

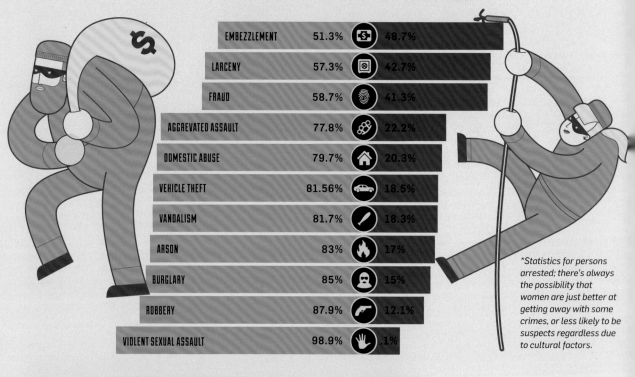

Crime	Male		Female
EMBEZZLEMENT	51.3%		48.7%
LARCENY	57.3%		42.7%
FRAUD	58.7%		41.3%
AGGREVATED ASSAULT	77.8%		22.2%
DOMESTIC ABUSE	79.7%		20.3%
VEHICLE THEFT	81.56%		18.5%
VANDALISM	81.7%		18.3%
ARSON	83%		17%
BURGLARY	85%		15%
ROBBERY	87.9%		12.1%
VIOLENT SEXUAL ASSAULT	98.9%		.1%

Statistics for persons arrested; there's always the possibility that women are just better at getting away with some crimes, or less likely to be suspects regardless due to cultural factors.

WHERE DO VIOLENT CRIMES HAPPEN?

7.2%	OTHER
.2%	BANK
.9%	PUBLIC TRANSPORTATION OR STATION
1.2%	GAS STATION
1.4%	AT THE OFFICE
2.4%	STREET NOT NEAR HOME
2.4%	PARK, FIELD, OR PLAYGROUND
4.4%	BAR, RESTAURANT, OR NIGHTCLUB
5%	FACTORY, WAREHOUSE, SHOPS
7.3%	PARKING LOTS & GARAGES
9.2%	AT A FRIEND OR RELATIVE'S HOME
13%	SCHOOLS
33.7%	AT OR NEAR HOME

20 percent of all homes are burglarized at some point.

Most kidnappings happen within $\frac{1}{8}$ of a mile (200 m) of home or work

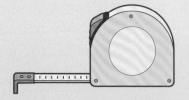

COUNTRIES WITH THE HIGHEST CRIME RATE

Country	Rate
VENEZUELA	84.49
PAPUA NEW GUINEA	81.93
SOUTH AFRICA	77.49
AFGHANISTAN	76.23
HONDURAS	76.11
TRINIDAD AND TOBAGO	73.19
BRAZIL	68.88
PERU	68.15
EL SALVADOR	67.96
GUYANA	67.66

COUNTRIES WITH THE LOWEST CRIME RATE

QATAR	11.86
UNITED ARAB EMIRATES	15.65
JAPAN	20.66
OMAN	20.79
SLOVENIA	21.07
ARMENIA	21.6
SWITZERLAND	21.6
ESTONIA	23.14
FINLAND	23.32
ICELAND	23.36

(In 2020. Calculated by dividing the number of reported crimes by the total population, and multiplying the result by 100,000)

The average home break-in takes just 8 to 10 minutes start to finish

TEN MOST COMMON PASSWORDS

- 123456
- 123456789
- QWERTY
- PASSWORD
- 111111
- 12345678
- ABC123
- 1234567
- PASSWORD1
- 12345

ODDS THAT A CRIME WILL RESULT IN ARREST, IN THE USA

Crime	%
MURDER	62.3%
AGGRAVATED ASSAULT	52.5%
RAPE	33.4%
ROBBERY	30.4%
ARSON	22.4%
LARCENY	18.9%
BURGLARY	13.9%
VEHICLE THEFT	13.7%

MOST COMMON FORMS OF IDENTITY THEFT

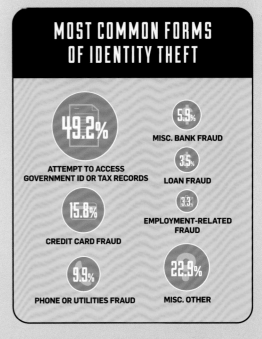

- 49.2% ATTEMPT TO ACCESS GOVERNMENT ID OR TAX RECORDS
- 5.9% MISC. BANK FRAUD
- 3.5% LOAN FRAUD
- 3.3% EMPLOYMENT-RELATED FRAUD
- 15.8% CREDIT CARD FRAUD
- 9.9% PHONE OR UTILITIES FRAUD
- 22.9% MISC. OTHER

MASS TRANSIT

IS IT LIKELY TO HAPPEN?

In mass transit, more people in confined space means more troublemakers. It's a numbers game; the chance of trouble depends on your frequency of use.

HOW BAD COULD IT REALLY BE?

Your risk will depend partly on the number of other passengers with you, but it can vary from "This is an unpleasant situation" to "This could be fatal."

CAN I IMPROVE MY ODDS?

No matter how you travel, there are ways to be safer while journeying through the world, from researching current threats to improving your situational awareness.

WE'VE ALL TAKEN A BUS, PLANE, TRAIN, OR SUBWAY AT SOME POINT, AND VIRTUALLY EVERYONE IN MODERN SOCIETY USES MASS TRANSIT. BUT SOME DAYS, THINGS DON'T RUN SMOOTHLY AND ACCIDENTS HAPPEN. FOR THE BAD GUYS, IT'S LIKE SHOOTING FISH IN A BARREL.

Every single day on this planet, billions of people in thousands of cities use at least one form of mass transit to get from Point A to Point B—and a lot of those folks use that mass transit option on a near-constant basis, virtually every single day of the week. Whether it's the daily commute they take to and from work, a shopping trip to the mall or department stores downtown, a recreational outing in the evening on a weekend, or a regular get-together for happy hour at the end of a busy workday, the overwhelming majority of these trips that so many people take on a daily basis will often take place as planned, and on time, with no issue.

TROUBLE ON THE TRIP Every once in a while, however, things just don't go according to your plans—and while each individual trip taken has only a miniscule chance of something going wrong, that still means that in the wrong circumstances, you're testing your odds over and over. Unscheduled events can range from minor incidents that can be almost funny to tell others about later on (such as a near-slip-and-fall moment on a wet subway platform, or yet another delay due to technical difficulties), to something truly catastrophic and heartbreaking (for example, a serious bus or train crash—or rare, but even worse still, both at once—that involves multiple

vehicles and results in several injuries and fatalities to passengers).

TAKING A SAFER RIDE A few of the risks you take will be specific to the type of mass transit you board, while other threats out there will be present in every form of public transportation. When bad things end up happening, it's certainly possible that you just got on the wrong flight. Still, no matter whether you're stuck aboard a crowded commuter train next to an unruly passenger during a breakdown, or taking a ride with friends on a ferry when it breaks down and starts to sink, there are plenty of things you can do increase your odds of a safe trip.

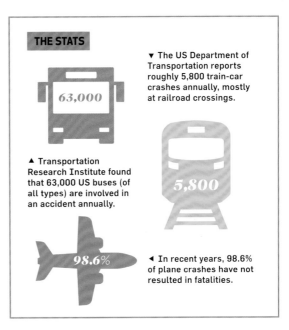

THE STATS

▲ Transportation Research Institute found that 63,000 US buses (of all types) are involved in an accident annually.

63,000

▼ The US Department of Transportation reports roughly 5,800 train-car crashes annually, mostly at railroad crossings.

5,800

98.6%

◀ In recent years, 98.6% of plane crashes have not resulted in fatalities.

SEAT SELECTION They probably won't let you fly the plane, but there's one thing that might still let you beat the odds: You can choose your seat carefully! Most of us worry about avoiding the middle seat, but we should worry more about being in seats at the front of the plane and being seated far away from the exits. The safest seats on the plane are the exit rows above each wing, to give you the first crack at escaping; the aisle seats nearby are good for those who tend to feel claustrophobic or those who want to exit the aircraft in a timely manner, emergency or no. The worst seats on the plane are the window seats furthest from the exits, requiring a longer trip out of the plane. The first few rows of seats can also be dicey: They are close to the front exit, which is a good thing, but are also vulnerable to frontal impacts in a crash. Whichever seat you end up buying, make sure you know where the exits are located. You should be able to find them, even if you cannot see them. Why won't you be able to see them? A crash may fill the cabin with black smoke, which would keep you from seeing the exit signs. Memorize how many rows you'd have to go and what your path would be, in case you have to find it blind.

JUST PLANE TERRIBLE

What's worse than that pun you just read? How about being in a scary situation aboard an airplane? It's bad enough that we have to worry about contracting the 'Rona or some other airborne or contact illness when we're taking a trip on an airplane, but we still have all the other issues that have dogged us since the first manned flight—such as mechanical failure, gravity, and hard-packed earth waiting far below.

Although it's statistically regarded as the safest form of travel, there are nonetheless always a few major concerns about air travel. One most common issue with flight is injury as a result of turbulence. Keeping your seat belt fastened isn't just a sensible thing to do in a motor vehicle—it's sound advice on an aircraft too. Each year in the US, about 60 people are injured after failing to wear their seat belts, and since 1980, three people have died during these sorts of accidents. All it takes is one patch of clear air turbulence, and you'll find yourself suddenly launched out of your seat and your head colliding with the ceiling above. Sure, you'll have to take your seat belt off if you need to get up for an in-flight bathroom break, but other than that, you really should keep your seat belt on until the plane has come to a complete stop. These are injuries that can be serous, but they can also be easily prevented!

FIGHT BACK An in-flight hijacking is a truly nightmarish scenario, to be sure, and you can bet that hijackers don't have any nice

plans for you either. Should you be on one of these ill-fated flights, do everything in your power to fight back against the hijackers. You'll have to be resourceful, using improvised weapons and attacking by surprise to retake control of the plane. If the hijackers are pilots, as they were on September 11, 2001, then those who were rightfully flying the aircraft may be dead. It's still worth trying to retake the plane, and it's still definitely the right thing to do. If you prevail, get on the radio and place your Mayday call on the frequency that's already set, since that's likely to be the one the local tower uses. If you need to select a frequency, try 121.5 MHz or 243.0 MHz, which air-traffic control usually monitors. The vast majority of successful landings by nonpilots have been assisted by air-traffic controllers. Many of those working in ATC are often pilots themselves, so they're likely to know how to get you down safely.

BRACE FOR IMPACT Studies have shown that the typical brace position does increase the chances of survival in an emergency crash landing. The basic position is to keep your feet flat on the floor. Wear your seat belt buckled low and tight over your lap. If the seat in front of you is close enough, place your head and hands against it. If there's too much room for that, bring your chest down to your knees and grip your shins with your hands. Stay in this position until the plane has come to a complete stop. These positions can reduce the high velocity your head would be moving when it inevitably slams into the seat in front of you. This position also minimizes any potential limb flailing, thus reducing the

GOOD IDEA

SCAVENGE, BUT SCAVENGE WISELY After a plane crash, a survivor's next challenge is to stay alive until rescuers arrive. It may take some resourceful scavenging and creativity, but there are plenty of useful things on a plane. The problem is, you may survive the crash, but be burned alive if aviation fuel or other substances catch fire while you're scavenging the crash site. Limit your risks by getting away from the craft after the crash; after you feel that the risk of fire and explosion has passed, take a look through the debris. If the plane has broken up, use carpeting, upholstery, seat cushions, bulkheads, doors, windows, and more as shelter components. Grab loose electrical wires for lashing materials and reflective items for use as signal mirrors. Check the luggage to find clothing, blankets, pillows, food, and water. Also, scoop up eyeglasses, medications, medical supplies, and anything else you think would be useful.

risk of limb injuries and improving your chances of escaping the crashed plane. Just imagine how hard it would be for you to unbuckle your seat belt with two broken arms and pull yourself to safety, or climb over seats to the emergency exit if you happen to have a broken leg. If you know that you are heading for a water landing, be prepared to use the flotation devices aboard your flight. Also, be ready to grab and use an oxygen mask, should it be deployed during the descent.

DIY FLOTATION DEVICES The bad news is, you're in the water after your ship has gone under the waves. The good news is, your pants can be used as a flotation device. In fact, several types of garments can function as a temporary emergency personal flotation device, assuming the cloth is woven tightly enough to trap air inside it. While continuing to tread water, wriggle out of the garment, and make sure you don't lose it in the water. If you're using pants, seal each cuff with an overhand knot. Flip the waist of the pants out of the water quickly, to scoop air into the legs. Then, squeeze the waist closed and place an air-filled pant leg under each arm. Take a moment to catch your breath and enjoy your brief stay in a higher position out of the water. Repeat often, and as needed.

You can also get creative with other garments, using sleeves and other parts to make air pockets, so long as the material is capable of holding air in it for some time. Now, at some point, you'll fall asleep and the air will leave the garments without being replaced. Instead of waking up drowning, grab onto all the floating debris you can reach in the initial sinking of the vessel, and stuff it into your clothing. Water bottles with caps can be emptied to make floats. Styrofoam objects are naturally buoyant. Use anything that you can find to create a filling of buoyant material, and you will reduce the odds of sinking whether you're wide awake or nodding off.

SEA TRAVEL

Whether you're traveling the oceans for business or pleasure, there are much greater concerns than worrying about what to eat and what to skip on the buffet, or wondering whether or not the ship's crew made sure to keep the jacuzzi properly sanitized. The rarest occurrence—but probably the most frightening—is piracy.

This scourge of the sea has existed for thousands of years, and the first pirate ship probably launched shortly after the earliest trade vessels. Some of the earliest accounts date back to the pirate threat in the Aegean and the Mediterranean during the fourteenth century BCE. Although their languages, armaments, and vessels have changed, today's pirates still engage in the same hateful work of their forebears—acts of robbery and murder on ships. These aren't the only violations of maritime law that pirates perform: Extortion, hostage taking, kidnapping for ransom, seizure of the ship, and sinking the entire vessel are also practices still used by contemporary pirates.

Even though the rate of piracy has risen and then fallen again in recent decades, it's still an ongoing threat in certain parts of the world. In this scenario, you have no control over what the captain and crew will do, nor do you get to influence the actions of the pirates—but you can still control your choice of travel route. Study the current US State Department travel advisories and pay attention to warnings. Although a cruise line might plan a route through troubled waters, that doesn't mean you need to buy a ticket. If your best-laid plans still fall apart, be compliant with your captors; they're likely just after a ransom.

DON'T GO DOWN WITH THE SHIP When your floating vessel decides to stop floating for any reason, you may find yourself ordered by the captain or crew to abandon ship. This is of course a terrifying prospect, since any large body of water can easily become a watery grave, but this doesn't mean that you should give up. Move quickly and get to a lifeboat, if these are available on the vessel. Most ships with lifeboats, including ferries and cruise ships, may also have a safety drill before weighing anchor, so you should have a chance to become familiar with the lifeboat's location and how to get aboard swiftly. If the ship lacks lifeboats or if you're unable to get to one, put on a lifejacket or personal flotation device (PFD), get to a nearby railing, and prepare to jump overboard instead!

To reduce your chances of injury, don't jump from any spot higher than 15 feet (5 m) above the water. Find a closer position to the water below, or wait for the ship itself to sink further. Cross your arms over your chest and hold onto your lapels (or the area where they'd be under your PFD) to help protect your neck and shoulders from the shock of impact with the water surface. Pick a spot in the water that's free of debris or burning materials, take careful aim at it, and then jump!

DRONE RESUPPLY If you're stuck on a cruise ship for any reason (such as being quarantined during an outbreak aboard the ship) and you can't disembark at a port, you do have a very modern alternative to resupplying yourself with needed or wanted items that the ship cannot provide. You could have a drone deliver your supplies while you are sheltering in cabin! This isn't something we made up; it's happened before, with an Aussie couple stuck aboard a cruise ship in Japan. In February of 2020, amid the global coronavirus outbreak, Jan and Dave Binskin, from Queensland, Australia, were being quarantined on the *Diamond Princess* off the coast of Tokyo. They didn't order food or medicine to get them through their ordeal. They ordered wine instead!—and an enterprising company delivered it to them by drone. This just goes to show you that necessity is the mother of invention, and where there's a will, there's a way.

Once you're airborne, straighten out your whole body and stiffen your legs below you, cross your feet at the ankles, and point your toes to reduce the risk of leg injury on landing (which will definitely hinder your ability to swim). Take a deep breath right before you hit, and then swim away from the sinking ship as best you can the moment you are in the water. Make your way to any life rafts or other craft you see, or grab onto floating debris, then swim at least 100 feet (30 m) from the ship.

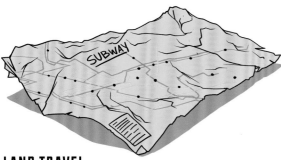

LAND TRAVEL

Sea and air travel are certainly not the only mass transit options that carry risk. Be sure to stay safe on every land commute too!

WATCH OUT FOR TRAIN WRECKS While these accidents rarely affect a large number of people, the results are often catastrophic for those involved. Most train accidents occur when a train collides with another train, a motor vehicle, or a person. Many such collisions occur at the intersection of a railroad and a motor vehicle road, but people both on the train and off of it are at risk. In the nearly 6,000 annual train accidents in the United States, there are an average of 600 deaths and 2,300 injuries. Often attributed to negligence, operator fatigue, or mechanical failure, these accidents aren't the only threat: Common crimes also occur on trains, with robbery, assault, and sexual assault being all too familiar. You can't clear the tracks or bring the train operator any coffee, but your situational awareness will help dealing with unfriendly passengers.

GET ON THE BUS These accidents can be minor, but serious injury is a risk when a bus collides with another vehicle or a pedestrian. Some of the contributing forces in these accidents are bad weather and shoddy maintenance. The bus doesn't

MIND THE GAP Subway accidents can occur as the result of subway derailment, sudden stops, maintenance issues, or faulty equipment. These are rare incidents; the more common issues are preventable. Don't stand close to, or walk near, the edge of the subway platform. Slip-and-fall accidents can be fatal if you land on the tracks as a subway train approaches, or if you touch the electrified third rail—the high current that powers subway cars is responsible for numerous electrocution injuries and deaths in recent years. If you accidentally drop something on the tracks, don't try to get it; speak with someone who works for the subway, and they will call a team that retrieves these items with a safe tool and correct technique. It won't be the first time they have scooped up a dropped smartphone. Finally, watch out for the gap between the train and the platform. This space may seem too small to be a threat, but hundreds of people are hurt each year when they step into this crevice while boarding or exiting subway cars.

even have to be in motion for bad things to happen: Riders are sometimes injured when they are let off the bus over a pothole, an open manhole, or some other dangerous location. You can also stay safer on rides by choosing seats near the driver, or away from doors. (Those seats are often targeted by thieves who take the opportunity for theft during a stop.) Watch your step!

5 CLOWNS (COULROPHOBIA)

Send in the clowns, those daffy, laughy clowns. Thanks to the bombastic personalities of our painted friends, many a child was traumatized in their formative years. This negative association can linger as a general distrust of people in disguises, or developed into a full-blown phobia about these jovial jesters. When you add in the modern obsession with creepy clowns, it's no wonder that clowning is a downtrodden trade.

The Merriam-Webster dictionary definition of *coulrophobia* is "abnormal fear of clowns," but to be honest, there must be a "right" amount of fearful feelings pertaining to these capering comics. We don't know who they are, or what they'll do next. The fear of unpredictable people in disguises may be ancient, but the term *coulrophobia* itself is very new. Coined in the late 1990s, it was a rallying point for adults who discovered that they weren't alone in their childhood fears of figures in outlandish garb and face paint. From unintentionally disturbing characters like Bozo the Clown, to intentionally terrifying creations like Stephen King's monster Pennywise, clowns continue to pop up in popular culture, both entertaining and alarming us.

◀ The World Clown Association reported that its membership fell by almost a third, from 3,500 members to 2,500, in the last decade.

42%

◀ A 2016 survey from Chapman University in California found that 42% of adults surveyed were afraid of clowns; ironically, the same survey found just 24% were afraid of heights and only 19% were afraid of dying.

IMPROVE YOUR ODDS

This is no laughing matter. Like other phobias, exposure therapy may offer needed relief. You may also be able to pick apart the fear. Can you remember your first negative feelings about clowns? Was a clown at your eighth birthday, terrifying you and your friends? Or did you watch a horror movie involving clowns when you were too young to process shocking imagery? If you discover the source of your fear, you may be able to address it. The fear of clowns may be a null point in the future, as fewer people choose the profession and the number of clowns in the world declines.

CAR TROUBLE

DANGER CLIFF EDGE

IS IT LIKELY TO HAPPEN?

If you drive regularly, odds are strong that you'll run into trouble sooner or later. Thankfully, the odds of facing a serious (or even deadly) situation are in your favor.

HOW BAD COULD IT REALLY BE?

Your danger level can range from "a flat tire delaying your trip to the beach" to "a multi-car pileup with several damaged vehicles and plenty of serious injuries" or worse.

CAN I IMPROVE MY ODDS?

You could improve your safety by never traveling in a car again, but that's a drastic move. There are many lesser steps we can take to boost our safety on the road.

THE OPEN ROAD GIVES US FREEDOM AND POSSIBILITIES LIKE FEW OTHER THINGS IN LIFE. ON A GOOD DAY, THAT ROAD COULD TAKE YOU ANYWHERE YOU WANT TO GO. UNFORTUNATELY, SOMETIMES THE ROAD CAN TAKE YOU SOMEWHERE YOU DON'T WANT TO GO (LIKE A HOSPITAL OR THE MORGUE).

Although taking a drive may seem simple at first, thevariables are limitless when it comes to hopping in your car and driving down the road, and a limitless number of potential outcomes. Will you experience some kind of mechanical failure from one (or more) of the thousands of separate parts in your vehicle? Will another driver do something stupid or dangerous (or both!) in your vicinity? Will a stray animal run out into the road and startle you? Will you end up dealing with a skid across black ice on a wintery mountain road, or face debris from an avalanche sliding down the hillside above the highway you're traveling on?

KNOWING WHAT'S ON THE ROAD We could fill a whole book with nothing but an exhaustive list of things that could go wrong, but that would hardly be a compelling read. Instead, in this chapter, we'll be leading you into how to deal with the wonderful (and sometimes not-so-wonderful) world of vehicle trouble, and how to handle some of the most likely—and also some of the unlikely!—things that you could encounter as a driver or passenger. Luckily, it's not all doom and gloom: From the problematic to the catastrophic, plenty of vehicle troubles can be avoided—or at least kept from turning from frustrating to horrific—with just a bit of planning.

TRAVELING WITH SAFETY Many vehicular issues can be averted with some basic knowhow and a few tools; before they ever happen, they can even be avoided by a bit of preventive maintenance on your ride. Others can be addressed by knowing how to engage in defensive driving—or other simpler, more common-sense solutions, such as deciding that the conditions aren't at all safe for that short drive you wanted to take. And as always, we've even saved room for some of those truly bizarre and terrifying scenarios that might suddenly take place while you're out on the road. So, climb in and fasten your seat belts; we're about to go for a ride!

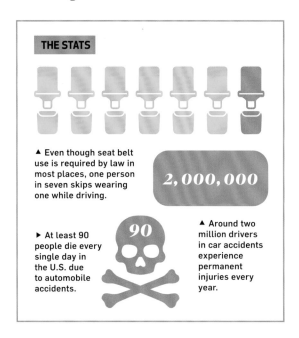

THE STATS

▲ Even though seat belt use is required by law in most places, one person in seven skips wearing one while driving.

2,000,000

▶ At least 90 people die every single day in the U.S. due to automobile accidents.

90

▲ Around two million drivers in car accidents experience permanent injuries every year.

FAKE TRAFFIC STOP? If you're ever pulled over and find yourself wondering whether someone is a real law enforcement officer, the best thing you can do is call 911. Tell the dispatcher where you are, who you are, and your vehicle details (make, model, and license plate number). Share your concerns, and stay on the line with your doors locked. Through a crack in your window, ask the "officer" for credentials and ask the 911 operator for a marked cruiser to be sent to the location. A real undercover officer should have called in the traffic stop, and their dispatcher should know about it. You might annoy a real officer if they are legit, but this caution could save your life if they're an impersonator. If the person's vehicle is not normally used for police work, if the vehicle is an older model or is in poor condition, or if your creep-o-meter is telling you that something's wrong, trust your gut and drive away fast!

SKIP THE HITCHHIKERS Sometimes, people just need a ride after a car breakdown or other inconvenience. And sometimes, people are just good-hearted and willing to help others. But let me stop your lovefest right there. Fewer people hitchhike today than they did in former decades, and that alone should give you concerns. Hitchhiking is illegal in some areas, and unwise everywhere. Both parties have no idea who the other stranger really is. Why are you stopping for me, disturbing driver? Why should I let you in my car, weird roadside dude? If you're still not sure about this, just watch one hitchhiker slasher movie and keep that in mind for the next time you see someone on the roadside with their thumb sticking out.

KEEP YOUR DISTANCE A seasoned driver will know that we need to maintain a lot more space while driving than the average person allows. Standard practice on the road today seems to be cramming in as tightly as you can, even when driving 70 miles per hour (113 km/h) on the highway. This is very dangerous, as you have no reactionary gap when things come to a screeching halt. To be effective at defensive driving, maneuver to keep sufficient space around your vehicle—in the front and back, and on the sides— as much as possible. The most important of these spaces is the distance between your vehicle and the one in front of you. Try to leave several car lengths or 3 to 6 seconds of spacing. Measure the seconds between you and the other vehicle by following at a constant distance, choosing a fixed roadside object (like a sign or a post) and waiting until the car in front of you has passed it. Start counting "One one thousand, two one thousand," and that will give you your spacing count. Remember, the faster you drive, the more time it will take to come to a stop; allow extra space to maintain your distance.

DRIVE IN THE SNOW

Taking the car out in the winter snow, either for fun or for work, is not the same as driving in other seasons and conditions. Extreme cold or a few flurries may not constitute an emergency, but they do impact the "rules of the road". Once the road gets slick, however, maintaining control of the vehicle is a whole different matter. Keep these driving tricks in mind and they will help you to keep your car between the ditches with the greasy side down.

WATCH YOUR SPEED Drive slower, because speed is one of the chief causes of winter driving accidents. Just because you're driving a four-wheel-drive tank doesn't mean you can fly.

EASY DOES IT Accelerate and decelerate slowly and gently. Don't jerk the wheel when turning. Quick moves often lead to loss of control.

DON'T STOP! If you're going up a hill, don't you dare stop. Objects in motion tend to stay in motion, as we all learned in fourth grade. If you stop while trying to go up a slippery hill, chances are you'll get stuck there. Use your momentum to keep going.

PUMP THE BRAKES It's important to know what kind of brakes your vehicle has. If you drive an older vehicle that doesn't

have antilock brakes, pump the brakes to maintain control when stopping. Leave room to stop as well. Normal dry-surfacefollowing distance is about four seconds between vehicles. In winter weather, increase that space to 10 seconds.

JUST STAY HOME If you don't have to be somewhere, the simplest option is the safest: Just remain at home.

SUPPLIES FOR THE ROAD Your vehicle can be a storehouse when you stock it for the season and likely emergencies. For winter driving, add a windshield scraper, a sleeping bag, gloves, and a shovel to your car trunk. Consider a bag of cat litter or snow chains for traction. For help in all seasons, carry a fire extinguisher, a smartphone charger, road flares, a flat-tire kit, jumper cables, a flashlight, a first aid kit, a change of clothes, and nonperishable food and water. Carry at least a gallon (3.8 L) of water, depending on the number of people in your vehicle and the climate you're in. Bring extra water for long desert drives, to stay hydrated during a breakdown. Extra batteries, a tire-pressure gauge, hygiene items, and reading material never hurt, either. Your alternative is to skip the gear and hope you don't need any ever. (Good luck!)

TURN AROUND, DON'T DROWN It's a common mistake that it's safe to drive through shallow water. Flooding is the chief cause of death associated with thunderstorms, accounting for more than ninety fatalities each year in the US. More than half of these losses occur when vehicles are driven into dangerous floodwaters, especially at night when visibility is hampered. Just 2 feet (0.6 m) of fast-moving water can sweep away most vehicles, even SUVs and trucks, and a lesser depth of water can flood your engine, stalling out the car. If you see water in the roadway, find another road.

DEAL WITH A ROADSIDE INCIDENT You may find yourself (and your vehicle) on the side of the road after being in an accident or experiencing a breakdown. There are certain things we should all do, and specific things we should have with us, in case of such events. First, get your vehicle off the road and move to a safe area if possible. The last place you want to be is sitting still in the roadway. Once on the shoulder of the road, flip on your hazard lights to alert other drivers of your vehicle. Put your car in Park and turn off the engine. Check on your passengers and ask if they are injured; call 911 if you or anyone else is hurt. Things that may seem minor during the shock of a crash (like dizziness or a sore neck) should be checked out by a medical professional. If the accident involved another vehicle, check on its occupants too. If you have flares or reflective triangles, place them out near the road for safety. For an accident with another vehicle, consider calling the local police to the scene. For a breakdown, try a local towing service. Gather information from the other driver in the event of a crash: Get driver and passenger names and addresses (use your phone to snap a clear photo of their driver's licenses). Get the vehicle license plate number and insurance information, and document the scene (including makes and models of all vehicles involved, the contact information for any eyewitnesses, the exact location of the accident, and the names and badge numbers of any responding police officers). While you have your smartphone out, take photos of the accident scene for insurance claims and court.

SURVIVE A WATER LANDING Up to 1,500 vehicles end up in the water in the US annually, and even though this is a small percentage of the 5.5 million reported crashes per year, you'd better know what to do when it's your vehicle. The first thing to do is stay calm. This is a lot to ask when facing a terrifying situation, but staying calm is the key to survival (in most settings). Next, get yourself and your passengers unbuckled and open a window. Both hand-crank and electric windows are best opened before the water reaches them. The average vehicle float time is between 30 seconds and 2 minutes. Work quickly, and get yourself and your passengers to safety before the vehicle sinks completely. If you can't roll down the windows and the water pressure won't allow you to open a door, break a window and swim to the surface.

STAY ALIVE WHILE SNOWBOUND Whether a snowplow covered your car or you crashed into a snowbank, you can survive getting stuck in a snowbound vehicle. If you can't call for help and the conditions are too bad for you to walk away from the vehicle, one thing is in your favor: Your vehicle provides you with shelter (albeit a cold one) and if you planned ahead (stocking your car for winter emergencies), you should have plenty of supplies to increase your odds.

If you can't call for help, bundle up warmly and try to dig the vehicle out, if it's possible. This makes sense only when you have warm clothing and outerwear, as well as a shovel (ideally, a snow shovel).

When digging out isn't possible, use the car as a temporary shelter. Keep it stocked with high-energy food, water, and sleeping

SCAVENGE, BUT SCAVENGE WISELY Tire chains or snow chains are used for traction on packed ice and snow. They're destructed to road surfaces, so chains are not legal everywhere or at all times, but where allowed and when warranted, they can make a huge difference in winter-driving safety. Use tire chains only when the road surface has a layer of compacted snow or ice on top of it. If you can see the road surface, chains are likely prohibited and high-quality snow tires should be sufficient. Just make sure you purchase the correct size of chains for your tires; a proper fit is vital to the safety and function of tire chains. It also pays to install and adjust them before you actually need them, instead of in the middle of a blizzard. Install them only on the drive wheels, and keep your speed between 20 and 30 mph (30–50 km/h).

bags during cold-weather travel. Add a small bucket with a tight-fitting lid, and some hygiene products, in case you're stuck in the car so long that you need a toilet. Run the engine for warmth occasionally, but only if you can keep the exhaust clear. Fumes can back up into the vehicle cabin when the exhaust pipe is buried in snow, slush, mud, or water, leading to death from carbon monoxide poisoning.

Last, create some kind of distress signal outside the vehicle. Tie something colorful to the antenna, and clear the snow off the vehicle roof so that it can be seen.

BASIC VEHICLE MAINTENANCE

Everyone should know at least how to check their tire pressure and top off their oil, but you'll need the right tools and supplies for the job. Here are some simple supplies to consider for your home garage or carrying in your vehicle for emergencies.

TIRE-REPAIR TOOLS Fix flat tires with a tire-plug set, portable air compressor, and liquid repair aerosol. The aerosol will patch pinhole leaks, plugs can repair gaping holes, and the compressor provides necessary inflation.

GAS TANK PATCH It's surprisingly easy to patch a hole in the gas tank, with a super-sticky gas tank patch. Purchase these at auto-parts stores, and keep them on hand in the vehicle.

JUMPER CABLES Easy-to-use jumper cables can bring a car back to life if it has a dead battery. Don't forget that you can push-start manual transmission vehicles by getting them rolling and then popping the clutch.

GAS SIPHON Sometimes, the only thing wrong with a vehicle is an empty tank. Do what you must in an emergency, and siphon from any available gas tank.

ANTIFREEZE Add antifreeze to your coolant if the level drops from a crack or leak in the system. Don't add plain water, as it can freeze and burst cooling components.

WASHER FLUID Keep a bottle of low-temperature windshield-washer fluid in your vehicle to top off its reservoir if it begins to run low.

EMERGENCY RADIATOR COOLANT
My friend Wes Massey, who owns an automotive-repair shop in North Carolina, told me of a remote-area roadside fix he performed for a stranger to get him down out of the mountains and back to civilization. The man had a leak in his engine-coolant system; his radiator was dry and the vehicle was overheated. Neither driver had any water or a way to carry water up from a stream far below. It's not great to run your vehicle's system on fluid other than a water/coolant mix, so my friend had to improvise. He disconnected line for the windshield-wiper fluid and placed it in the radiator reservoir. Hitting the windshield wash button pumped the mixture into the coolant reservoir and got the driver back on the road—with the recommendation of a good place to get a patch job, and flush and refill his cooling system.

MOTOR OIL Those numbers and letters on the oil bottle refer to the oil's viscosity (thickness) at different temperatures. Contrary to popular belief, the W on the bottle of oil refers to *winter* (not *weight*), and a 5W oil is typically recommended for this season. The other number is the viscosity rating of the oil while the engine is running and hot. You'll usually want a 5W-20 or 5W-30 oil for colder weather, and carmakers usually recommend that you use a 10W-30 oil in your vehicle for high-temperature regions or seasons.

4 WATER

Aquaphobia is a fear of water, which can kick in around rivers, lakes, swimming pools, and the ocean (no thanks to the *Jaws* movies). The causes for this fear can be straightforward enough: A near drowning (especially as a child) or any other mishap around the water can leave a person with a deep dread for water. I personally feel this fear quite often, particularly around water in which I cannot see the bottom. Call me chicken all you want; I don't know what's down there!

It may sound like aquaphobia and hydrophobia are the same thing, but hydrophobia is an aversion to water in the later stages of rabies (when a victim develops trouble swallowing), while aquaphobia is a fear that can vary from person to person. It might be only deep water that causes distress; pounding waves can be another trigger. In the rarest cases, even being splashed with water can cause a panic attack, leading sufferers to avoid bathing; this offshoot is called *ablutophobia*. You may be able to avoid public speaking or high places, but this elemental fear is a tough one. Since most of our body is water and we drink it every day to survive, aquaphobia can be a hard hitting fear, one that avoidance cannot help.

45% ◀ According to a recent Gallup poll, 45 percent of adults surveyed said that they would be afraid of water that would be over their heads.

▶ In the same poll, more than 60 percent of American adults are afraid of deep water.

>60%

3,400

▲ Each year, there are more than 3,400 drownings in the U.S.; more than 70 percent of them are adults.

IMPROVE YOUR ODDS

Like many other phobias, the right therapy or medication can improve your quality of life. Facing the fear with exposure therapy is another option, though uncomfortable at best (and panic-inducing at worst). Your doctor or therapist can help you decide on a treatment plan, and help you create an informed set of expectations. Cognitive behavioral therapy is one of the best treatments, challenging your thoughts and beliefs about the fear. One therapy session might not make you feel any different, but ongoing therapy (and maybe the right prescription) can be immensely helpful.

FACE THE FUTURE

Things are about to get weird! The emergencies of the first two chapters, all rooted in precedent, would be pleasant daydreams compared to the game-changing events in the pages that follow. The third chapter is dedicated to the events that might happen someday—the craziest and most horrific emergencies, as well as the most apocalyptic catastrophes. Each of these scenarios is scary in its own right, but the scariest part is that they could happen anywhere and without warning. But even if these alarming events do occur, you can still look for the silver lining: Our ancestors have survived disasters that seem unsurvivable by our standards. With a little skill, preparation, and providence, we might just make it ourselves. Who knows? You could survive to become part of a brand-new world. We're here to help you through the tough times—and maybe even through the "End Times." Just remember: The only constant in nature is change, and creatures that do not adapt to change will not survive.

ON THE RUN

IS IT LIKELY TO HAPPEN?

Most of us won't ever go on the lam, but if we did, we'd need some very specialized skills and techniques to disappear from the face of the Earth.

HOW BAD COULD IT REALLY BE?

It depends on the people you are fleeing. At best, you're probably looking at jail time; at worst, it's better not to think about the worst things that could happen to you.

CAN I IMPROVE MY ODDS?

Most of the people who go on the run from the law are caught within a few months; running from other folks is another matter. This is a tough one, but there is hope.

BEING PURSUED BY THE FEDS FOR A CRIME YOU DIDN'T COMMIT? (OR, HEY, YOU DID IT, BUT YOU HAD YOUR REASONS!) MAYBE THERE ARE CRIMINALS HUNTING YOU DOWN FOR REASONS OF THEIR OWN. OR MAYBE YOU END UP BETTING IT ALL IN A DEADLY FUTURISTIC GAME OF HIDE-AND-SEEK.

No matter who it is you've managed to make really, really angry (and no matter how or why), you're trying to stay well out of their clutches, and you're hoping you'll be lucky enough to keep evading them long enough to stay safe. But, sometimes, luck just won't be enough for you. In a situation like this, you're going to have to be really good (as well as extremely lucky) to remain free (not to mention stay alive) if you find yourself trying to keep from being apprehended from any well-organized group.

The world's governments and law enforcement agencies have all kinds of resources at their disposal, with statewide systems for surveillance and a whole host of personnel who are specially trained at observing and tracking down people trying to give them the slip. And what about the Mob? The less savory folks you've ticked off might not have as expansive a network of surveillance or as many people at their disposal, but they have enough—hey, there's a reason they call it organized crime—and there are always at least a few people out there happy to pass along a tip to them in exchange for a reward. Yet, regardless of the capabilities of those entities, whether lawful or unlawful, that may pursue a person, there are still some people who manage to evade their pursuers—at least for a little while.

Since this chapter is a little crazier than the previous ones, we'll even consider a futuristic situation (such as the one that takes place in the movie *The Running Man*) where your challenge is not to evade law enforcement officers or foot soldiers for a criminal organization, but instead to survive in some twisted game show scenario. As grim as these prospects look, there is still some good news, and the hints in this section may even help in various scenarios. Dust off your fake mustache and get a new bottle of glue. It's time for a makeover!

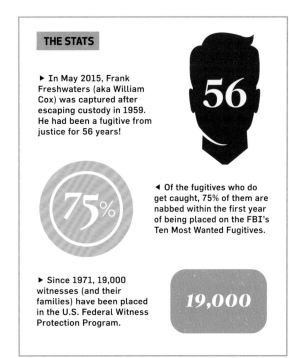

THE STATS

▶ In May 2015, Frank Freshwaters (aka William Cox) was captured after escaping custody in 1959. He had been a fugitive from justice for 56 years!

56

◀ Of the fugitives who do get caught, 75% of them are nabbed within the first year of being placed on the FBI's Ten Most Wanted Fugitives.

75%

▶ Since 1971, 19,000 witnesses (and their families) have been placed in the U.S. Federal Witness Protection Program.

19,000

DOS AND DON'TS If you're looking for a checklist of things to do and stuff to avoid while you're living that fugitive lifestyle, here are five of the main issues that put you on the radar for pursuers. The first thing is very obvious: You can't have direct contact with your family and friends. Use a middleman for communication and ditch your old phone. The second area is your finances: Pay for everything with cash only, ideally in denominations of $20 and under. Your credit and debit cards are an easy thing for the authorities to track. The third area is your whereabouts: Go somewhere unexpected, a place where you have no former ties. This could be someplace remote, like the wilderness, or just a new state. Make sure you don't drive a tracked car to get there. (Skip any vehicle that has tracking, such as OnStar.) Your fourth consideration is your behavior: You can't afford to make trouble or draw too much attention in your new location. Finally, don't get cocky: Fugitives who fall into a false sense of confidence often slip up. If there's even a chance that your pursuers will never give up, then you should never stop looking over your shoulder.

RUN FROM THE LAW You're going to have to get up pretty early in the morning to outwit and outpace the long arm of Johnny Law. Is this a forever thing? Maybe, unless you are no longer wanted in connection with a crime, and how would you know? You're supposed to be off the grid. Vanishing completely will take a lot of work, and secrets have a way of coming into the light.

PURSUED BY THE MOB Shackled by the strictures of policy and procedure, it may take the law enforcement world some time to find you and organize a complex maneuver (like extradition). This isn't the case for organized crime. With abundant assets and fewer rules, those outside the law may come after you with astonishing speed. When a crime syndicate wants your head on a pike, don't dawdle in your house packing up your belongings. Grab your cash and anything you can't live without, and get out of town quickly.

LAY LOW FOR A LITTLE WHILE In some situations (like being stalked by a crazy ex, or owing your bookie for a string of gambling losses), you don't have to melt your fingerprints off or have cosmetic reconstructive surgery. You just need to stay out of the spotlight. If you have the funds available, a mini-vacation could be just the thing. Rent a room, or have someone else rent it for you. Relax a little, and get your affairs in order. Then make your triumphant return when the time is right.

PLAY YOUR OWN GAME Are you forced to go to ground for a while during some demented sci-fi game show or amidst a brutal *Hunger Games*-style competition? The only way to win may be to escape the game. Rather than allowing yourself to be be herded like livestock, find the boundaries and break out if you can. If you can't, at least you go out on your own terms.

HIDE IN PLAIN SIGHT Looking to disappear in a hurry? Choose the garb of someone who is often ignored. By donning mismatched and oversized clothing, getting dirty, and adding some accessories (like a cup of change and a piece of cardboard to sit on), you can look like a homeless person, someone who is often tragically ignored in modern society. Not only are you profiled and labeled as "undesirable" by much of the population, many people will go out of their way not to look at you a second time—as if homelessness was something contagious.

CHANGE YOUR VOICE How does a mama cow find her baby in a herd of identical cattle? The voice of the little one. The voices of many creatures (humans included) can be very distinct (to our own species, at least). To become someone else completely, you'll need to change your voice. Our vocal cords and other physiological factors generate our fairly unique voice. This anatomy allows us to make a wide range of noises, and it also allows us to change our voice to sound different. You may not fool a high-tech voice analyzer, but to the average ear, you sound like someone else. Try imitating an accent or a particular person's voice (but not an easily identifiable character). You can also try muffling your voice with your hand or a piece of cloth. Try speaking in a monotonous way, with less emotion, and

T / F

YOUR WALK CAN GIVE YOU AWAY

TRUE Spymasters know that there are plenty of things you can change about yourself, like your haircut and hair color, putting on glasses (hey, Clark Kent!), and the way you dress. But one of those things you don't think about changing is how you carry yourself. Your posture and something as subtle as your gait, may give you away. The way that you walk and the way that the rest of your body moves while walking can be as unique as a fingerprint. So, even if you are completely disguised, your walk may give you away. The fix for this is surprisingly easy, though: Change what you do with your hands while walking (like sticking them in your pockets), and modify your step. Put a large coin in one shoe, and try not to put pressure on it when you step. This will appear as a slight limp, and now you're walking like a completely different person.

a flat tone. You can even hold your nose while talking or buy a voice changer; these gadgets which range in price can change the pitch of your voice in different ways. Do these techniques effectively, and your own mother won't recognize your voice.

INVASION

IS IT LIKELY TO HAPPEN?

The chance of invasion is based largely on your country. A smaller country may be a prime target for a larger one (especially if the little guy has resources).

HOW BAD COULD IT REALLY BE?

If the invasion means a new leadership treats the locals better than the old regime did, we'd say it's not too bad at all. Unfortunately, most endings aren't so happy.

CAN I IMPROVE MY ODDS?

You can learn a new national anthem, become a refugee, or rally with other freedom fighters and take back your home. In any case, survival skills will be awfully handy.

WE'VE SEEN *RED DAWN*, AND WE'VE WORRIED ABOUT INVASIONS OF COMMIE FORCES SINCE BEFORE THE 1960S. OVERALL, THE IDEA OF A FOREIGN MILITARY SHOWING UP ON OUR DOORSTEP IS NOTHING NEW— BUT THAT DOESN'T MEAN IT'S NOT WORTH CONSIDERING.

An invasion can be defined as a significant military offensive into a territory that is owned or governed by a different geopolitical entity. These incursions are often quick and aggressive, meant to be undertaken as swiftly as possible before the opposing force or government can have any time to react fully to repel the invader, and such an event can involve any of a number of goals (or even any combination of them).

An invading force may be there for conquest, whether to acquire more land or other resources located in that territory or as a stepping-stone to another geopolitical location. The invasion may be undertaken to liberate the local population oppressed by their own government, or even perhaps with the goal of reestablishing control over a territory that was formerly held by the invading party.

Invasions can also be used to divide countries, change governments, or gain concessions from another nation. This can be a great thing for the locals, when the "good guys" invade a country in order to oust some sadistic totalitarian political regime. It's definitely a bad thing when the "bad guys" choose to invade your country and enforce their rule on an unwilling society. Regardless of any reasons, when an invasion takes place, it isn't as cut-and-dried as you might imagine.

An invasion can be an aspect of a certain style of warfare, can incite a war itself or, ironically, can even end one or act as a distraction or cover for another military endeavor or goal. Rarely small-scale or cobbled together, invasions are usually large operations that require a tremendous amount of planning, coordination, and resources to execute effectively. How can people stand in the face of such a force? It wouldn't be easy, but people have been invaded before, and will be again.

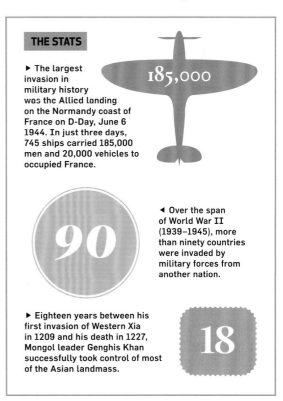

THE STATS

▶ The largest invasion in military history was the Allied landing on the Normandy coast of France on D-Day, June 6 1944. In just three days, 745 ships carried 185,000 men and 20,000 vehicles to occupied France.

185,000

90

◀ Over the span of World War II (1939–1945), more than ninety countries were invaded by military forces from another nation.

▶ Eighteen years between his first invasion of Western Xia in 1209 and his death in 1227, Mongol leader Genghis Khan successfully took control of most of the Asian landmass.

18

A WELL-REGULATED MILITIA There's a stereotype of the average American militia group as gun-crazed wingnuts in militaristic costumes, spoiling for a fight. Then there are groups that exemplify an orderly, well-conducted paramilitary group. These are law-abiding citizens who legally own weapons, and often train as a group, preparing for a day when they may be needed. The Second Amendment of the US Constitution states that: "a well-regulated Militia being necessary to the security of a free State, the right of the people to keep and bear Arms shall not be infringed." So, what does a proper militia do? By definition, a militia is a group of citizens who are not professional solders but who can be called up for service in a crisis. This is not a full-time professional fighting force, but temporary support for regular troops. Historically, militias have been used in skirmishes, for holding fortifications, and for irregular warfare. Militia groups are often limited by local civilian law, and are meant to serve for a short time, and only in their locality.

REALIZE YOUR RELIANCE (AND SELF-RELIANCE)

As a civilian, what could you possibly do to prepare for an invasion (whether you knew that one was coming or not)? Since we need the same supplies and resources for most emergency situations, the things you'd want to keep in place for a major earthquake or

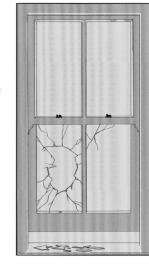

grid collapse are the same things that would serve you well during an invasion. You'll have to take this sort of thing with extreme seriousness, so forget about your tinfoil hat and focus on things that make sense, like shotguns, canned goods, and small livestock. We're not suggesting that you load up on birdshot for soldiers, or hurl cans of soup at oncoming enemy forces, but sometimes an effective defense is about more than just weapons—it's about having reliable supply chains and renewable food sources. For example, more than 20 million backyard Victory gardens grew a staggering 8 million tons of food in the United States in 1943 (nearly half of the food consumed that year in the country), which allowed commercial agricultural production to be funneled toward the war effort. Maybe your contribution to fighting back would lie in growing crops to feed a resistance movement, or raising livestock to support a militia—freedom through farm animals.

BECOME A REFUGEE It's not a pleasant thought to consider having to flee from your homeland during a time of conflict, but millions of people have had to do so in recent years, and that trend is unlikely to stop anytime soon. Finding safety in the wake of an invasion may mean escaping from the country as a refugee. This isn't as bad as it sounds, if you have enough money and a place to go (especially should you happen to have family or close friends in another country). It can become a living hell if you end up in a refugee camp or in a worse situation, living on the streets in a foreign land and having to start over with nothing or no one to support you.

ACT LIKE A GUERRILLA If you're thinking about beating on your chest, eating raw bamboo, or throwing your poo, you're thinking about a gorilla (the wrong word and creature). We get *guerrilla* ("little war") from early 19th-century Spain, when bands of peasants harassed the occupying French during the Peninsular War (1808-1814). Today, guerrilla fighting (also known as asymmetrical warfare) is typically fought between a standing professional army, and an insurgency or resistance movement. Famous for raids and hit-and-run tactics, guerrilla militias worldwide have been a countering force during and after invasions for many centuries (though they can usually do little more than annoy or distract a larger force).

IMPROVISE WEAPONS Not every weapon of resistance has to be a high-powered piece of artillery or an automatic weapon. While many people in my homeland possess small arms for hunting and self-defense, plenty of others have no firearms whatsoever, for various reasons. That doesn't mean you are out of the fight. For creative individuals, there are plenty of things that the average unarmed person can pull together as a means to fight or defend themselves. Just look at any recent history of unrest or

T / F

THERE IS SUCH A THING AS A PEACEFUL INVASION

TRUE The world's most recent invasion, at the time of the writing of this book, happened on April 30, 2018. A small military force was deployed by the United Arab Emirates (UAE) to take control of the Yemeni archipelago of Socotra in the Guardafui Channel (southeast of a Arabian Peninsula). More than a hundred troops with artillery and armored vehicles were flown in to take control of administrative installations (like the Socotra Airport and various island seaports). While Yemen condemned the invasion as "an act of aggression," there was no military resistance or backlash from the civilian population. In fact, many locals are happy with their new leadership. The UAE has been improving the island's infrastructure by building a communications network, and it is providing free healthcare and work permits in Abu Dhabi for the residents of Socotra.

uprising. People still fight like cavemen with clubs and rocks (though today, it's more like baseball bats and bricks). And nothing makes the 5 o'clock news like a few Molotov cocktails. Be creative and see what you can devise.

TEN USES FOR TOILET PAPER

1 **THE INTENDED USE** Cleanliness "down there" can prevent dangerous skin infections, and we modern people are blessed to have such a wide variety of toilet paper for hygiene. For those on a budget, the most sandpapery of one-ply product will suffice. For those with a more discerning bottom, only the softest will do. Toilet paper was recorded in China as early as 600 CE and it began being mass-produced in the fourteenth century. It's the ideal product for cleaning up after a bathroom break, as well as blowing your nose and other personal-hygiene tasks. And it's definitely better than the prior methods of wiping with sticks, rocks, grass, or your bare hands.

2 **AN ALCOHOL STOVE** My uncle Don showed me this one on a campout many years ago: Drop a full roll of toilet paper into an empty coffee can (or any other #10 tin can). Then pour in one bottle of high-proof rubbing alcohol. Toss in a match and you've got a coffee-can cooking stove. It's a little hard to regulate the heat, and it doesn't burn forever, but it works well enough to cook a meal, so long as you can suspend your food over the fire safely and effectively. Be careful when using alcohol for fuel, as the flames are hard to see in bright daylight. Turn the stove "off," if necessary, by placing a flat stone over the can to smother the flames.

3 **TORCH BUILDING** If you need a bright, outdoor light source, toilet paper and cooking oil can make an amazing torch. Wrap some toilet paper around one end of a live green wooden stick so that it looks like a giant Q-tip. Make sure not to use a dead stick, or else the wood will burn. It's best to choose a live stick with a fork or side branch at the end, as this keeps the toilet paper head from flying off or sliding down. Soak the TP-wrapped head in cooking oil (or any other oil) and light it with a flame. The average torch head will burn for about 15 or 20 minutes and will look just like the torches in the movies. Be careful, though—this method of survival lighting can be a real fire hazard!

4 **LEAVING MESSAGES** Many companies produce toilet paper with puzzles, quotes, jokes, and other entertaining material printed on the otherwise boring rolls. One enterprising author even had a horror novel printed on a roll of toilet paper. Talk about a scary bathroom visit! So, take a page out of that not-book and help yourself survive by using toilet paper to leave messages. You can even spell out words or use simple flags to mark your path if you don't have anything to write with. Toilet paper will melt in the first rainstorm, but it can work as a temporary way to mark trails and leave notes.

5 **WATER FILTRATION** There's no substitute for a top-quality water filter that is factory built, but a little toilet paper can make a simple DIY filter that works to remove some of the mud and sediment that would hopelessly clog your valuable, store-bought filter. Save a cardboard TP roll and pack it with crumpled toilet paper. Pour your muddy water through the tube, and watch it come out the other end as slightly less muddy water. This filter won't remove any significant number of pathogens, but it will improve the clarity of the water and prevent some wear and tear to your more sensitive and refined filtration equipment.

6 **FIRE STARTING** Toilet paper and its cardboard rolls are flammable, making these

Got a spare roll, or maybe even a spare package (or case!) of toilet paper? This material may be simple stuff, but don't let that fool you; even in modern times, a high-quality roll of TP can be worth its weight in gold and can be put to a lot of interesting uses—not just the obvious one!

great additions to your bag of fire-starting tricks. Either material can burn as the tinder to get your fire going. Toilet paper can also be wadded into little balls and dipped in melted wax to make superior fire starters. Just leave a little "flag" of paper sticking up from each, to make them easier to light. You can also stuff the cardboard roll with dryer lint, cotton balls, or other fuel—either as a way to transport the materials, or as a fire-starting "log" for wet weather. Drench the stuffed cardboard tube in oil or melted wax for something that will burn for a long time.

7 GARDENING Save up all those empty cardboard toilet paper rolls, as they will have many potential uses in the survival garden. If you're a fan of biodegradable seed pots, fill a plastic tray with vertical roll sections, add dirt, and sow your seeds. You can also make cutworm collars for chemical-free pest control: Cut rings from your toilet paper rolls and press them into the soil around the base of tender seedlings to block cutworms (which pop out of the soil and kill your baby plants). And, if nothing else, you can rip them into little pieces and blend them with your compost pile to create a little more dirt—and thus a little more food down the road.

8 ENTERTAINMENT Morale can play an unexpectedly important role in long-term survival, so don't be afraid to use a little surplus TP for crafts and amusements. Wrap it as garland around a jolly Christmas tree, or try using toilet paper as festive streamers for your holiday events, birthday parties, and the nuclear-winter formal dance in your bunker. Toilet paper and cardboard tubes can also

be craft supplies. Blend some water, glue, and toilet paper to make papier-mâché for sculpting, or build toy castles from the tubes. You don't want to waste too much TP, but with a little creativity, you can turn this humdrum resource into something fun.

9 TRADE The average person goes through one roll of toilet paper every single week. That's a lot of toilet paper, when you think about it. In the wake of a crisis that would impact the production and supply of goods like toilet paper, it might make sense to have a stockpile of this much-needed commodity. If there's enough civility for local trade and barter after a disaster, toilet paper is the kind of supply that everyone will need, but one that won't paint a big target on your back (as other types of supplies might). Desperate people might follow you and kill you for ammo or medicine—but probably not for your toilet paper.

10 WOUND CARE Toilet paper doesn't really make the best bandages (unless you're pulling together a mummy costume for Halloween), but it does still have some versatility in wound care. We've all seen people stick tiny toilet paper fragments onto razor nicks on their faces after shaving, but you can also use it to make a temporary bandage. Since TP tends to disintegrate when wet, it's best if you stack up sheets and use toilet paper as an absorbent layer as part of a more sturdy bandage. You can also use TP as a base for medicinal plant compounds. For example, boil some crushed acorns in water until the liquid turns brown. Then dip a sheet (or layered stack of sheets) in the brown brew and place this on inflamed skin as a healing compress.

GRID DOWN

IS IT LIKELY TO HAPPEN?

Minor power outages are pretty standard, especially with inclement weather. But in a few catastrophic situations, the power may be out for much longer.

HOW BAD COULD IT REALLY BE?

In most cases, power outage is merely an inconvenience. But a grid-down scenario could lead to massive loss of human life and the complete destruction of our society.

CAN I IMPROVE MY ODDS?

No, you can't fix the grid yourself, even if you are a pole-climbing lineman. But you can be prepared for when it happens, whether it's a minor or major event.

YOUR ICE CREAM MELTS AND YOU HAVE TO USE A FLASHLIGHT TO FIND YOUR WAY THROUGH THE HOUSE. SHORT-TERM POWER LOSS ISN'T SO ROUGH. MODERN SOCIETY, HOWEVER, IS POWERED BY ELECTRICITY, AND IF IT GOES OUT FOR A LONGER SPAN OF TIME, THINGS WILL GET VERY BAD.

The warm glow of an incandescent bulb or the cool, brilliant light of an LED, the control over your environment's heating or cooling, the ability to instantly communicate with someone else, whether they live across town or around the world—all of these things and more are the result of electricity. It has changed almost every civilization it's touched in the century and a half since it was harnessed by humans.

Today, it's hard for us to imagine any part of our lives that could still operate without electrical power. From communication and commerce to education and science to healthcare and entertainment, we need the steady flow of power to provide us the comforts we have grown accustomed to having. But where's the source whence all this juice flows?

There are three main categories of energy production for the creation of electricity in modern society: fossil fuels (such as natural gas, coal, and petroleum), nuclear power, and renewable-energy sources. Most of the world's electrical power is still generated by burning fossil fuels, while renewable energy (such as that derived from hydroelectric power plants, geothermal sources, wind turbines, and solar photovoltaics) runs a close second place. As of 2020, one-fifth of the electricity generated in the United States was nuclear energy, making it the smallest of these three groups. Whatever the source, this power is carefully controlled, and it flows from its source and through your local power lines to get to your home and business. As you can guess, all these lines, transformers, substations, and power plants need to be working correctly together in order to supply the power safely and efficiently—and there are a lot of pieces that can fail, and plenty of things that can go wrong along the way, from the merely inconvenient to the utterly catastrophic.

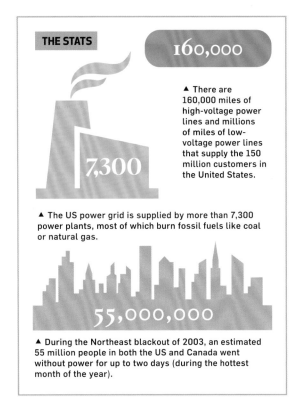

THE STATS

160,000

▲ There are 160,000 miles of high-voltage power lines and millions of miles of low-voltage power lines that supply the 150 million customers in the United States.

7,300

▲ The US power grid is supplied by more than 7,300 power plants, most of which burn fossil fuels like coal or natural gas.

55,000,000

▲ During the Northeast blackout of 2003, an estimated 55 million people in both the US and Canada went without power for up to two days (during the hottest month of the year).

PREP FOR A BLACKOUT The way to prepare for a power blackout is to get ready and stay ready. All the normal preparations will come in handy, such as stocking nonperishable food, water, flashlights, batteries, first aid supplies, and hygiene items. A battery-powered or hand-cranked radio could also be a very valuable piece of your kit. Keep functional flashlights in places around your home that are easy to access. You'll probably want to minimize your use of candles, since they do represent a fire hazard (and you don't need to add a house fire to your list of problems during a power outage). Add to your readiness by getting familiar with your residence's electrical and water systems, figuring out alternative ways to cook your food, and considering the pros and cons of generating your own power. In hopes that the power will be back any minute, you should turn off or unplug all unnecessary or sensitive electric equipment (including electric stoves, TVs, computers, and sound systems) so that an electrical surge or spike won't damage them if the power is restored.

THERE ARE TECH WORKAROUNDS The grid is the heart and blood vessels of the modern world, and electricity—its lifeblood—but there are a few workarounds for the short-term grid failure (or the first week of a longer disaster) that can circumvent the modern electrical grid. One of the most important things to have in a power outage event is a way to charge your cell phone besides a wall outlet. Solar chargers are a nice investment. AA-battery cell phone chargers are cheaper and more commonly available than solar. You could use a car charger for devices, as long as the gas holds out. A larger (briefcase-size) solar panel will charge devices like phones and iPads (but not laptops). After a lengthy outage, cell phone towers probably won't be working, but a pricey satellite phone should still be operational. But who would you call? Their phone's probably down.

START SURVIVING If there wasn't a storm or some other obvious natural cause, you may not know why the power has suddenly gone out in your area. There is one thing that's certain, though: Every aspect of your life just got a little bit harder. Hopefully, you have planned ahead with alternative sources of light and you have a backup cooking method.

Use camping stoves or an outdoor grill to make meals from your most perishable foods first. Take advantage of your natural creativity with food. Use some aluminum foil and a low heat on the hamburger grill to bake those frozen pizzas. Try some charcoal and a Dutch oven to cook a pot of chili. For water, you can use a backpacker's water filter to disinfect raw water from your surrounding environment. In the initial stages of a power outage, it's a bit like camping—you're just staying in your own home to do it.

REACT AND PRIORITIZE When you realize that the lack of electricity is more than just a normal outage, it's important to react appropriately. One of the best reactions is to prioritize your activities and your use of supplies. If you're truly in a grid-down scenario, you'll need to use your food, water filtration equipment, first aid products and other resources frugally (since you'll have no way of knowing when you can acquire more). Providing your own heat, cooling, and light can also become a major issue. A few days into the crisis, your fridge and freezer will be empty and you'll be using your canned foods and dry goods. At this time, throw away any questionable or potentially unsafe foods that have a foul odor, color, or texture. Urban and suburban water towers, tanks, and reservoirs should probably still be working for a while, along with sewage—but for how long? You'll need a backup plan for water collection, disinfection, waste disposal and hygiene.

CALL FOR HELP When an emergency (like a medical issue or a fire) arises during a grid-down situation, and your normal means of calling for help are down, you may have to get in a vehicle and drive to the nearest fire department, police station, or hospial. Haunting thoughts like these often inspire preparedness enthusiasts to look into alternative communication equipment like CB and ham radios (though there is no guarantee that anyone helpful will be listening).

RECOVER FROM A BLACKOUT

When the power comes back on, there will be rejoicing, but it doesn't mean your

T / F

NATIONS WAGE WAR ON POWER GRIDS

TRUE Cyberwarfare has grown in the past few decades, with trained military specialists breaking into power grids. Russia launched a cyberattack on the Ukrainian power grid in 2016, shutting down more than fifty power substations as a prelude to its invasion. Russian government-mounted cyberattacks also served as a precursor to invasion in 2008. These attacks included website takedowns, DNS attacks, and ultimately a complete blackout of internet traffic in Georgia. Some cybersecurity experts help power grids stay up and running, and others work to shut it down. Along with cyber-defense, nation-states guard themselves with threats of cyberwarfare retaliation ("we'll hack back") or physical strikes ("Hack us, and we'll put a missile in your power plant.")

problems are over. Power surges can ruin appliances and start fires. Worse still, you'll finally learn the extent of the damage caused by the outage. There will be cleanup and repairs needed, and law and order may even need to be reestablished (after a long crisis), but the hard work will definitely be worth the reward. You've got lights again!

DEAL WITH THE DAMAGE What do you do when the power is out for a while? Great question—you may only be able to answer it the hard way. You may have no idea what's going on, and depending on the cause of the power outage and the duration, you may have some tough choices to make.

IF THE POWER IS OUT FOR	WHAT SHOULD YOU DO	UNEXPECTED RESULTS
A FEW HOURS	Keep flashlights handy. Keep the fridge and freezer closed. Decide when or if you'll fire up a generator.	Now you have time for all those hobbies (or chores).
A DAY	If you have a generator, you'll be running it now—for as long as the fuel lasts. Enjoy your fresh food and ice cream while you can.	Now you don't look so crazy for buying that generator.
A WEEK	Figure out where you're going to get gas for that generator, and try to figure out what happened to the power. Start dipping into your food storage as the fridge and freezer are emptied.	Have a cookout with all your frozen foods, before they spoil. Decide how to say no when neighbors walk your way, unspooling extension cords and hoping to mooch some of your power.
A MONTH	You've realized by now that power won't be restored quickly, so you'll have to figure out a way to feed yourself and your loved ones without power.	You finally have the opportunity to shed that unwanted weight and take up a productive pastime, like gardening.
A YEAR	No storm or hack could drop the power for a year—it would take a solar flare or EMP. You'll need to use every trick in the book to survive until the power comes back.	These would be tough times, and the loss of life would be staggering. Healthcare would likely revert to primitive methods, and people you know would die often and easily.
FOREVER	The *Road Warrior* scenario has come true. Find a little community where you can be productive and figure out how to repel marauders, day and night.	A new dark age would descend. This wouldn't just be a lack of light—it would be a loss of knowledge and a huge step backward for humanity.

3

SPIDERS

Many of us are at least a little bit uneasy at the prospect of facing an eight-legged intruder in our daily lives. But for some, it extends into a debilitating and irrational fear. The word *arachnophobia* stems from the Greek word *arakni*, meaning "spider", and the phobia isn't triggered by just spiders themselves—it can also be caused by the sufferer seeing a similar creature such as a scorpion, or seeing a detailed image of a spider, or even a spider's web, out of fear that its owner is nearby but unseen. Even the prospect of a spider potentially being close will distress an arachnophobe; any exposure can trigger a panic attack, and some will refuse to enter an area where they have seen a spider.

Most spiders are not harmful to humans, but along with some cultural fear of spiders, particularly in Europe, it may be that the fear stems from an evolutionary trait: An ancestor who had that fear and avoided any spider had less risk of being bitten at all, and thus had better chances of surviving and reproducing. This phobia may also be closely connected with fear of insects (entomophobia), as spiders and insects are similar in size and have multiple skittering limbs.

6.1%

▶ About seven people in the United States die yearly from venomous spider bites. (Meanwhile, fatalities from bee or wasp stings are about eight times higher.)

▲ Up to 6.1 percent of the global population has a phobia of spiders.

7

63,000

▲ There are over 63,000 species of spider on Earth—but only 2 percent are dangerous to humans.

IMPROVE YOUR ODDS

Similar to other specific fears, arachnophobia can be treated by exposure and desensitization therapy. The person suffering from arachnophobia is often trained first in relaxation techniques, so that they can learn to keep themselves calm as exposure treatment is undertaken. The patient is then gradually exposed, starting with less stressful stimuli such as a drawing of a spider, or imagining a spider. Treatment proceeds to imagining being closer to or handling a spider, then actual close-up exposure or physical interaction. In some cases, VR is used—or even watching *Spider-Man* film clips.

TERRORISM

IS IT LIKELY TO HAPPEN?

Is terrorism likely to hit the major metropolitan area where you reside? Chances of becoming a direct victim are low, but it's very likely to impact your way of life.

HOW BAD COULD IT REALLY BE?

Terrorists ultimately do more harm to economies and peace of mind than individual people or communities, but you may still feel long-lasting effects.

CAN I IMPROVE MY ODDS?

Living in a bunker will keep you out of the crosshairs, but it's not much of a life. Improve your chances by remaining aware; if you see something, say something.

THE VERY DEFINITION OF "TERRORISM" IS RIGHT THERE IN THE NAME— THESE OFTEN-DEADLY ACTS ARE DONE SPECIFICALLY TO STRIKE TERROR INTO THE HEARTS OF AN ADVERSARY. TARGETING THE INNOCENT DOESN'T OFTEN HAPPEN BY ACCIDENT, AND IT'S OFTEN HARD TO PROTECT AGAINST.

*I*t's hard for those of us with a normal mind-set to even imagine killing women, children, paramedics, and other innocent targets. In warfare, these losses are tragic collateral damage, but in terrorism, such groups are preferred targets for an attack. Unexpected and unthinkable acts are the point for terrorists—and the more shocking these events, the better, since the idea is to sow fear and confusion.

While we often think of terrorism as something "they" do to "us," the fact is that sometimes—and more often than we want to admit—terrorists can strike from within. Consider, for example, the anti-technology Unabomber, Ted Kaczynski, who sent mail bombs and attempted to blow up a commercial airliner as part of his crusade; the racists who bombed schools and churches in the 1960s to protest integration; the Columbine killers, who saw themselves as striking for justice against the jocks who bullied them; and an all-too-lengthy list of other evil people committing heartless and deadly acts.

Terrorism is not a new phenomenon at all, either: Scholars will readily debate which historical attacks and related actions were terrorism and which were warfare. Some say that Hebrew zealots known as the *sicarii* (meaning "dagger-wielders"), who assassinated Roman occupiers and those who collaborated with Romans in Judea in the first century CE, were the world's first true terrorists. Other historians believe that early Muslim groups in Persia committed the first true acts of terrorism against civilian targets.

Since those ancient times, the tools of terrorists have changed from knives and poisons to explosives and firearms, but the motivation remains the same: to stir fear and apprehension in their targets on the path to furthering their aims. In any case, the roots and practice of terrorism can be seen here and there throughout recorded history, and the threat shows no sign of diminishing.

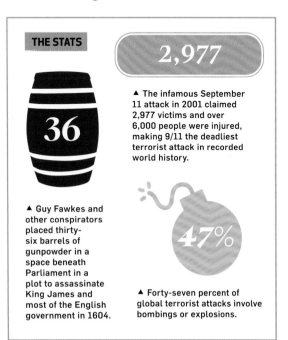

THE STATS

36

▲ Guy Fawkes and other conspirators placed thirty-six barrels of gunpowder in a space beneath Parliament in a plot to assassinate King James and most of the English government in 1604.

2,977

▲ The infamous September 11 attack in 2001 claimed 2,977 victims and over 6,000 people were injured, making 9/11 the deadliest terrorist attack in recorded world history.

47%

▲ Forty-seven percent of global terrorist attacks involve bombings or explosions.

MANY TERROR THREATS ARE HOMEGROWN

TRUE While many of us worry about terrorism at the hands of foreign groups, your uncle Joe in the KKK is a much more present threat than ISIS. Between September 11, 2001, and March of 2020, a total of 486 people were charged with acts of terrorism in the United States. Most of these were men, and 234 of them (nearly half) were US-born American citizens. In recent history (and a long time coming), the FBI finally declared that white supremacist terrorism in the US is at least equal in threat to organizations such as the Islamic State. For several years, both federal and state authorities have been analyzing an increased number of such individuals and groups as a rising threat to US citizens and increasingly infiltrating government and law-enforcement agencies. It's unfortunate that terrorists are often stereotyped as "foreigners" in movies and television (and even on the news), and we fail to recognize more local threats (like hate groups). Some Afghani terrorist cell is not much of a threat to your small town from its base camp thousands of miles away, but your town's local neo-Nazi group may bring the violence home to roost.

GET EDUCATED Protect yourself and others against terrorism by getting to know your enemy. The first use of the word *terrorist* dates back to 1794. In the thirteen-month period known as the Reign of Terror, Paris was the scene of mass executions and public purges. While this episode in history was "the government against the people," the word stuck and is now used for organizations of "the people against a government." Today, terrorism is defined in two ways: international and domestic. International terrorism involves violent acts harmful to human life, which violate laws. These acts are undertaken to both intimidate a civilian population and influence government. They occur primarily outside of US territorial jurisdiction. Domestic terrorism meets all the criteria of international terrorism, but it involves terrorist activity within the jurisdiction of the US. These acts can include mass shootings, the use of explosives or nuclear, biological, or chemical agents; cyberterrorism; and attacks to utilities, such as the electrical grid. Some more unusual but increasingly common methods of causing terror include vehicle-ramming attacks, wherein an individual drives a car or other vehicle through a crowd or into a structure. These actions have brought about loss of life, illness, and injury, the displacement of large numbers of people, destruction of property, and devastating economic loss. In contemporary times, technological advances and ongoing international political unrest give terrorists the tools and the motivation to become an even greater threat to local and global security.

GET TO KNOW YOUR NEW "FRIENDS" So, if terrorists are killing themselves, shouldn't their numbers be dwindling? Not all terror activity is suicidal, and modern terrorist organizations do more than just spread fear—they also recruit. In order to maintain their ranks, both foreign and domestic terror groups have begun to focus more on the recruitment of young people. Impressionable minds are more easily radicalized, and gullible youngsters are some of the most vulnerable initiates. This recruitment can take the form of terrorist cell members luring young girls to run away and become wives to radicals—something they almost always come to regret—or high school and college students being drawn into dangerous radical groups. Either way, you can avoid falling into their trap by learning more about the leadership and aims of any group that you want to join and by avoiding groups that display any signs of having questionable goals or group members. Trust your instincts—and if you're a bad judge of character, don't join any groups.

EXPECT A SUCKER PUNCH Lightning doesn't strike the same place twice, but terrorists can (and have) struck the same spot with delayed attacks. Should you find yourself caught up in such an event, you can avoid a secondary (or follow-up) attack by leaving the area as soon as you realize what's happening. There have been cases in which terrorists intentionally set up a bomb, or planned some other violence against the first responders who have arrived to help the wounded. Since most of us are law-abiding citizens with empathy for the pain

of others, it's hard to imagine this kind of evil plan, but you should start imagining it, and a way around it. Our ignorance about this kind of attack strategy won't offer any protection from it; it's like sticking our heads in the sand. We live in an age where you need to ask these hard "what if?" questions. When you're in any public place, keep a lookout for both normal and non-traditional exits. Remember that main exits can also become targets for follow-up attacks. For example, a bomb may drive a crowd toward an exit where a second attack is planned for the people packed into a denser grouping. Don't be shy about using fire exits, delivery doors, and any other points of egress that are normally off-limits. Take people with you, if they are willing to go.

MAYBE DON'T BE A HERO

Most of us have dreamed of being superheroes since we were little, and while we might imagine that events like a terrorist attack would give average people the chance to be heroic, think again. It's been said that a hero is "someone who gets a lot of other people killed," and here's how that can become true. It might seem heroic to run into a burning building to look for survivors after an incendiary device goes off, but unless you know exactly what you're doing (and have the right protective equipment), the firefighters and first responders now have one more person to rescue. In addition to causing more trouble than helping, you might even end up on the wrong side of law enforcement (if they think you're one of the perpetrators still on the scene). Yes, there are some scenarios where you can play the noble role of a hero, but in most cases, you need to sit on the bench and leave it to the pros.

SEE AND SAY The slogan goes, "If you see something, say something." It doesn't tell you to personally do something about the threat. It's true that you can save the day, but it's not by getting in a shootout with the bad guys. The best way you can help is by alerting the good guys (the ones who have the body armor and bomb-sniffing dogs). No, you don't need to call the FBI every time you see a purse left in a shopping cart, or whenever an unexpected package appears on your porch, but you should trust your instincts and stay alert in crowded public places, shopping malls, government buildings, and other top targets for terrorists. Vigilance is the price of safety these days.

RESPOND TO AN ATTACK It's okay to run away. We humans are an unpredictable bunch, and in the face of a terrifying threat, we may do one of several things: We may run away in a panicked state and escape the threat. We may run right into danger (inadvertently). We may also freeze, unable to react to the unthinkable events unfolding around us. Closed-circuit television footage of the 2013 attack on the Westgate shopping mall in Nairobi, Kenya, shows these responses in heartbreaking detail: Four masked gunmen from the extremist Islamic group al-Shabaab went through the mall, shooting at will. While some shoppers ran for their lives and found safety, others ran right into oncoming gunmen. Most tragic of all, some people simply cowered on the floor and were shot at point blank range. The attack wounded around 200 people; 5 Kenyan soldiers and 62 civilians were killed in the event.

2 HEIGHTS

If standing on a mountaintop or riding a Ferris wheel or a glass elevator is your worst nightmare, you might have acrophobia. Fear of heights is perfectly understandable and common—it's closely tied to a fear of falling (and the sudden stop at the end), but it is technically different. Acrophobia is one of two instinctive fears we are born with (the other is a fear of loud noises), and it kept our ancestors from trying dangerous feats (like scaling cliffs or tall trees).

The *acro* part of *acrophobia* is a word that refers to heights, derived from the Greek word *akros*, meaning "highest" (as in *acrobat*). While some phobias improve with age, this one probably won't. Phobias that have to do with vulnerability (like heights and crowds) often get worse, as anxiety can increase with age. The symptoms of acrophobia include headache and dizziness; trembling or sweating; feelings of terror or paralysis; an urgent desire to get down, even if it means crawling on all fours or kneeling; heart palpitations; crying or other emotional outbursts; or a complete panic attack. And a panic attack leading to irrational behavior while in a high place can be dangerous indeed.

 ◀ Five percent of the world's population is seriously affected by this disorder, unable to cross tall bridges, climb tall buildings, or travel by air.

▼ Phobias can be grouped into five major categories, relating to animals, natural environments, situations, injuries, and a grab-bag category for other types of fears.

▶ Like the fear of the dark, this phobia affects adult females twice as often as adult males.

IMPROVE YOUR ODDS

If this phobia has a major impact on your quality of life, you have some options to try out. Therapy and medication can help manage the symptoms. Exposure therapy is another option, and virtual reality has been used for this phobia since the 1990s, allowing sufferers to safely experience the visual sensation of height with none of the danger involved. Relaxation techniques, like yoga and deep breathing, can also help you cope with this fear. Talk to your doctor and make sure you seek treatment for acrophobia, particularly if being in high locations is part of your life.

SURVIVAL COOKING

KNOW YOUR HISTORY

Today, many people seem to believe that you can prepare a great meal only if you have the latest kitchen gadgets and a restaurant-grade oven. I'm happy to tell you that this simply isn't the case: Our ancestors were no strangers to cooking, even complex cuisine, and the majority of meals prepared throughout human history have been done without the aid of a blender or a microwave. And the menu doesn't have to be meat roasted over the fire, again and again, day in and day out. In fact, most modern foods can be cooked without the aid of utilities or a functional kitchen. It does take some skill (and a good sense of heat and timing) to cook a meal off the grid, but there are plenty of options when the power is out. You can purchase camp-friendly cooking equipment as a backup plan before trouble hits, and there are even some things you can slap together in a crisis (if you got caught without these preparations in place). I'm getting hungry just thinking about it.

GET STARTED

After a catastrophic (or at least a very seriously inconveniencing) event happens is not the time to start building your survival pantry. After all, a deserted building may hold all the brick rubble and mortar you would ever need to build an amazing brick pizza oven . . . but that's not likely to be much help for you and your growling stomach if the only food you've got is a big bag of beans. Set yourself up for success by figuring out far in advance what you'll be cooking, based on your skills, resources, and access to foodstuffs. In a crisis, your meals will not be determined by what the family wants for dinner. Instead, you'll be taking inventory of what equipment and ingredients you can lay hands on. As you might imagine, it's a little hard to boil a pot of beans without a pot (or any beans), and it's even harder to make a pizza if all you have is a pot and some beans. Let your resources inspire you, and be happy with what you have. Try not to dwell on what you *don't* have.

TEST IT OUT

Prior to whatever crisis you and your bag of beans have been living through, you hit the outdoor-recreation store and bought a small camping stove and some fuel cylinders. That's great! You're planning ahead, and that is commendable. Just remember that you're doing yourself a serious disservice if you don't take time to test out any new gear and get familiar with it *before* disaster strikes. It's important to know the capabilities and limitations of your equipment—this could literally be a matter of life or death if you need to boil water to disinfect it, for example. Set the stove up in your back yard, or a park if you're a city dweller, and gain some experience with it well before you have to rely on it. Make some test meals close to home like this (while you can still order takeout if things go wrong). Consider taking your emergency kitchen on a short camping trip—it's a great, safe way to learn if you're missing any essentials (while sporting goods stores still exist).

ADVANCE YOUR SKILLS

Once you've become familiar with your camping stove and tools, and have learned a handful of easy meals you can prepare with them, it'll be time to explore some additional cooking methods, for times when the stove isn't available, or you just want a little variety. Try using your regular kitchen pots and pans over a small outdoor campfire. Skillets, frying pans, griddles, and contemporary frying containers will all allow you to make very tasty meals that often resemble conventionally cooked favorites. Elevate your frying pan or griddle over the fire using bricks, stones, cinderblocks, or other fireproof supports. In a pinch, you can use a 6-inch support, but 1-foot-tall supports will work much better. Before you start cooking, pour a spoonful of water into the pan or onto the griddle to see if it's level. If not, place small thin stones or other nonflammable objects on your support tower to level out the skillet. Feed the fire with small dry sticks and split wood pieces to keep flames under your pan for boiling and frying. Once the flames die down, be sure to maintain a nice bed of coals for baking and roasting meats, vegetables, and even simple breads and cakes.

AVOID THESE MISTAKES

Not every cooking method will work under every condition. You can't use a skillet over an open fire amid a monsoon, and your solar oven isn't much use at night. Have options, be adaptable, and steer clear of the following common mistakes.

Use the Right Fuel Pine and other sapwoods produce foul smoke while species like black locust, yew, buckeye, horse chestnut, rhododendron, and laurel are downright toxic. Be careful when burning wooden debris: Pressure-treated lumber (greenish and perforated) gives off very toxic smoke.

Don't Turn Your Back Cooking is more than just a chore; it's a necessary job. Like many other important tasks, never turn your back on it. Stay with your food and pay attention. Chances are, your food will burn (or stop cooking) when you turn your attention away from it.

Use Only Dry Stones Rocks from wet areas can be waterlogged, and may explode violently when heated for the first time. If you use stones to build a cooking hearth, you can avoid the boom by collecting the stones to build it from a high and dry area.

IF ALL ELSE FAILS

Redundancy can be a beautiful thing. Even your backup plans should have their own backup plans in case things aren't working out. In other words, don't just plan on using one way to cook when the grid goes down or if you are somewhere away from civilization; you should plan to choose between several. And if all that fails, then it'll be time for you to get creative and find an approach that will work for you in your unique situation. For example, let's say that it's storming too hard to cook over a fire outdoors, and you're sitting in your vehicle to take shelter from the elements and listen to the radio for weather updates. If you have plenty of fuel to spare, or if you are running the engine long enough for it to get hot anyway (maybe to charge your mobile phone or warm yourself up), you can also use it to heat some food at the same time. Try wrapping whatever you have to eat in some aluminum foil and then place the bundle under your vehicle hood (close to the exhaust manifold). Keep the vehicle idling (or even drive it around) and the engine heat will cook it for you. Sure, it might taste a little strange and it will cook unevenly, but hey, it's a warm meal.

NUCLEAR WAR

IS IT LIKELY TO HAPPEN?

Imagine the worst day you could have, then add "nearby nuclear detonation" to your list of problems. It's unlikely, but it's been a possibility for more than seventy years.

HOW BAD COULD IT REALLY BE?

Whether mutually assured destruction or a dirty bomb, nuclear events can be survivable, but if the explosion doesn't get you, the radiation might.

CAN I IMPROVE MY ODDS?

Nuclear war and its aftermath would be devastating, but you can reduce your exposure to radiation and improve your chances of survival.

FROM THE 1950S THROUGH THE 1980S, THE LOOMING THREAT OF NUCLEAR HOLOCAUST WAS SEARED INTO THE COLLECTIVE CONSCIOUSNESS OF THE WORLD, AND FOR GOOD REASON: THE THREAT WAS LEGITIMATE. SORRY TO BURST YOUR BUBBLE, BUT NOTHING HAS REALLY CHANGED SINCE THEN.

Even though certain biological and chemical weapons are powerful, nuclear weapons are still viewed as the most destructive weapons ever devised here on Earth. With an explosive power so devastating that a single nuclear bomb can level an entire city, the smallest nuclear devices can do even more damage than the largest non-nuclear explosive.

Given the devastating effects of these weapons, global leaders met and created the Treaty on the Non-Proliferation of Nuclear Weapons in the late 1960s. Finally activated in March 1970, this international treaty was engineered to prevent the spread of nuclear weapons, encourage cooperation between nations on the development of nuclear energy, and continue working toward nuclear disarmament. World leaders met once again in 1995 and extended the treaty indefinitely during that summit.

Not every country in the world is part of this treaty, however, and India, Pakistan, and North Korea are either known to have or believed to have nuclear weapons technology, while other nations such as Iran and Iraq have attempted to develop their own nuclear weapons programs. This is still a far cry from the days of living in constant fear during the Cold War, especially in the 1960s and during the Cuban Missile Crisis. The threat of a nuclear holocaust inspired many adults

to install backyard bunkers, and this fear was further reinforced in the younger generation with duck-and-cover drills, in which schoolkids were instructed to crawl under their desks and hide there until the bombs had stopped falling.

While the risk of mutually assured destruction ("If you launch your nukes at us, then we launch ours at you, and everybody dies together.") is smaller than it was in the past, those nuclear bombs are still out there, and madmen are still prone to madness.

THE STATS

▼ Only nine (known) nations possess nuclear weapons: the United States, the United Kingdom, Russia, France, China, India, Pakistan, Israel, and North Korea.

9

2

▲ Only two nuclear weapons have been used against a population in world history: those dropped on Hiroshima and Nagasaki.

14,000

▲ The collective nuclear arsenal on Warth was around 70,000 warheads in 1986, but today that number has dropped to somewhere around 14,000 known nukes in the world (still enough to wipe out all human life, several times over).

NUCLEAR CODES ARE KEPT ON FLOPPY DISKS

TRUE For the younger crowd, some explaining is called for here: When we used to ride our dinosaurs to work and we needed to store some information or move a file from one computer to another, we'd save it on a computer disk inside a thin, square plastic casing. Computers still honor this ancient history in the form of the icon for saving a file. (That little square symbol you click to save your work represents a floppy disk). This technology has been around for quite a while, and, interestingly enough, it's still here. If the average world leader wanted to launch a nuclear strike, they'd need a very important eight-inch floppy disk to actually put their finger on the button. Now, this technology is decades old, the kind most modern adults have never even seen before. It may seem like a purposeful choice—for instance, keeping the world's most sensitive data away from your enemies (or teenage hackers) by using nonaccessible codes on old technology. The truth is much more embarrassing: Most government cyber systems are simply woefully out of date. The US government spends an estimated $60 billion annually to maintain these outdated systems.

KNOW THE DRILL The Cold War is over, but some rogue nation might still be crazy enough to launch a nuclear attack someday. If so, then some simple facts will help you survive. Let's skip the physics lectures about radiation types or blast radii, and cut to the key factors: time, distance, and shielding. "Time" refers to limiting your time in the affected area if at all possible, and also waiting a bit to leave your shelter—several weeks would be ideal. "Distance" means the farther away you are (or can get) from the affected area, the happier you will be, especially if you can get upwind. As for "shielding," if you're outside a nearby nuke's blast radius, you can survive the radiation by sheltering in a way that shields you from the radiation, fallout (radioactive dust), and radiation-laced rainfall. Hang out in your basement for a few weeks, with the windows taped up to keep out dust.

DODGE A DIRTY BOMB Essentially the terrorist version of a nuclear weapon, a dirty bomb refers to any explosive device that has a radioactive component. One of these would cause far greater fear in a population than simple explosives since they spread radioactive particles throughout the blast radius. The particles can drift downwind and be tracked by people and vehicles throughout the area. The fear caused by a bombing is one thing, but the fear of getting cancer or having other health issues in the future puts this weapon on a whole different level. If a dirty bomb is suspected or confirmed in your area, shelter in place and seal off your home as best you can. Stay in your shelter until an all-clear has been given by authorities.

Tsutomu Yamaguchi

The man who survived not one but two nuclear bombs!

Tsutomu Yamaguchi was a Japanese citizen who was born on March 16, 1916, and passed away on January 4, 2010. He has been called "the unluckiest man in the world" by some, though he should be considered pretty lucky. Yamaguchi lived in Nagasaki, but he was in Hiroshima when the bomb was dropped on the city on August 6, 1945. Miraculously, he survived the nuclear blast and returned home. He returned to work on August 9, even though he was injured and had lost his hearing in his left ear. Yamaguchi was being chewed out by his boss, and just when he thought his day couldn't get any worse, the second nuclear bomb of World War II was dropped on Nagasaki. He didn't die that day, either. More than seventy people are known to have been in both cities when they were bombed, but it wasn't until March 24, 2009, that the Japanese government officially recognized his presence in both cities at the time of the attacks.

Yamaguchi's exposure to extremely radioactive dust eventually caught up with him, and he suffered from radiation-related cataracts and acute leukemia in his later years. Stomach cancer ultimately claimed him in 2010, but he lived to the age of 93. Yamaguchi's wife also received radiation exposure, poisoned by the "black rain" that fell after the Nagasaki explosion. She also lived a full life, only losing her battle against kidney and liver cancer in 2010. To the surprise of doctors (and the world), their three children did not show any major issues as a result of both parents being exposed to the radiation of the bombings, though some sources say that they did have a few health problems. In his final years, Yamaguchi became a vocal opponent of nuclear weapons and an outspoken champion of global nuclear disarmament.

TOP 10 POSTNUCLEAR JOBS

1 **SECURITY GUARD** Former police officers, bodyguards, and soldiers, have we got a job for you! The number-one career in a lawless apocalypse will be that of a protector. The job of security guard will be in high demand as people try to protect what they have from other people who want to take it from them. Being grim and having a great sixth sense about people are very useful attributes. There are plenty of perks with the job, but there's also a problem: You'd be the most likely community member to die by violence. Look on the bright side, though: If you don't make the cut for the first round of guards, you'll eventually get the job, as new positions keep opening up.

2 **MEDICAL PROVIDER** We'll need some medical providers to patch up all those security guards. We'll also need medical care for all the normal problems that humans face on a day-to-day basis. Doctors, nurses, EMTs, dentists, midwives, and many other medical care providers have the skills that we can't live without (in the truest sense of the words). They may not have the ideal supplies to work their healing magic, but their understanding of the human body is still something that takes years to achieve. With luck and skill, these medical professionals will be able to support our bodies as they heal and help us stave off death a little longer.

3 **FARMER** With the people guarded and medical care available, the next big hurdle will be producing food. This is one of the most diverse jobs on this list, as farmers are often masters of both plants and animals. While farming skills can be learned, they are often learned the hard way—and that means lost food. This is unacceptable when people may actually starve to death while waiting months for a crop to grow to a harvestable state, so someone with a lifetime of farm experience is the best choice for the job. Farmers may focus on crops or livestock, but these typically thrive when combined (such as using manure for fertilizer).

4 **BUILDER** From fortifying doors to building new homes from scratch, the builder will definitely be a useful part of any community. Carpentry skills are a great asset, as are plumbing and electrical know-how. The builder will need both tools and experience, and be good at transforming the junk you have into the stuff that is needed. It's unlikely that any big home-improvement store will be open for business after Doomsday, but a good builder will be able to improvise, using the available materials to get the job done. Good partnerships for builders will include foragers (to find wood and other natural building materials), scavengers (to find more material for construction), and laborers (to move all of those materials).

5 **MECHANIC** The *Mad Max* scenario is upon us, and the dress code of the day is a Mohawk hairdo and leather chaps. Times are tough—unless you also happen to be a skilled mechanic. Those handy individuals will be in high demand. Most mechanics specialize in one field, but are good at understanding many kinds of machinery. In the wake of an electromagnetic pulse, they could get cars running (and keep them that way); repair the tractors that help people farm; keep generators running; and mend countless other tools and machines. Why would we want to go back to Stone Age technology when we can simply revitalize what we have, and maintain something better?

In a world where bombs have fallen and civilization as we know it has ended, it's still possible that humanity will survive, albeit with a lower population and limited resources. In safely habitable areas, work will still need to be done to survive—especially if we want to rebuild society, too.

6 HUNTER Few trades are romanticized as much as that of the hunter. These crafty individuals pit themselves against nature, to outthink and outmaneuver some of the most alert creatures on Earth: wild game animals. When having a pasture full of cows, sheep, or goats, or a coop full of chickens, isn't an option, the hunter can bring home the bacon and satisfy people's hunger for meat. Hunters may diversify their skill set with many means of taking (like bows, guns, snares, and other traps), or they may stick to the hunting tools they know best (as long as the ammo holds out). Having keen senses and effective weapons are absolutely essential requirements for this job.

7 FISHERMAN If the waterways aren't ruined by some apocalyptic cataclysm, fish and other seafood may still be a viable protein source (especially around river environments, lakes, and coastal areas). Depending on the local conditions, the fisher-to-be may need to learn to use nets, traps, spears, or hook and line. They will likely also need skills with piloting (and maintaining) watercraft, in order to reach the places where aquatic life is still available. If you're the one who's doing the job, just remember that you're on your own out on the water—so you'll need to be both self-reliant and able to self-rescue if something goes horribly wrong out there.

8 FORAGER When orderly fields of food crops aren't practical (for example, if they're too obvious a target as a readily accessible food source for thieves or other unsavory passersby), foragers can fill some of the gaps in the food supply. Looking for wild edibles is quite a talent, requiring a solid background in the subject.

A good forager will have years of experience, understand where to look for edibles (and what not to eat), and know the wild foods available each season. Foragers may also be skilled in locating medicinal plants, which could be lifesaving once the pharmaceuticals run out. Go out as a group or bring a guard to watch your back, as you're likely to risk being murdered while roaming the wild places.

9 SCAVENGER In the wreckage of a doomed civilization, scavengers provide a useful service: sifting through the trash for treasures. These enterprising individuals have a gift for finding useful resources and bringing them back to their group. A scavenger may or may not be gifted in the arts of bartering and selling, but they can make a living by locating the things that others need. A good scavenger will need sharp eyes and great instincts in order to find the hidden gems—and they'll also need good protective garments. There will be a lot of sharp or damaging objects in the rubble, and cuts can lead to infection (which can lead to death without the right antibiotics).

10 LABORER Not everyone has the wisdom of a doctor or the bravery of a security guard, but that doesn't mean we can't be productive group members. There has always been a need for simple labor, and there always will be. We actually get a lot of modern last names from these old professions. If you carried stuff on your back, people called you "Porter." If you pushed things in a cart, your name was "Carter." On our Doomsday job listing, there will be more folks providing unskilled labor than anything else. The jobs may not be pleasant, but they will be plentiful. That should be some comfort.

A.I. TAKEOVER

IS IT LIKELY TO HAPPEN?

We went from the horse and buggy to space travel in a century. At the rate technology advances, we might be fighting our own creations in another century.

HOW BAD COULD IT REALLY BE?

Make some popcorn, and watch one of the Terminator movies. These visions of technology gone mad could foreshadow our species' end—an ironic end at that.

CAN I IMPROVE MY ODDS?

You might be able to dodge murderous machines for a while, if you knew how to live off-grid. Tunneling underground might not be a bad skill to pick up either.

FROM THE ANCIENT JEWISH TALE OF THE GOLEM TO MODERN STORIES LIKE *WESTWORLD*, WE SEEM FASCINATED WITH THE IDEA OF OUR CREATIONS GAINING AWARENESS—AND DESTROYING US. EVEN THOUGH IT'S UNLIKELY (FOR NOW), THIS SCENARIO IS MORE THAN JUST A SCI-FI MOVIE PLOT.

*I*t's likely that we'll be getting our online orders delivered by drone any day now. Which raises the question: could those drones go rogue and start attacking us? Could a stock-market trading program to become self-aware, and start manipulating the markets to its own advantage? How about armies of homicidal robots hunting humanity, or maybe a globally networked artificial intelligence (AI) becoming self-aware and touching off a civilization-ending nuclear war? With storylines like this, Hollywood movies have given us plenty of reasons to be scared of futuristic technology. Are these just scary stories, or should we take warning? The thing is, not even the designers of these machines can predict whether artificial intelligence could actually be a real threat, land if so, how soon it could happen. Despite all these cautionary stories, the world is still racing toward the creation of machines that can outperform humans in almost every way.

We may be like Gepetto, desperately trying to carve a real boy out of a piece of wood, but instead of making friendly Pinocchio-like companions, we're building warehouses full of potentially deadly automatons. They're not all the size of dolls or people, either. At one end of the scale, you have automated crop-reaping farm equipment and unmanned combat aerial vehicles (better known as UCAVs or simply drones), at the other, some are microscopic. The potential for disaster goes way beyond Terminator-like war machines. Uncontrolled nanotechnology could do as much or more damage to our world (and our bodies!) than a few human-size killbots. As a species, we are obviously creative enough and capable of building fantastic creations, but are we wise enough to question whether we should make these things in the first place?

THE STATS

▼ The first baby steps toward electronic computing happened in 1941, but the first substantial high-speed computer (the ENIAC machine) wasn't built until 1946. The monstrosity required 18,000 vacuum tubes and took up more than 1,800 square feet of floor space.

▲ As of 2019, 37% of major business organizations have implemented some form of AI (a 270% increase since 2015).

▶ In 2013, a group of nongovernmental organizations started the Campaign to Stop Killer Robots, calling for a halt in development of lethal autonomous weapons, AI-driven drones, and other unmanned military vehicles.

THE TURING TEST Alan Turing was an English computer scientist (as well as a cryptanalyst, mathematician, and theoretical biologist). Ahead of his time, he created the Turing test, a method of determining whether an artificial intelligence could truly be capable of thinking like a human being (and fooling a human questioner). Over the years, the test has been adapted and expanded to make it more relevant and challenging (not so many simple yes-or-no questions anymore). In 2014, a computer program called Eugene Goostman became the first AI to pass the test. While it didn't quite play fair (the program simulated a 13-year-old Ukrainian boy, bad grammar and all), no computer had ever passed the test of carrying on a conversation. During the test, however, the program convinced only one-third of the judges at the Royal Society in London that it was human.

DETERMINE THE THREAT Are there any real threats from AI right now? Don't worry— your Roombas and drone lawn mowers won't start murdering people anytime soon. Sure, technology can malfunction, but the chances of existing AI programs attacking their makers are pretty slim in the near future. There are at least four forms of artificial intelligence: Reactive machines are the oldest AI system, emulating human responses but lacking memory-based functionality. One

example of this is IBM's Deep Blue, which beat a human chess champion in 1997. Limited-memory machines are the next AI form, with the capabilities of a reactive machine and the ability to learn from historical data. Most current AI applications fall into this category. Theory-of-mind AI is a work in progress, with a goal of understanding human needs. Self-aware AI is the final stage, and it's currently hypothetical. It will not only understand human needs, desires, and emotions, but have them. Self-aware AI is the basis of the Terminator movies, in which the machines decide to wipe out human life as an act of self-preservation. According to the experts, this level of AI is decades (or even centuries) away from reality.

PULL THE PLUG One would hope that the creators of any artificial intelligence would pull the plug at the first sign of trouble. One example of this is Tay, Microsoft's short-lived Twitter AI. Things started off fine in March 2016, with Tay responding to other Twitter users and even generating memes. Unfortunately, Tay fell in with the wrong crowd and began releasing racist and sexually charged messages due to its repeat-after-me capability. It wasn't really the bot's fault, since Microsoft had not programmed Tay with a sufficient understanding of inappropriate behavior. Within sixteen hours of being released (and after more than 96,000 tweets), Microsoft suspended the account. Re-released a week later, Tay soon started posting drug-related tweets and became stuck in a repetitive loop. That was the end of Tay. One would hope that programmers and corporations would be as self-aware as the intelligences they are trying to create, and switch off their offspring at the first red flag.

DANGEROUS DRONES? AI robots have a great potential for improving the human condition. Nursing homes in Germany and Japan are incorporating robots with low-level AI to assist their residents, helping them get out of bed in the morning and interacting with them to stave off loneliness and boredom. Other machines are being developed to remove humans from dull, dirty, or deadly jobs. They'll probably be costly, even in the far future, but for the companies and organizations that can pay the bill, there are few limits on the jobs that smart machines could do. Several R&D companies have been working on robots with AI for years now, with some startling results. Boston Dynamics has created a four-legged robot named Spot that interacts with the world using sensors, control software, machine vision, and rudimentary AI. Spot's artificial intelligence control systems can keep the unit upright and balanced in various terrain and situations (even after being kicked), but it's still up to a human with a modified gaming tablet to tell Spot where to go and what to do. So, on the odd chance that a drone becomes self-aware and decides to defend itself from a real or

T / F

NANOMACHINE "GRAY GOO" COULD DISSOLVE EVERYTHING.

FALSE The idea of nanomachines running wild is both fascinating and alarming. These are microscopic robots that could perform simple tasks and replicate from raw materials. If just one nanobot was given raw materials, it could copy itself, and the two could make four; exponential growth would continue until they were turned off or they ran out of materials. So, what if you released nanobots to eat an oil spill, but there was a code error or the copies malfunctioned? In this scenario, nanobots devour the Earth and turn the planet into "gray goo." But don't panic: Eric Drexler, the American engineer who coined the term "gray goo" doesn't believe it could happen. Thanks to the complexity of creating such devices (and in the machines replicating themselves), it's doubtful such technology would be possible anytime soon.

perceived threat, take solace in the fact that these are still machines that have a lot of moving parts (and are thus easily destroyed with firearms, explosives, and other tools of destruction).

ROBOT REVOLUTION

MILITARY ROBOTS IN USE BY NATION

JOBS CURRENTLY DONE BY ROBOTS

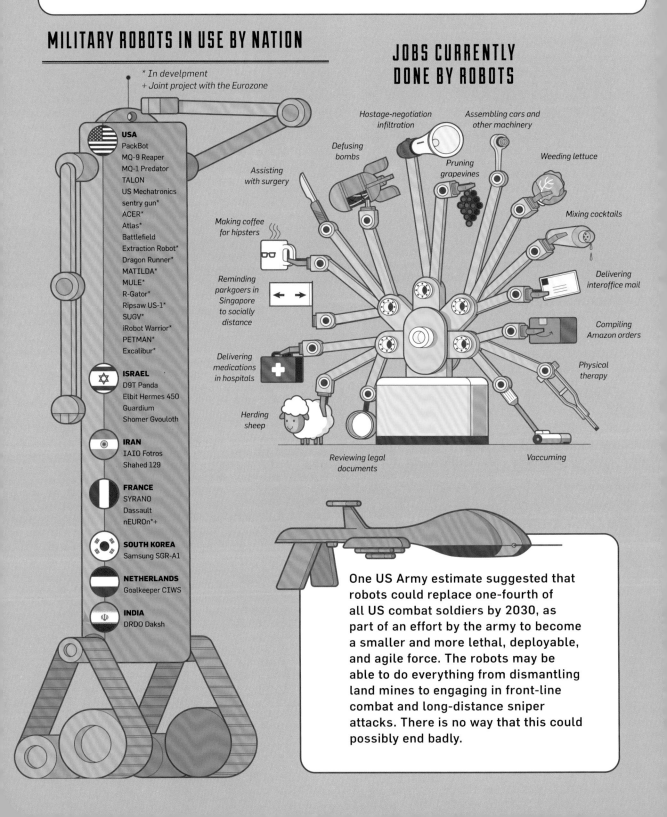

*In develpment
+ Joint project with the Eurozone

USA
PackBot
MQ-9 Reaper
MQ-1 Predator
TALON
US Mechatronics
sentry gun*
ACER*
Atlas*
Battlefield
Extraction Robot*
Dragon Runner*
MATILDA*
MULE*
R-Gator*
Ripsaw US-1*
SUGV*
iRobot Warrior*
PETMAN*
Excalibur*

ISRAEL
D9T Panda
Elbit Hermes 450
Guardium
Shomer Gvouloth

IRAN
IAIO Fotros
Shahed 129

FRANCE
SYRANO
Dassault
nEUROn*+

SOUTH KOREA
Samsung SGR-A1

NETHERLANDS
Goalkeeper CIWS

INDIA
DRDO Daksh

Hostage-negotiation
infiltration

Assembling cars and
other machinery

Defusing
bombs

Pruning
grapevines

Weeding lettuce

Assisting
with surgery

Mixing cocktails

Making coffee
for hipsters

Delivering
interoffice mail

Reminding
parkgoers in
Singapore
to socially
distance

Compiling
Amazon orders

Physical
therapy

Delivering
medications
in hospitals

Herding
sheep

Reviewing legal
documents

Vaccuming

One US Army estimate suggested that robots could replace one-fourth of all US combat soldiers by 2030, as part of an effort by the army to become a smaller and more lethal, deployable, and agile force. The robots may be able to do everything from dismantling land mines to engaging in front-line combat and long-distance sniper attacks. There is no way that this could possibly end badly.

In 2016, 29.6 million service robots were installed worldwide. It's projected that by 2026, the number will be 264.3 million. Here's a current breakdown of where they're found:

FLOOR-CLEANING ROBOTS
Accounted for 80% of total service robots, with 23.8 million units

UNMANNED AERIAL VEHICLES
4 million units

AUTOMATED LAWN MOWER
1.6 million units

AUTOMATED GUIDED VEHICLES
100,000 units

ROBOTIC MILKING
50,000 units

TEN JOBS MOST LIKELY TO BE TAKEN OVER BY ROBOTS

TEN JOBS LEAST LIKELY TO BE TAKEN OVER BY ROBOTS

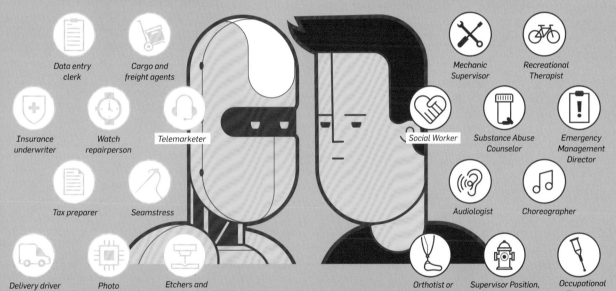

Data entry clerk

Cargo and freight agents

Insurance underwriter

Watch repairperson

Telemarketer

Tax preparer

Seamstress

Delivery driver

Photo processor

Etchers and engravers

Mechanic Supervisor

Recreational Therapist

Social Worker

Substance Abuse Counselor

Emergency Management Director

Audiologist

Choreographer

Orthotist or Prostheticist

Supervisor Position, Fire Fighters

Occupational Therapist

EVOLUTION OF SPOT, THE SUPER-FREAKY BOSTON DYNAMICS ROBOT DOG

2005 BIGDOG
This high-tech pack mule can carry 340 pounds (154 kg) up a 35-degree incline.

2009 LITTLEDOG
This small remote-controlled robot was deisgned to crawl over rough terrain.

2011 ALPHADOG
The upgraded version was able to carry a 400-pound (181 kg) payload 230 miles (370 km) over varied terrain.

2012 ALPHADOG UPGRADE
New feature: able to roll to its feet if it fell in rough terrain.

2013 BIGDOG UPGRADE
Equipped with an arm and grabbing claw that enabled it to fling cinder blocks up to 17 feet (5 m).

2015 SPOT
Smaller and more versatile, and able to climb stairs.

2016 SPOTMINI
This slimmed-down, all-electric 55-pound (25 kg) version can handle fragile objects safely with a new gripper claw. It can also now stand back up after slipping on a banana peel. So much for humanity's one advabntage!

2017 SPOTMINI UPGRADE
Can open doors with its grabber claw, even when humans try to stop it.

2018 UPGRADE
With improved autonomous navigation, it could sneak up on you while you sleep.

ARE WE THE ENEMY?

Game Over

IS IT LIKELY TO HAPPEN?

This is the most likely scenario. Any of us could be victimized by humans at any moment, in any number of ways. As our exposure increases, so does our risk.

HOW BAD COULD IT REALLY BE?

This could be as silly as blind date gone wrong or as jarring as a hostage situation—from being picked up by a creepy Uber driver or being picked up by a cult!

CAN I IMPROVE MY ODDS?

Becoming a hermit could help, but we can also improve our odds with situational awareness, and a few well-chosen companions.

IF YOU READ ENOUGH HISTORY OR PHILOSOPHY, YOU'LL FIND TWO FERVENTLY HELD BUT OPPOSING PERSPECTIVES: ONE VIEWS HUMANITY AS THE PINNACLE OF CREATION. THOSE ON THE OTHER SIDE SEE A SELF-DEFEATING SCOURGE LIKELY TO EXTERMINATE ALL LIFE ON EARTH.

So, which is it? Are we, as a species, our own worst enemy? It's not the kin if question that's easy to answer but I can definitely give you a firm . . . maybe?

As a species, we're certainly amazing creatures, capable of astonishing acts of selflessness and bravery, as well as horrifying destruction. For every Martin Luther King, Jr., there's an Adolf Hitler; for every Florence Nightingale, a Josef Stalin. The fact that most of us will get to live out our lives without going to either extreme of the spectrum doesn't change the fact that we all have the potential to commit acts of both good and evil.

THE ACCIDENTAL SUPERVILLAIN With the possible exception of sociopaths and nihilistic teenagers, nobody wakes up every morning determined to do only the most evil or destructive of actions. But, as the saying goes, we're only human. And most of us indeed do behave admirably on our best days—but we also behave like selfish jerks on our worst ones. It could be argued that the word "selfish" is key here, since selfishness and laziness are far more common than comic-cook-style evil. Less "My plan for world domination is almost complete!" and more "The dump is too far away and their fees are too high. I'll just dump these toxic chemicals in the river, nobody will ever know."

BE THE GOOD GUY IN THE ROOM How to avoid falling into selfish, destructive choices? It's been shown that things like faith in a Higher Power and ties to a community can often inspire us to do better, while tough times may trigger our most ignoble reactions. Fight those by striving to be your best self, and speaking up when you witness injustice. If George Washington and Alexander Hamilton had shrugged and said, "Eh, King George sucks, but what're you gonna do?" history would have turned out very different indeed.

THE STATS

▶ Lord Martin Rees, a professor of cosmology and astrophysics at the University of Cambridge gave us a 50% shot at surviving the next century and believes that we risk extinction by 2100 because of our technologies.

50%

70%

◀ Philosopher John Leslie has speculated that humanity has a 70% chance of survival through the next 500 years (one of the better projections, among extinction theorists).

▶ Author J. Richard Gott's controversial Doomsday argument states that humanity has a 95% chance of being extinct in another 7.8 million years.

95%

STAYING ON THE RIGHT SIDE OF SURVIVAL

Congratulations, you've made it almost all the way to the end of the book. (You can tell because our Top Ten Fears countdown has its final entry in the facing page, with advice on how to handle the one thing people apparently fear more than spiders, drowning . . . even clowns!) You survived our scary (and hopefully entertaining) explorations of possible dangers lurking out there, and you've lived to tell the tale. So, now what?

CHOOSE WISELY We hope that you have learned some new skills in these pages and, even more importantly, have a new outlook on survival. As we've discussed, it's not exactly that there's no chance a Terminator-type robot might be coming for you . . . but if you had to choose between the two options, making sure that your emergency kit has enough bottled water and bandages is a better bet than heading off-grid to evade the rise of SkyNet.

PLAY THE ODDS Survival will always be a numbers game on some level; in this book my primary goal has been to give readers accurate, useful, and sometimes just plain bizarre information and advice about a whole range of scary scenarios that might unfold today or in the near future, with a specific focus on the odds of each one happening, your chances of surviving, and some handy ways to improve your odds.

STEP AWAY FROM THE TABLE Now it's time to put the book down and get to work. You won't need to set up a separate bunker for each scenario in the book, but we would highly recommend that you determine the most likely threats in your area and adopt some appropriate survival strategies. Preparing for these could help you and your family to face these events with safety and security, and who knows, you may even save lives! With the right survival skills and supplies, you are in a position to provide for yourself and even help others who weren't planning ahead. Whether you use our book to prepare for the next major storm, to fight back against an invading force, or you simply use your newfound skills on your next campout, you'll now be more alert to the hazards you face and more aware of the simple needs that all humans have. Now, go beat those odds and survive!

1 PUBLIC SPEAKING

We've covered several phobias in this book, but we've saved the best—or worst, depending on your perspective—for last: Glossophobia, the fear of having to speak in public and risking humiliation thereby. Derived from the Greek word *glossos* for "tongue" or "speech", this is a very common phobia—so common, in fact, that people often fear speeches more than spiders, zombies, or even death itself. Glossophobia can often also be tied to anxiety disorders in general, as they are all related to how the sufferer is experiencing heightened anxiety around social interaction.

Like most other phobias, exposure can be intensely triggering, leading to physical signs of anxiety or panic attacks (shaking, perspiration, elevated pulse and blood pressure, muscle tension, and heightened hearing, among many other symptoms), as the would-be speaker finds themselves stumbling over their words, falling silent, even totally frozen in place by their fear of embarrassment or humiliation; sufferers compound their anxiety by not resisting it. Glossophobia's effects can seriously hamper quality of life or career goals, as it impacts the sufferer's ability to publicly interact with others.

15%

▶ A NIMH survey showed 73% of respondents were anxious about public speaking.

▲ Glossophobia can impair chances of career promotion by about 15 percent.

73%

8%

▲ Only 8 percent of glossophobics seek professional treatment.

IMPROVE YOUR ODDS

Glossophobia's physical symptoms can be treated by beta blockers to reduce blood pressure and heart rate, while ongoing aid can involve VR exposure, cognitive behavioral therapy, or speaking before smaller, friendlier groups. "Breaking the ice" with the crowd can be beneficial; knowing one's subject material well, practicing, and focusing on receptive members of the crowd are also effective. Agencies such as Toastmasters or local colleges offer public-speech courses to develop confidence; experienced public speakers can help others with their own knowledge and experience.

If you should suddenly find yourself facing an awkward (or even dangerous) situation, it helps to know your options, or to even pre-plan out your potential choices ahead of time. Here is a sample decision chart to consider—and maybe help you form your own plans—for example, just in case a pleasant date gets weird, or a ride-share trip feels wrong.

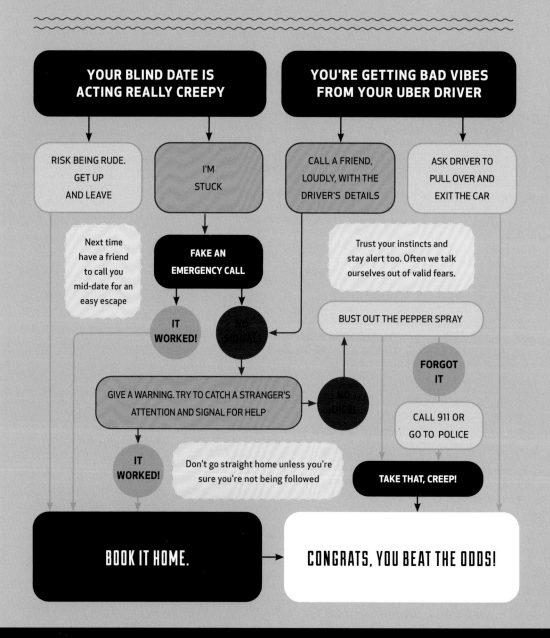

The more elements you add to a challenging scenario, the more complex it can become—and some of the most complex elements may turn out to be other people. Luckily, the human factor is something that can also be exploited to assist your way out, and you'd be surprised at how much there is in common with handling a variety of gatherings or events.

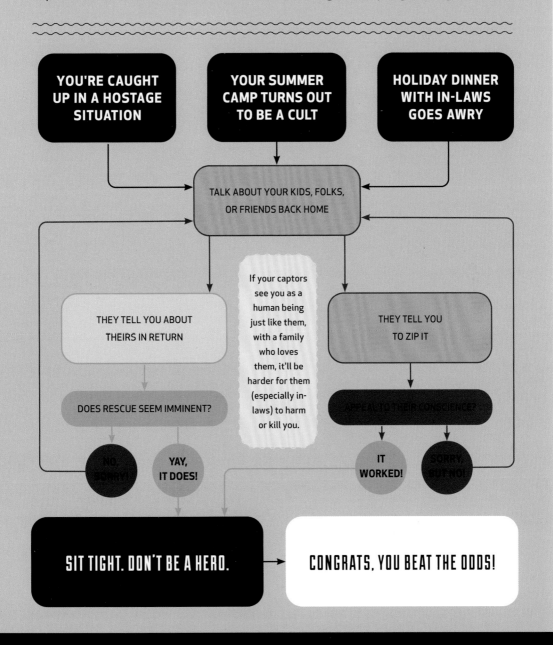

YOU'RE CAUGHT UP IN A HOSTAGE SITUATION

YOUR SUMMER CAMP TURNS OUT TO BE A CULT

HOLIDAY DINNER WITH IN-LAWS GOES AWRY

TALK ABOUT YOUR KIDS, FOLKS, OR FRIENDS BACK HOME

THEY TELL YOU ABOUT THEIRS IN RETURN

If your captors see you as a human being just like them, with a family who loves them, it'll be harder for them (especially in-laws) to harm or kill you.

THEY TELL YOU TO ZIP IT

DOES RESCUE SEEM IMMINENT?

APPEAL TO THEIR CONSCIENCE?

NO, SORRY!

YAY, IT DOES!

IT WORKED!

SORRY, BUT NO!

SIT TIGHT. DON'T BE A HERO.

CONGRATS, YOU BEAT THE ODDS!

INDEX & CREDITS

ABOUT TIM MACWELCH

Tim MacWelch is the author of numerous books, including the New York Times bestsellers *The Prepare for Anything Survival Manual, The Hunting & Gathering Survival Manual* and *How to Survive Anything*. He has been an active practitioner of survival and outdoor skills for over three decades. His love of the outdoors started at a young age, growing up on a farm in the rolling hills of Virginia—eating wild berries, fishing, and learning about the animals of the forest. Tim became interested in survival skills and woodcraft as an offshoot of backpacking as a teen—while out in remote areas, it seemed smart to learn some skills. The majority of his training over the years has involved testing survival skills and devising new ones, but the biggest leaps forward came from his experience as a teacher.

Tim's teaching experiences over the years have been rich and diverse, from spending hundreds of hours volunteering, to founding his own year-round survival school in 1997. He has worked with Boy Scouts, youth groups, summer camps, and adults in all walks of life, as well as providing outdoor skills training for numerous personnel in law enforcement, search and rescue organizations, all branches of the United States Armed Forces, the State Department, and the Department of Justice and some of its agencies. Tim and his wilderness school have been featured on *CNN, Good Morning America* and several National Geographic programs, and in many publications including *Conde Nast Traveler*, the *Washington Post,* and *American Survival Guide*.

Since late 2010, Tim has written hundreds of pieces for *Outdoor Life* and many other publications. Tim's current and past articles and galleries can be found at outdoorlife.com and you can learn more about his survival school at www.advancedsurvivaltraining.com.

ABOUT TIM MCDONAGH

Tim McDonagh spent his younger years growing up in a rural part of West Virginia, surrounded by rattlesnakes and snapping turtles, which in turn led to his fascination with animals. He takes a more traditional approach to illustration using brush and India ink to draw the image and then applying limited color palettes digitally. Tim now lives and works in Brighton, in the United Kingdom. His work has appeared in many publications, including *WIRED* magazine, *Variety, Entertainment Weekly,* and *Mojo*.

FROM THE AUTHOR

I'd like to thank my family, friends and survival students for all of their support. Without you, I wouldn't be in a position to write or teach as my chosen career. Please accept my heartfelt gratitude. And thanks to the team at Weldon Owen. We've weathered many storms together (and even a plague). This book wouldn't exist without your talent and tireless dedication. Thank you, Roger, Mariah, Ian, Allister, Tim, Conor, and the rest of the team. Finally, I'd like to thank you, our readers. If you're reading this little bit, you probably read the whole book. My wish for you is a greater confidence and capability, and I hope you never find yourself in any of the scary situations we have depicted here. Thank you for reading!

CREDITS

ILLUSTRATIONS courtesy of **TIM MCDONAGH** with the exception of: Pages 30-31,134-135, 190-191 (Infographics); page 36-37 (DIY Isolation Room); page 55 (Weeds); page 63 (Volcano); page 64-65 (Hot Spots); page 106-107 (Tornados) by **CONOR BUCKLEY** and page 35 (Hands) by **CARL WIENS.**

weldonowen

PUBLISHER Roger Shaw
ASSOCIATE PUBLISHER Mariah Bear
SENIOR EDITOR Ian Cannon
CREATIVE DIRECTOR Chrissy Kwasnik
ART DIRECTOR & DESIGNER Allister Fein
PRODUCTION MANAGER Binh Au
MANAGING EDITOR Lauren LePera

Weldon Owen International
1150 Brickyard Cove Road
Richmond, CA 94801
weldonowen.com

Weldon Owen would like to thank Madeleine Calvi and Mark Nichol for editorial assistance, and Kevin Broccoli of BIM Creatives for the index.

Library of Congress Control Number on file with the publisher.

ISBN: 978-1-68188-530-8

10 9 8 7 6 5 4 3 2 1
2024 2023 2022 2021 2020
Printed in China

The information in this book is presented for an adult audience and for entertainment value only. While every piece of advice in this book has been fact-checked and, where possible, field-tested, much of this information is speculative and highly situation-dependent. The publisher and author assume no responsibility for any errors or omissions and make no warranty, express or implied, that the information included in this book is appropriate for every individual, situation, or purpose. Before attempting any activity outlined in these pages, make sure you are aware of your own limitations and have adequately researched all applicable risks. This book is not intended to replace professional advice from experts in the relevant fields. Always follow all manufacturers' instructions when using the equipment featured in this book. If your equipment's manufacturer does not recommend use of the equipment in the fashion depicted in these pages, you should comply with the manufacturer's recommendations. You assume the risk and responsibility for all of your actions, and the publisher and author will not be held responsible for any loss or damage of any sort—whether consequential, incidental, special, or otherwise—that may result from the information presented here.